P9-EDK-566

Responsible
Police
Administration

Responsible Police Administration

Issues and Approaches

LEE W. POTTS

The University of Alabama Press

Library of Congress Cataloging in Publication Data

Potts, Lee W., 1949–
   Responsible police administration.

   Bibliography: p.
   Includes index.
   1. Police administration—United States. I. Title.
HV7935.P67   1983   363.2'0973   82-16059
ISBN 0-8173-0140-2

Contents

Tables

Figure

Responsible
Police
Administration

1 Responsible Police Administration

An Overview of the Issues

The government process was once thought of as having two separate and distinct functions: first, politics—the articulation of the public will, and second, administration—the implementation of that will (Goodnow, 1900:22; W. Wilson, 1887:198). In the past half century, it has become clear that administrators—those who execute or enforce the law—play a vital role in government beyond implementation of laws. Police executives, for example, make vital decisions about policy implementation. But as administrators use more initiative in executing policy, it becomes increasingly vital to ensure that their actions fall within the bounds articulated by the representatives of the people.

Administrative responsibility as a legitimate expression of the public will is of great relevance to the function and performance of the police. Because the police are among the government officials closest and most important to the public, the problem of responsibility is especially important to and contentious for police administration.

This book will examine several approaches to responsible police administration. It will focus first on traditional external controls—legal and bureaucratic—on police behavior. It will then examine contemporary alternatives that assume responsibility to be a problem of representativeness and professionalization. Finally, an approach to improving the existing system to provide responsibility that does not require restructuring of the police function or of police agencies will be discussed.

Inquiry into the nature and systematic evaluation of alternative measures for achieving responsibility has been inhibited primarily by a persistent concern with controlling rather than directing the police. In large part this impasse is a consequence of a longstanding tension between the role of the police and beliefs about the nature of democratic society. Subsidiary problems generated by this basic problem are narrow conceptions of administration, of leadership, and of the police role in society. These problems must be examined before the efficacy of the various alternative approaches to developing responsible police can be evaluated.

The Paradox of Police Power in a Democracy

Democratic government rests on a paradox. The citizenry is expected to be able to control the government. But the people expect the government to assure social order and stability and to organize collective action for the attainment of socially significant goals. These activities in turn require a measure of control over the citizenry. Recognition of this paradox has existed since the very beginning of the American republic. In the *Federalist Papers,* No. 51, James Madison asserted that the great difficulty in framing a government is, first to "enable the government to control the governed and in the next place, oblige it to control itself" (1787:123).

Because government personnel possess the tools of coercion, the citizenry's control over the government depends, to a large extent, on the cooperation of the government. This dilemma applies not only to the government as a whole but also to the executive agencies. For some agencies, such as the police, this is a practical problem, not simply a philosophical issue. The paradox of requiring institutions of social control to be controlled themselves is strikingly manifested with regard to the police.

Police officers are among the few civilian government officials who are uniformed and, therefore, highly visible. They are among the few civilian government officials who are armed. They are readily identified as enforcers of the law. They possess the power of life and death. Many people see them as the embodiment of the government's coercive power. Perhaps most significantly, they exercise their power in direct personal contact with individual citizens.

The police are thus caught up in the paradox of democratic government. The basic premise of democracy is that the people are capable of ruling themselves. The basic premise of policing is that social regulation is necessary. Under the democratic ideal, the government, including the police, is expected to serve the public. Yet, as law enforcers, while the police are serving the public in an abstract sense, they are quite the opposite of servants in the concrete. Although the police do much more than enforce the law, the fact that they are uniformed and armed makes their coercive role dominant. Physical coercion is, after all, the mechanism by which the government compels subordination of individual interests to the common interest of the society.

The essential challenge to those who are charged with oversight of police operations is to ensure that the power of the police is constrained within proper boundaries. In a democracy, these boundaries are assumed to be set by the desires of the public. But in complex modern societies there are many public wills because there are many publics. The position that the first duty of the government is to govern requires determining the collective goals of society and mobilizing the organized power of society to pursue and attain those collective goals. To achieve those goals, government must provide the social harmony and peace that ensure a productive communal life. In an ideal society, shared values and beliefs lead to intermeshing of individual interests and a high degree of consensus about social purposes. In the real world, there arises a need for institutions of authoritative interpretation of values and for machinery to enforce those interpretations.

A primary question in a democratic society, therefore, is: Who controls the institutions of interpretation and enforcement? The need to control must be balanced by the need to assure that the answer to the question is "the people." The quest for government responsibility represents the attempt to balance government's coercive power and its responsiveness. The proposition that the people are capable of self-government carries with it the corollary that "whoever claims to be the guardian of the collective social interest is a dangerous man" (de Jouvenel 1957:129). He is dangerous because he has put himself above the people.

For the agencies of the government, and especially for the police, the question of the boundaries of control presents a grave problem. There is an inherent element of distrust of the police as guardians of social order in a democracy. This distrust is intensified because history has taught the need for skepticism about claims by governments to be serving the public interest. The wielders of government power have emphasized the first element of Madison's dichotomy: the acquisition of power to control the governed. On the other hand, Americans place a positive value on limited government. Nearly a century ago, Woodrow Wilson observed that one of the most salient features of the evolution of Anglo-American political culture has been "controlling rather than energizing government" (1887:206).

This brings us back to the issue of how police operations should be constrained. Specifically, how can the exercise of police power be held in conformance with the values, beliefs, and wishes of the citizenry? The question of responsiveness then becomes the question of responsibility, which relates to the administrative process.

The Administrative Process

An examination of the administrative process must begin by identifying some basic assumptions about public agencies. First, it is assumed that police departments and all other public agencies exist for a purpose that was perceived before the agency was established. Therefore, it is assumed that the ends sought are not determined by the agency. The agency, however, may have some latitude in defining operational objectives.

Once established, an agency is subdivided into various operational components. One set of these components is focused on operations; these are line units, which perform the duties associated with the societal ends prescribed for the agency. In police departments these subdivisions include patrol, criminal investigation, traffic, and juvenile units. A second set of components is developed to contribute to overall departmental goals; these are staff units, which perform the essential task of acquiring the raw materials that make it possible for the line to perform. Staff units include planning, personnel, and financial management. Staff and line units could meet the needs of organizational performance only if it were assumed that societal ends and agency objectives are essentially the same. In fact, some mechanism is needed for translating the diffuse expectations about ends into relatively specific operational objectives. This is the function of the administrative level of police departments.

The administrative level is concerned with providing direction for the department. The essential task of administration is to make decisions about what the department is doing, about what it should be doing, about internal management, and about relations with the public and with government superiors. The administrators mediate relations between the department and the outside world and among units within the department. They identify operational objectives to meet societal expectations. They use information about organizational performance to determine whether the objectives are being approached. They take corrective action when the department goes off course. They use information about internal relationships to determine whether organizational maintenance is secure, whether the organization can adapt to changing circumstances, and whether the line has sufficient raw material to provide effective operation rather than being absorbed in the pursuit of organizational and subunit mainte-nance. (On this perspective on the administrative process see Church-man, 1968; Emery and Trist, 1972a, b; Thompson, 1967.)

From this perspective, leadership becomes the obverse of responsi-bility. Responsibility lies in using power in conformance with the val-ues, attitudes, and expectations of the public and instilling commitment to the goals throughout the agency. The key elements of concern are social ends and societal values.

The linking of leadership and the administrative process helps to clarify the distinction between police administration and police man-agement which will be maintained in this book. Administration is to be seen as the broadly based process of guiding an agency toward its goals. It involves analysis of the role of the agency's personnel and operations in setting policy, as well as analysis of the way an agency executes the policies that have been set for it. In other words, the administrative process is the process of translating generalized goals of public policy into operational guidelines for specific agencies, hold-ing the agency to conformance with the guidelines and social norms, adjusting the guidelines to reflect changing circumstances (including changes that are the direct or indirect consequences of agency task performance), and adjusting the agency's course to correspond with the changed guidelines. Administration deals with relative instability.

Management, by contrast, deals with relative stability. The manage-ment process involves the use of organization resources for agency task performance. Management works with givens. Policy is set at the administrative level and carried out at the operational level. Manage-ment seeks to ensure that the two are in harmony. This does not mean that a line of demarcation can be drawn between the administrative process and the management process. Administrators are managers. Managers have an impact on and a necessary role in the administra-tive process. The two processes, administration and management, are conceptually distinct. Police management is an integral element of police administration that cannot be disregarded in analysis of the administrative process. But it is only an element of the administrative process.

In spite of the widespread agreement on the need for administra-tive responsibility, there has not been a commonly agreed-upon method for ensuring responsibility. There has been almost no con-cern for ensuring institutional leadership. Nevertheless, the quest for police responsibility has been implicitly at the center of developments in police administration. In fact, it may even be said that the essential dynamic of police administration comes down to the quest for responsibility.

The Importance of Institutional Leadership

The concept of institutional leadership—articulation of the basic mission of an institution in conformance with public desires and enduring social values and integration of a commitment to that mission into the processes and operations of the institution—is of great importance for the police. Administrative leadership involves mediation between the department and significant outside interests and among subunits of the department. Mediation requires clear thinking and the power of persuasion. The administrators of a police department must be able to demonstrate to external power holders and the general public that the department is serving the public interest and is a meaningful component of local government. At the same time, they must be able to maintain the integrity of the department. Policy direction cannot be left entirely to outside interests just as it cannot be left entirely to police professionals.

The problem of mediation between departmental-professional interests and external interests and the crucial need for an affirmative articulation of the police mission assume tremendous importance in police administration. The police absorb a large share of local government finances and must demonstrate that they deserve the costs. A more fundamental problem involves the ambiguity of the police as a coercive institution in democratic society.

For mayors, city councilmen, and other public officials the costs of police service are a readily apparent indication of the political significance of the police. The International City Management Association has reported that the police function accounts for approximately 30 percent of municipal employees and approximately 33 percent of the municipal payroll. In each of these categories police employment is second only to education (which accounts for about 31 percent of employees and 36 percent of payroll) (1979:183–86). In municipal government criminal justice operations, police protection accounts for almost 90 percent of full-time equivalent employment and approximately 85 percent of expenditure (Bureau of Justice Statistics, 1982:9, 39).

The cost factor is especially significant to officials because the police function is extremely labor-intensive. Nationwide, wages and salaries amount to 86 percent of the expenditures for police protection, even though other factors vary. For example, Memphis, Baltimore, and Dallas each has approximately the same population. They have very different police-population ratios and per capita police costs. The number of police officers per one thousand population are 1.46, 2.28, and 3.96, respectively. Per capita costs are $38.66, $57.82, and $108.27, respectively. Yet the percentages of the police budget expended on salaries are 86.0, 86.1, and 86.0 respectively (Heaphy, 1979). During the 1970s expenditure on police protection increased faster than number of employees and payroll increased faster than expenditure (Bureau of Justice Statistics, 1982:19).

A budget may be looked upon as a statement of priorities with price tags attached. The more money allocated to a given function, the more valuable that function should be. The police function does seem to be accepted as vital to local government. It receives the second largest share of the budget, and is often believed to be justified in receiving increases in appropriations. There are no national data on compliance by local officials with requests for increases, but Arnold J. Meltsner (1971) found that during the decade of the 1960s the Oakland Police Department made requests for low-level increases compared to other municipal departments but received comparatively high-level increases. Such an allocation would indicate a relatively high level of legitimacy. The legitimacy of high-level expenditures on the police is also indicated by the commitment of the federal government to provide financial support for local police service. During the years 1971–79, the Law Enforcement Assistance Administration (LEAA) was authorized to spend more than $7.6 billion to aid state and local government criminal justice operations. The largest portion of that assistance has gone to police.

The irony of the situation is that the commitment of government to the police has tended to obscure the need for high-quality police leadership. The public concern over street crime, which was roused in the mid-1960s and continued into the 1970s, provided an almost automatic incentive to increase police financial support. Local officials were pressured by the public to combat crime by providing more and better police service. The federal government, responding to the same public pressure, undertook the "war on crime," which had its most vivid manifestation in the creation of the LEAA. The grants of federal money further spurred local expenditure.

Under the circumstances, the second aspect of the need for institutional leadership—the problem of police role ambiguity—remained unaddressed by most police administrators.

Police Role Ambiguity

The police have benefited from their close identification with law enforcement. Concern about crime led to investment of scarce resources in police protection because the police are believed to be the primary social institution for enforcing the criminal law. This identification of law enforcement and policing has developed without reference to the social reality of policing. In no way can it be argued that law enforcement is all there is to police work.

Identification of the police mission must have the social reality of policing as a primary point of reference. The social context of police work may be said to lie in the patterns of expectations held by the public about how and when police power should be used. To clarify this context it is necessary to go beyond the declaratory public sentiment that the police enforce the law and to examine the occasions upon which citizens seek to mobilize the police, the patterns of police-public interactions, and the police officers' orientations to their tasks.

One of the most common findings of the volume of data developed on the police in the late 1960s and early 1970s was the falseness of the belief that law enforcement dominates police work. In an analysis of calls to the Syracuse, New York, Police Department Elaine Cumming et al. (1965) found that less than one-third of the calls related to what they labeled police control functions while nearly one-half were classified as calls for support. James Q. Wilson (1975) found that only about 10 percent of the calls in Syracuse resulting in the dispatch of a patrol car involved law enforcement. Albert Reiss's (1971) analysis of calls to the Chicago Police Central Communications Center identified only about one-third as law-enforcement-related. Thomas Bercal's (1970) comparison of dispatched calls in St. Louis and Detroit found a higher proportion of crime-related calls (39 percent in Detroit and 51 percent in St. Louis), but the data included dispatches in response to burglar alarms, which are generally false alarms.

Rather than being primarily a law enforcement officer, the average policeman (the patrolman) is primarily a peace officer (Banton, 1964). His time is spent performing public services such as directing traffic and escorting vehicles or performing social welfare services such as dealing with the mentally deranged, attempted suicides, domestic crisis intervention, and neighborhood disputes. The problem of role ambiguity arises particularly with regard to these social duties.

Not only do the police have multiple roles, but there is conflict among those disparate roles. As law enforcement officers, the police find their coercive role to be paramount. As peace officers, they most often find their public servant role to be paramount. An individual may have difficulty in adjusting from one role to the other, especially because in the law enforcement role, officers are accustomed to meeting resistance and hostility that require them to protect themselves from physical assault. Even in the peace officer role, where their presence is meant to resolve or preclude disputes, they may find themselves the object of hostility. When called upon to intervene in disputes, the police often must act as instrumental negotiators (Cumming et al., 1965), using their personal authority and the authority of their position to work out provisional solutions to disruptive situations. They do not solve the problem that gave rise to the situation; they only attempt to stop the conflict in progress. But here the problem of role ambiguity may become especially acute. When involved in crime fighting, officers can rely upon the criminal law that defines acts held to be illegal to support and guide their activities.

In fulfilling the peacekeeping function, however, police officers have no such guidance and support. Their main concern is with restoring relative calm, not with comparing a law to observed behavior and making an arrest. A law may have been violated. Laws regarding disorderly conduct rest upon the premise that a condition such as public order exists and can be diminished. But there is no unambiguous definition of public order. Unlike criminal law enforcement, the instrumental negotiator role focuses not on guilt but on blame. Since blame and not guilt in a legal sense is the issue, citizens requesting police assistance want something done to settle the dispute but may not necessarily desire that their adversaries be arrested (J. Q. Wilson, 1978:57).

Because as peace officers the police often lack firm guidelines on how to proceed, they find their authority problematical, and they find little opportunity for self-validation. People call on them for help but turn on them when they give it. Perhaps even worse, although the public calls on them to perform service and instrumental negotiator duties more often than it does to apprehend criminals, the public image of the basic police function is law enforcement. Professional training and professional opinion tend to reinforce that image. Consequently, for the police officer "real police work" is law enforcement. Service is not real police work and may be resented as a petty interference with the important task of policing.

The problem of role ambiguity is a challenge both to police responsibility and to police leadership. It is a challenge to responsibility because the public places a high value on service work and the peace officer role. The patterns of expectations about when police should be mobilized, as demonstrated by calls for police service, indicate that to be responsible, the police have to be able to play the peace officer role. Yet overt legitimacy for police operations is placed on law enforcement.

In providing leadership, police administrators have to persuade their officers that social service is a vital part of their role, that they have a social mission that extends beyond law enforcement. That mission is the preservation of social order. The police are among the few government services available twenty-four hours a day, seven days a week, three hundred sixty-five days a year. They can respond within a few minutes. They are empowered to impose order on situations without having to contend with immediate interference. Their power may extend to any disruptive situation.

To focus on law enforcement is to distort the picture of the police role. Effective police officers have to know more than crime-fighting techniques. They have to know how and where to obtain expert information on a wide variety of emergency situations. Individual commitment to developing the appropriate skills and to acquiring the appropriate information cannot be expected without an institutional commitment to reward the effort to become a proficient peace officer. Demonstrating that commitment to rewarding well-rounded police officers is the internal aspect of reducing the effects of role ambiguity.

Leadership also involves external efforts to minimize role ambiguity. Police administrators who are to be institutional leaders have to be able to educate officials and the public about the capabilities of the police. They need to be able to attempt to bring public expectations in line with departmental capabilities. They have to attempt to secure official and public acceptance of the peace officer role to the same extent that that role is expected to be played when called for by the public. At the same time, ironically perhaps, steps must be taken to stress the limitations of the police. The police cannot solve the problems of crime and criminality. Nor should they be expected to be the last-resort social-crisis institution. The failures of the welfare system, public education, and socialization cannot be overcome by redefining nonconformance to be criminality and calling it a law enforcement problem.

The Role of Leadership in Responsible Administration

The key to police administrative responsibility lies in the patterns of relationships between individual police officers and the departmental policy-making and managerial structures, between the police leadership and the elected representatives of the public, and between the policeman on the street and the members of the public with whom he deals. These relationships can take a wide variety of forms. The responsible exercise of police power is not reducible to a simple problem of individual behavior. Social expectations, legal powers, occupational culture, organizational arrangements, disciplinary and rule-making procedures, and professional orientations of the police all interact.

It is the task of police administration to assure that the patterns of interaction conform to the principles of democratic government. The exercise of power has to be in line with the values of the public. Institutional leadership is of great importance in translating those values into operational guidelines. But in the process of articulating the police mission, institutional leaders influence both the police department and the public. They do not simply point the way and inspire their followers to follow. They educate and persuade. They match public sentiment to departmental capabilities and reconcile the two.

The police are a unique institution. Other social institutions exist to promote peace, order, and security but do not at the same time provide emotional support. The police, of all government institutions, have been beset by agonizing predicaments arising from a lack of a clear definition of their role. The need for public education about the capabilities and limits of police power is not a new problem but as long as money was rolling into police departments because of public pressure to decrease crime, there was little incentive for most chiefs of police to attempt to identify an overall police mission. The illusion that the police are primarily crime-fighters served the interests of the police hierarchy. Those police chief executives who took a broad view of the police mission and sought to impart that view to police operations often found themselves out of the profession or out of a job (Potts, 1980).

The Law Enforcement Assistance Administration no longer exists, and federal law enforcement agencies are concentrating on white-collar and organized crime. Local police are unable to prove that the billions of dollars spent during the past decade and a half have had a negative impact on crime. Police executives will have to work harder to justify claims for their share of scarce local resources. The challenge for the 1980s and beyond will be to earn public and official confidence in police performance. Institutional responsibility will have to be proved. To do so requires that institutional leadership be provided. The former is an indispensable ingredient in securing public and official confidence, which is essential for building, maintaining, and communicating responsibility.

Many mechanisms for securing police administrative responsibility have been developed. The problem is that little effort has been directed at explicating their limitations and potentials or at explicating the consequences of coexistence of not necessarily compatible assumptions about responsibility. The chapters that follow will provide such explication and will lead to a scheme for integration of the various mechanisms and premises.

2 Responsibility as a Problem of Obedience I

Legal Control of the Police

Theoretically, the easiest resolution to the problem of administrative responsibility is to prevent independent action by officials. Historically, this was the earliest approach. Law enforcement officers and all other public officials were ministerial agents of the king and merely carried out instructions. They were not expected or allowed to exercise their own judgment about how or when to act. Obedience was equated with responsibility. The situation could hardly have been simpler.

In modern democracies, the law may be considered a sovereign authority in society. Faith in the rule of law is usually considered one of the hallmarks of democratic society. The principles that no man is above the law, that everyone is equal before the law, and that ours is a government of laws not of men are widely proclaimed to be essential features of the American system. The primacy of law can be related to administrative responsibility by holding that the elected representatives of the people enact laws that express the desires of the public regarding the duties and prohibitions of the government.

From this perspective, there is no burden on an official to interpret his role or his duty. He is simply to do what the law requires and not do what the law forbids. The common law maintains that the law is the sole determinant of proper police procedure, as was stated by Lord Denning of the Court of Appeal in England in the case *R. v. Commissioner of Police of the Metropolis; ex parte Blackburn* (1968). Albert R. Blackburn had challenged police enforcement policy on gambling. The court ruled that a chief constable, as all other constables, is the servant of the law: "The responsibility for law enforcement lies on him. He is answerable to the law alone." Nor does the law recognize police discretion. At common law the police officer is sworn to uphold the law. He is presumed to have no other duty and to have no right to enforce laws selectively. He is the servant of the law with ministerial duties. In the eighteenth century, Sir William Blackstone stated that a peace officer who is present "when any felony is committed is bound by law to arrest the felon on pain of fine and imprisonment" (1765: Book 4, chap. 21).

In the United States, this interpretation of police duties is backed up by statute. According to the laws of most states, a policeman is required to arrest any person committing a crime of which he is aware. Illinois law, for example, states that it is the duty of every peace officer, "when any criminal offense or breach of the peace is committed or attempted in his presence, forthwith to apprehend the offender and bring him before some judge" (Rev. Stat., chap. 125, sec. 82). Blackstone's statement applied expressly to felonies; the Illinois statute has been interpreted to apply to misdemeanors as well as felonies (*People* v. *Davies*, 1934).

Enforcement of these common law principles is left to the courts as articulators of legal mandates. Court action against offending police officers can come in several ways. Police officers may be subject to criminal prosecution, both for misconduct (just as private citizens who violate the criminal law may be prosecuted) and for failure to fulfill their formal ministerial role. Blackstone's statement on police duty explicitly noted that failure to arrest is subject to fine and imprisonment. The penalty for failure to perform a mandatory duty under Illinois law is forfeiture of office and a fine and/or imprisonment up to five years (Rev. Stat., chap. 38, sec. 33-3). The United States Congress has affirmed this common law principle for District of Columbia police officers. Members of the Metropolitan Police Department are bound to arrest all lawbreakers or be subject to criminal prosecution leading to possible imprisonment for up to two years (D.C. Code Ann., sec. 4-143, Supp. III, 1970).

Police officers are also subject to civil liability for negligence or unacceptable conduct. Again, liability is not a new concept. Common law existing at the time the United States became independent of Britain held that if a public officer is guilty of neglect or breach of duty, "the party aggrieved shall have an action on the case, for damages assessed by a jury" (Blackstone, 1765: Book 3, chap 9). While negligence is actionable simply because it represents a danger to the public, misfeasance and nonfeasance are actionable because they represent a form of breach of contract. A police officer who fails to do his duty or misuses his position is guilty of violating the trust of those who employ him—the public.

The courts may take direct action against police misconduct. The courts may issue common law writs or injunctions prescribed by statute to review and control police conduct. They may also make use of a judicial tool, the exclusionary rule, created by the United States Supreme Court. The Court has decreed that officers of the law may not violate the law in order to apprehend criminals. The exclusionary rule provides that any illegally obtained evidence must be excluded from admission in a criminal trial.

In this chapter and the next, the various legal controls on police behavior and police practices will be examined. The forms of misconduct that are open to criminal prosecution, civil liability, and the exclusionary rule will be presented. Finally, the effectiveness of legal liability as a mechanism to secure police administrative responsibility will be evaluated. Before addressing the forms of legal oversight, however, the legalistic issue which is most contentious in contemporary American society—the legitimate dimensions of the police use of deadly force—must be discussed.

The Police Common Law Right to Use Force

As a general rule, a police officer may use whatever force is necessary to make an arrest. At common law this has historically included the right "to break open doors and even to kill a felon if he cannot otherwise be taken" (Blackstone, 1765: Book 4, chap. 11). It has also been a longstanding principle of common law that homicide is justifiable if an officer in the execution of his duty "kills a person that assaults and resists him" (Blackstone, 1765: Book 4, chap. 12). Additionally, police officers have the same right as any other citizen to use deadly force in self-defense or to prevent bodily injury to another person.

The greatest controversy in police use of deadly force has arisen with regard to the fleeing felon rule: the principle that use of deadly force is always legal when instrumental in apprehending a suspected felon. The only limiting condition under this rule is that no lesser amount of force could have subdued the suspect successfully. Several problems of definition in this rule are pointed out by critics. One is that many crimes are now felonies that formerly were not. Literal application of the old rule makes it legitimate to use deadly force against nonviolent offenders such as bigamists, perjurors, and panderers. A related problem of definition is that, in most areas, it is a felony to flee from arrest, even if the original offense is a misdemeanor. American courts have held that it is "better to allow one guilty

only of a misdemeanor to escape altogether than to take his life"
(*Reneau* v. *State*, Tenn., 1879). But as recently as 1962, an Australian
court ruled that someone fleeing from arrest for a misdemeanor for
which he may be arrested without a warrant may justifiably be killed if
there is no other way within the situation to take him into custody (*R.*
v. *Turner*).

According to the National Center for Health Statistics' Division of
Violence Statistics (1979) 3,082 citizens were killed by police officers
between 1968 and 1976. This figure represents an average of 342
deaths per year. To some people this is unacceptable. They blame the
high total on the looseness of the limitations on police use of deadly
force. Nevertheless, it is unclear how to resolve the problem. In the
ten-year period 1971-80 more than 1,100 police officers were killed in
the line of duty and more than 56,000 assaults on police officers were
reported (FBI, 1981).

Although the propriety of using deadly force to make arrests is
controversial, there is general agreement on the right of a police of-
ficer to use deadly force when he has reasonable grounds to fear for
his life or that of another person. It is extremely difficult for anyone
other than the officer to evaluate the necessity for using force. Police
officers often confront disruptive and hostile crises or emergency sit-
uations requiring a quick response, and they cannot weigh every fac-
tor in determining how to respond. Especially in apparently life-
threatening circumstances, the officer must decide in the heat of the
moment whether a perceived threat is serious enough to require a
drastic response. Judges have been extremely hesitant to make an
after-the-fact determination that an officer overreacted to a perceived
threat. The guiding principle for judges was laid out by United States
Supreme Court Justice Oliver Wendell Holmes in the 1921 case *Brown*
v. *United States*. His words have been incorporated directly into Aus-
tralian case law. Even though hindsight indicates that lesser force
would have averted the danger, it does not mean that force was unrea-
sonable: "Detached reflection cannot be demanded in the presence of
an uplifted knife" (*R.* v. *Howe*, 1958).

As a partial check on police use of excessive force, common law
recognizes the right of citizens to resist unlawful arrests. Citizens may,
in all cases of excessive police force, exercise self-defense, whether the
police action is lawful or unlawful. That right applies only to self-
defense from physical harm, however, and does not extend to self-
defense from infringement of liberty. The general principle is that
police orders are to be followed, even if they are later found to have
been unlawful. A defendant in a criminal case may be exonerated
from charges of resisting arrest if he shows the arrest itself to have

been unlawful. Nevertheless, he is subject to sanctions for the violent form such resistance may have taken. As testimony to the contemporary necessity of prompt, decisive police action, at least seven American states have by statute rejected the common law right to resist unlawful arrests.

In spite of the erosion of citizens' rights to use force to resist unlawful arrests, the public outcry that frequently follows a police shooting of a fleeing suspect, and legal arguments that use of deadly force against suspects amounts to denial of due process of law, the common law right of police officers to use deadly force against fleeing felons as well as to defend life remains essentially intact. In a highly armed society in which criminals often do not hesitate to shoot police officers, felons are justifiably regarded as dangerous people. The crimes for which they are wanted may not have been crimes of violence, but that does not mean they are not violent people or that society is not at risk if they are allowed to escape apprehension. American police are empowered to protect themselves and the public. To do so they are frequently compelled to use deadly force. The task is to ensure that force is used responsibly. That is one of the tasks of the courts in judicial review of police behavior and police practices. A blanket rejection of the power of deadly force cannot be expected.

The rest of this chapter will focus on the mechanisms available for judicial oversight of the police.

Police Criminal Liability

Police officers are criminally liable under the same terms as other citizens for most common crimes. A police officer who commits a burglary or a robbery is subject to the same conditions of arrest and prosecution as anyone else. For certain other common crimes police liability hinges on the relationship between the act and official duty. For homicides and assaults the issue is whether the officer acted within the scope of his duty, under legally sanctioned conditions, with proper restraint, and without malice or caprice. If these conditions are met, the force is generally justified. If these conditions are not met, the officer is subject to prosecution for murder, manslaughter, assault, battery, or criminal trespass with the same liability as a private citizen. This discussion of police criminal liability will focus on those offenses defined as requiring the participation of a public officer.

Criminal Liability under State Law

Many states have statutes providing criminal penalties for false arrest, false imprisonment, malicious prosecution, trespass, and assault and battery that may be invoked against police officers who exceed their authority. At least as long ago as 1603, English courts held that a law enforcement officer could not break into a house, even when armed with a valid warrant, unless he first identified himself and stated his purpose (*Semayne's Case*). In 1724, a sheriff was fined for "the unnecessary terror and outrage" caused by an arrest made upon a warrant when he broke down a door "without telling what they were or wherefore they came" (*Waterhouse* v. *Saltmarsh*). These offenses are far more commonly treated as civil matters and will be discussed fully in the next chapter.

More strictly criminal charges lodged against police concern corruption, usually extortion and bribery. Bribery and extortion both involve at least two parties. Bribery rests on a solicitation by a citizen of an agreement between a citizen and an officer to engage in a corrupt practice. The solicitation or agreement, not the act solicited or agreed to, constitutes the offense. The act itself need not be consumated, nor need it be within the officer's scope of duty. Extortion, in contrast, rests on a demand by an officer that something of value be provided to him in exchange for some alteration in his behavior connected with his official capacity. An officer is guilty of extortion if he asks for money or property either to perform or to refrain from performing his duty. He is equally guilty if the agreement is made or the transaction is effected through an agent, so long as he is aware of it and does not attempt to prevent it. A police officer would not be guilty of extortion if he demanded money to secure a government service not provided by the police department.

Two other corrupt police practices subject to criminal prosecution are obstruction of justice (if an officer willfully prevents or impedes legal processes in order to protect himself or another individual) and perjury (willfully and falsely testifying as to material issues in a legal proceeding, either judicial or administrative, if the latter is expressly covered by statute). For perjury, it is not enough that the testimony be false; it must be knowingly false, have a corrupt purpose, and be material to the point in question. That is, it must be directly relevant to the matter in controversy and calculated to affect the determination of the issue at hand.

Bribery, extortion, obstruction of justice, and perjury are corrupt practices that may be engaged in by any public official, not just police officers. Offenses dealing with search and arrest warrants, however, relate almost solely to police malpractice and are not usually considered forms of police corruption. There are four major offenses of this type: malicious procurement of a warrant, execution of an invalid warrant, improper execution of a valid warrant, and conducting a warrantless search or making a warrantless arrest without probable cause.

Only eighteen states have statutes governing these matters, and all of them define the offenses as misdemeanors. The most widely proscribed violation in this group is malicious procurement of a warrant. Two states provide specific penalties. Under Alabama law, an individual who improperly secures a warrant is subject to imprisonment in a county jail for up to one year or to six months hard labor and/or a fine of no less than $25 and no more than $500 (Ala. Code, Title 15, sec. 99). Under Florida law, the available penalties are imprisonment up to six months and a fine not to exceed $500 (Fla. Stat., Sec. 933.16).

Police officers are criminally liable for improper execution of a valid warrant in only twelve states. Improper execution of a warrant occurs when it is served at the wrong time (some warrants are day warrants), in the wrong jurisdiction, without following other limitations, or is executed with unnecessary severity. Again, specific punishments for violation of such code provisions are generally not stated except that the violation is identified as a misdemeanor. Only Florida prescribes the available penalties for officers who are convicted of the offense. The officer is liable to suspension or removal from his position as a peace officer and to penal sanctions of up to six months in jail and a fine of $500.

Eight states have enacted laws providing criminal liability for knowingly executing an invalid warrant. It is a criminal offense for a police officer to conduct a warrantless search without probable cause in only five states. As with the other related statutes, most states with laws against warrantless searches do not prescribe punishment except to identify the offense as a misdemeanor. The only exception is Virginia, where liability includes a fine of no less than $50 and no more than $500 and/or imprisonment in a county or municipal jail from one to six months.

Criminal Liability under Federal Law

Several federal statutes provide criminal liability for federal law enforcement officers that are similar to the state laws discussed above. There are also federal statutes that apply to law enforcement officers at the state and local levels. The latter group of laws are most directly relevant to this discussion, but the laws regulating federal agents will be addressed briefly, as a point of comparison with state codes.

The United States Code contains statutes regulating arrest, search, and seizure which are similar to the few existing state laws. State and federal laws differ in that the federal laws explicitly identify the sanctions that may be imposed (unlike the usual state laws, which merely classify such offenses as misdemeanors). Each of the federal statues covering improper execution of a valid warrant and improper procurement of a valid warrant prescribes the same penalty: "Whoever, in executing a search warrant, willfully exceeds his authority or exercises it with unnecessary severity shall be fined not more than one thousand dollars or imprisoned not more than one year" (18 U.S.C. 2234).

The law covering warrantless searches is more complex than the similar state laws and is more complex than the two previously cited statutes. It also provides for greater variety in penalties. It states that an officer, agent, or employee of the United States, engaged in the enforcement of any law of the United States, who searches any premises used and occupied as a private dwelling without a search warrant or who maliciously and without reasonable cause searches any other building or property without a search warrant, shall be fined for a first offense not more than $1,000 and, for a subsequent offense, not more than $1,000 or imprisoned more than one year or both. The section does not apply to any person serving a warrant of arrest; arresting or attempting to arrest a person committing or attempting to commit an offense in his presence, or who has committed an offense in his presence, or is suspected on reasonable grounds of having committed a felony; or making a search at the request or invitation or with the consent of the occupant of the premises (18 U.S.C. 2236).

The federal statutes on improper execution of a warrant and improper procurement of a warrant are worded similarly to the state statutes. In both cases the laws are briefly worded and presume that the conditions constituting improper behavior are known without having to be spelled out in the statutes. The federal law on warrantless search, contrarily, specifies the significant dimensions of the offense and delimits conditions that qualify the general proscriptions. This law provides an example of how state laws could be made less general and presumably more enforceable. The most important similarity between state and federal laws is that both sets require the same elements to be present to constitute an offense. Under either jurisdiction, the prosecutor must be able to prove that the officer's conduct was knowing, malicious, or both. The officer's intention, not just his objective conduct, is at issue. He must be shown to have acted so as to deprive a citizen of his rights. Federal law is more severe in its penalty structure than is state law. While state codes generally subject violators to a maximum fine of $500 and/or incarceration up to a maximum of six months, the United States Code allows fines up to $1,000 and/or imprisonment up to one year.

The federal criminal laws that are directly applicable to police misconduct involve police corruption and police action intended to deprive citizens of their rights under the United States Constitution. The primary device for federal criminal litigation of police corruption or "racketeering" is the Hobbs Act. This act provides for a fine of up to $10,000 and/or imprisonment up to twenty years in a federal penitentiary for obstructing, delaying, or affecting commerce by robbery or extortion. Section b.2. of the act defines extortion as obtaining property from another, "with his consent, induced by wrongful use of actual or threatened force, violence or fear, or under color of official right" (18 U.S.C. 1951). The police are vulnerable under this law because "color of official right" includes receiving money or property in return for nonenforcement of the law.

The antiracketeering law is also backed up by two additional laws that have been used in police corruption cases. The federal perjury statute and the federal statute covering false sworn statements have been used against police officers attempting to conceal or cover up corrupt practices which are contrary to federal law. The perjury statute is most often invoked against officers who lie to or mislead grand juries. The false statement statute is most often invoked against officers who lie to or attempt to mislead investigative officers. The perjury law requires corroboration to prove "beyond a reasonable doubt" that the misinformation was willfully given (18 U.S.C. 1621); the false statement law allows proof of intent to be shown through introduction of two contradictory statements. (No other support for the charge is required except that the statements were of such a nature that one of them must logically be untrue [18 U.S.C. 1623.c.].) The penalties for conviction under 18 U.S.C. 1621 are a fine of up to $2,000 and/or imprisonment up to five years. The penalties under 18 U.S.C. 1623 are a fine up to $10,000 and/or imprisonment up to five years.

The other major source of police criminal liability under federal law is the Civil Rights Act of 1871 (also known as the Ku Klux Klan Act of 1871). The statutes contained in this act are 18 U.S.C. 241 and 18 U.S.C. 242. Both of these statutes were enacted under the authority provided to Congress by section 5 of the Fourteenth Amendment of the United States Constitution. The amendment provides: "No state shall make or enforce any law which shall abridge the privileges or immunities of citizens of United States; nor shall any State deprive any person of life, liberty or property, without due process of law; nor deny to any person within its jurisdiction the equal protection of the laws" (sec. 1). Section 5 provides for congressional power of enforcement by appropriate legislation.

Sections 241 and 242 of the United States Criminal Code are intended specifically to punish deprivation of due process of law and equal protection of the laws. Section 241 applies to private conspiracies to deprive citizens of their rights. Originally directed against the Ku Klux Klan, it makes it a federal crime for two or more individuals to go upon the highway or private property in disguise to injure, threaten, oppress, or intimidate a citizen in the enjoyment of his rights. The agreement, not the action taken, constitutes the offense. Conviction under 18 U.S.C. 241 is liable to a fine of $10,000 and ten years imprisonment, or both.

Section 242 applies directly to police officers. It creates a federal misdemeanor for state officers acting to deprive individuals within their jurisdiction of civil rights. If the violation of rights leads to the death of the individual acted against, the penalty may be life imprisonment. The statute was intended to prevent Klansmen from avoiding prosecution under Section 241 by claiming that they were, in fact, "special deputies" enforcing the law and not conspirators violating the law. Nevertheless, the law is clearly worded and was intended to prevent bonafide peace officers from violating individual rights. The law specifies: "Whoever, under color of any law, statute, ordinance, regulation, or custom, willfully subjects any inhabitant of any State, Territory, or District to the deprivation of any rights, privileges, or immunities secured or protected by the Constitution or laws of the United States, or to different punishments, pains or penalties ... shall be fined not more than one thousand dollars or imprisoned not more than one year, or both; and if death results shall be subject to imprisonment for any term of years or for life."

Unlike section 241, this section applies to inhabitants, not just citizens. It covers all rights secured or protected by federal law and the United States Constitution. In *United States* v. *Classic* (1941), the Supreme Court defined the "color of law" provision: "Misuse of power possessed by the virtue of state law and made possible only because the wrongdoer is clothed with the authority of state law is action under color of law." In other words, a police officer is liable under section 242 even if he is not acting within his scope of duties and even if he is acting directly contrary to state law. The test is whether he was known to be an officer. His position, not his actions in a specific case, creates his liability. Furthermore, if an officer is involved in a conspiracy with private individuals he is liable under both section 241 and section 242.

If he is involved in a conspiracy with other officers only, he is liable under 18 U.S.C. 88, which provides for up to two years imprisonment for conspiracy to commit any federal offense.

Section 242, with its broad proscription of violation of civil rights, may be seen as a legal barrier to any form of police street justice. Any police action that violates due process could fall under that statute. An arrest without probable cause, improper use of a warrant, coerced confessions, illegal searches and seizures, and all other conduct that contravenes proper procedure in the administration of justice is potentially a misuse of power under color of law to deny an individual his rights. Since it is a criminal matter, however, intent must be proved. Mere negligence would not be actionable.

Enforcement of Police Criminal Liability

A significant number of offenses could provide the basis for criminal prosecution of police officers who violate the bounds of responsible administrative behavior. To evaluate the effectiveness of criminal liability as a mechanism for ensuring responsible behavior, it is necessary to examine the record of enforcement of the criminal law as it relates to the police.

Enforcement of State Law

State criminal prosecutions of police violations of individual rights (as distinct from common crimes such as burglary and from corrupt practice such as extortion) have been few and widely dispersed in time and location. The primary offenses related to abuse of authority germane to the exclusionary rule or to personal injury other than physical assault are false imprisonment and trespass. Each of these may be subsumed under the common law criminal offense of official oppression, which involves an individual who, while exercising or under color of exercising his office, inflicts injury other than extortion upon any person.

In an early American case it was ruled that if an officer makes an arrest without a warrant, he does so at his own risk. If it turns out that no felony has been committed, he faces criminal prosecution (*State* v. *Clark*, Del., 1793). Nevertheless, the United States Supreme Court has determined that the prevailing standard is the common law rule: an officer may validly arrest without a warrant anyone who commits an offense in his presence or anyone whom he has reasonable grounds to believe has committed or is about to commit a felony (*U.S.* v. *Watson*, 1976). The test of reasonableness is the prudent person test, that is, the officer must be able to demonstrate that the facts before him at the time of the arrest were such that a person of ordinary care and prudence would be led to believe that the offense had been committed (*Stacey* v. *Emery*, 1878). In other words, the officer must have only probable cause to believe the person arrested has committed a felony. He does not have to be certain.

False imprisonment criminal liability for police officers may arise from acting upon an invalid warrant, making a misdemeanor arrest without warrant and without witnessing the offense, or making a felony arrest without probable cause. Police officers are immune from false imprisonment prosecution when they act on warrants which are apparently valid. Only if an officer fraudulently procures a warrant may he be convicted. Excluding use of fraudulent warrants for purposes of extortion, there seems to have been only one successful prosecution of an officer for an arrest made pursuant to a valid warrant. In that case the officer illegally attempted to take an individual into custody. When the individual fled, the officer secured a warrant for resisting arrest. Since the initial detention was illegal, the warrant was void and the officer was guilty of false arrest (*Montgomery* v. *State*, Tex., 1943). There also appears to have been only one successful criminal prosecution of officers for false imprisonment based on a warrantless misdemeanor arrest, and the convictions were overturned on curious logic. False imprisonment is either a high-grade misdemeanor or a felony, but in this case the officers made the illegal arrest for violation of a municipal ordinance. The California Court of Appeals stated that the officers would not commit an offense of a more serious character than that which they accused the person arrested of having committed (*Ex parte Dillon*, 1919). The clear pattern is that only arrests without probable cause and with malice may give rise to criminal conviction of police officers.

There have been even fewer successful prosecutions of police officers for trespass than for false imprisonment. In 1822 a constable was convicted of criminal trespass for forcing open a door to serve a civil process (*State* v. *Armfield*, N.C., 1822). In 1876 two officers were indicted for criminal trespass, but the trial court sustained a demurrer to indictment which was upheld by the Arkansas Supreme Court (*State* v. *Leathers*, 1876). The only two twentieth-century convictions of police officers for trespass actions were prosecuted on other grounds. In the New York case of *People* v. *Summers* (1903), officers had occupied a tobacco store for eleven days on the pretext of the code requirement that they inspect such establishments. The officers were convicted of oppression. In a 1920 South Carolina case turning on search and seizure questions, an officer and chief of police were convicted of assault. They had taken a suitcase from a porter in a railway station in the belief that its owner was transporting liquor. They had no probable cause and no search warrant, and the state supreme court upheld their convictions (*State* v. *Wagstaff*).

Enforcement of Federal Law

The general pattern of nonenforcement that prevails at the state level is even more evident at the federal level. No federal officer has been convicted under 18 U.S.C. 2234, 18 U.S.C. 2235, or 18 U.S.C. 2236. Lack of vigilance or the hidden nature of violations of citizens' rights may account for the small number of state convictions and the absence of federal convictions of federal officers. The small number of convictions of police officers for violating the Civil Rights Act of 1871, however, has resulted from the United States Supreme Court's very narrow interpretation of the requirements of Section 242, that guilt rests on having acted under color of law willfully to deprive an individual of rights secured by federal law.

The leading case outlining the scope of criminal liability under Section 242 is *Screws* v. *United States* (1945). M. Claud Screws was the sheriff of Baker County, Georgia. He and his deputies were convicted by a federal court of violating the civil rights of a black man who had been arrested for theft. The victim had allegedly reached for a gun and had used insulting language. He was beaten with fists and a blackjack until he was unconscious, and he later died. Evidence was presented at the trial that Screws had a longstanding animus toward the victim and had threatened to "get" him.

The indictment leading to Screws's conviction charged that the victim had been deprived of "the right not to be deprived of life without due process of law" and "the right to be tried, upon the charge on which he was arrested, by due process of law." The conviction was appealed on the grounds that the law was unconstitutional because it was vague. The Supreme Court ruled that the claim that "rights . . . secured by the Constitution" was not illegally vague; in fact, the rights attendant upon due process of law and equal protection of the law were sufficiently known. The decision by Justice William O. Douglas noted, however, that the definitions of due process rendered by the Court were "broad and fluid." Under the circumstances, he admitted, use of "the customary standard of guilt for statutory crimes" would place local law enforcement officers on "treacherous ground." Justice Douglas believed that, if that customary standard were used, an officer could be found guilty by virtue of violating some aspect of due process defined by the Court after the act. Therefore, he reasoned that it was necessary to read Section 242 more narrowly than other statutes. The alternative he settled upon was to "construe 'willfully' as connoting a purpose to deprive a person of a specific constitutional right." The result of this construction was that, although a helpless person was beaten to death in a "shocking and revolting episode in law enforcement," the conviction of his attackers was overturned.

The essence of the Court's ruling was that conviction under Section 242 required that the defendant be proved to have specifically intended to deprive the victim of a constitutional right. A generally bad purpose was not sufficient. Since it was not clear that Screws' intent was to deprive his victim of due process, he was acquitted at his retrial.

The interpretation that liability under Section 242 requires specific intent to deprive of rights rather than a general intent to harm which involves deprivation of right has had a chilling effect on enforcement. In the few cases that have arisen under Section 242 the element of specific intent was clear. Justice Douglas, in *Screws*, had used as a prototypical example of willfull deprivation of rights the 1879 case *Ex parte Virginia* in which a Virginia state judge had continued to bar blacks from jury duty after the United States Supreme Court had declared the practice unconstitutional. The 242 cases subsequent to *Screws* have been based on actions that clearly violate due process requirements. They usually deal with what Justice Douglas labeled in *Screws* "trial by ordeal"—the substitution of physical coercion or punishment for legal process and judgment.

The incidents in the prosecutions under Section 242 illuminate the difficulty involved in making a case under the section. In each case the behavior of the officers was so clearly contrary to due process that little doubt could exist about intent. For example, in *United States* v. *Lynch* (1951), a private detective who had been issued a special police officer's badge and who was assisted by a regular sworn police officer was convicted for beating four individuals until they confessed to thefts. In *Miller* v. *United States* (1962), police officers were prosecuted for attempting to coerce confessions by intimidating the suspects with dogs and by beatings. In *United States* v. *Price* (1966), the sheriff of Neshoba County, Mississippi, a deputy sheriff, and a police officer were prosecuted for releasing three civil rights workers from jail and killing them with the purpose of punishing them.

The Exclusionary Rule

Although there has been limited use of criminal liability to secure police responsibility in conformance with the rule of law, judges have been very willing to use their oversight power through the so-called exclusionary rule to exclude from trial any evidence gathered by illicit police practices. The exclusionary rule only became an issue of public concern in the 1960s following several celebrated decisions by the United States Supreme Court. Most notable were probably the *Mapp* (1961) and *Miranda* (1966) decisions. These cases became famous because in them the Court imposed the exclusionary rule on local police. The rule had been accepted at the federal level eighty years earlier. Anglo-American criminal procedure has always allowed judges to exclude some matters from admission in evidence. It has long been accepted that hearsay is inadmissible, that examination and testimony must be relevant, and that only best evidence may be admitted. The exclusionary rule as it applies to control of police practices is controversial because it excludes direct, relevant, best evidence.

Development of the Exclusionary Rule

The exclusionary rule has been developed to provide a mechanism for judicial protection of citizens' rights under the Fourth, Fifth, and Sixth Amendments to the United States Constitution. The Fourth Amendment states that the right of the people to be secure "against unreasonable searches and seizure, shall not be violated." The Fifth Amendment provides that no one "shall be compelled in any criminal case to be a witness against himself." The Sixth Amendment provides that in all criminal prosecutions an accused person "shall enjoy the right . . . to have the assistance of counsel for his defense."

The first federal criminal case involving the exclusion of illegally obtained evidence was *Boyd* v. *United States* (1886). It was not until 1914 in *Weeks* v. *United States* that something approaching a rule was stated. In *Weeks*, the Court ruled: "The tendency of those who execute the criminal laws of the country to obtain convictions by means of unlawful seizures and coerced confessions should find no sanction in the judgements of the Courts which are charged at all times with the support of the Constitution."

Two primary reasons were advanced by the Court for supporting the exclusionary rule in subsequent decisions. First is the "clean hands" rationale, holding that the enforcers of the law must not be allowed to violate the law even to catch criminals. If the government's officers are permitted to win cases by "dirty" methods, they dirty the law. Perhaps the best statement of this view is Justice Louis Brandeis's dissent in *Olmstead* v. *United States* (1928): "If the government becomes a law breaker, it breeds contempt for law." To declare that the government may commit crimes to secure convictions of private criminals "would bring terrible retribution," and the Court should resolutely reject that pernicious doctrine. Three decades later, Justice William J. Brennan echoed that sentiment when he declared in *Jencks* v. *United States* (1957) that the interest of the government "is not that it should win cases but that justice shall be done."

The second rationale advanced to support the exclusionary rule is the one most directly at issue in examining police responsibility. In the 1948 case, *United States* v. *Di Re*, Justice Robert H. Jackson countered the claim that the exclusion of illicitly obtained evidence made law enforcement difficult and uncertain, stating that the Constitution had been designated "to place obstacles in the way of a too permeating police surveillance." The intent of the Fourth Amendment is, he said, to protect free people from a graver danger "than the escape of some criminals from punishment." This rationale rests on the premise that the exclusionary rule will deter police from irresponsible behavior because "illegal searches and seizures will not be undertaken if they will have no meaningful effect" (*United States* v. *Schipani*, 1970).

In spite of the importance attached to the rule by several justices of the United States Supreme Court, the Court was slow to extend it to cover state officers in state trials. One reason for the hesitance to impose the rule on the states may have been the fact that it is not an obvious element in due process. When serving as a judge of the state of New York, the customarily liberal Justice Benjamin N. Cardozo rejected the rule. In *People* v. *Defore* (1926), he stated that the federal ruling in *Weeks* was unreasonable because it makes no sense that "the criminal is to go free because the constable has blundered."

Another reason for the hesitance to extend the rule is that it is not based on common law. Only in the United States have judicial officials been given a broad mandate to exclude illicitly obtained evidence. A 1955 decision by the House of Lords in Great Britain (the Law Lords sit as the highest court of appeal in Britain) held that, in determining whether evidence is admissible, the only test is its relevance, not how it was obtained. The trial judge always has discretion to disallow evidence that operates unfairly against the accused, but illegally or improperly obtained evidence is not of itself to be excluded (*Kuruma* v. *The Queen*, 1955). In Scotland the position is that "irregularity in the obtaining of evidence does not necessarily make that evidence inadmissible" (*Lawrie* v. *Muir*, 1950). The court must consider the reliability of the evidence and the nature of the misconduct.

The Supreme Court of Canada has denied that a trial judge has discretion to exclude evidence just because of impropriety or illegality by the police in obtaining the evidence. In the case *R.* v. *Wray* (1971), a trial judge had excluded admission into evidence of a murder weapon that had been discovered as a result of an illegally obtained statement. The Ontario Court of Appeals upheld the exclusion on the grounds that the courts should suppress evidence that brings the administration of justice into disrepute (the dirty-hands rationale). Justice Ronald Martland, writing the opinion for the Supreme Court, held that the fairness of the trial and not the administration of justice in general is the proper concern of a judge; therefore, exclusion of evidence can only be based on ensuring that the trial is fairly conducted.

In Canada, Australia, New Zealand, Scotland, England, and Wales the right of the judge to exclude evidence obtained improperly is recognized, but it is also recognized that the right is to be exercised only in extreme circumstances. Evidence obtained by illegal searches and seizures and wrongfully obtained confessions is admissible if relevant and reliable. Technical violations of procedure do not automatically lead to exclusion. In other words, it is considerd abhorrent that a criminal go free because the constable has blundered. The police officer's errors are to be dealt with by means other than excluding good (that is, relevant and reliable) evidence.

The Exclusionary Rule since 1961

In 1961, the Supreme Court of the United States rejected both its own precedent in *Wolf* v. *Colorado* (1949) and the generally accepted principles of common law. In an otherwise insignificant case, *Mapp* v. *Ohio*, the Court decreed that the ruling in *Weeks* applied to state officers. In the *Mapp* case, Cleveland police officers broke into Mrs. Mapp's home on the basis of information that she and her daughter were harboring a fugitive and were in possession of gambling materials ("policy paraphernalia"). After a thorough search of the home uncovered neither the fugitive nor the gambling materials, Mrs. Mapp and her daughter were arrested for illegal possession of "obscene material." The appellate courts of Ohio upheld the conviction, and the case went to the United States Supreme Court. The Court split 6-3 with the majority holding that under the Fourth Amendment "all evidence obtained by searches and seizures in violation of the Constitution is . . . inadmissible in a state court."

The Court left little doubt about the implications of the *Mapp* decision for the belief that police responsibility could be secured through judicial oversight. Six years earlier, the California Supreme Court had stated in *People* v. *Cahan* (1955) that the exclusionary rule was necessary at the state level to control police behavior because "other remedies have completely failed to secure compliance" with constitutional provisions. The United States Supreme Court concurred and in rehearing a companion case to *Mapp* (*Linkletter* v. *Walker*, 1965), it stated that, as applied in *Mapp*, the purpose of the exclusionary rule "was to deter the lawless action of the police."

Once the exclusionary rule had been extended to cover physical evidence, it was only logical to extend it to cover oral evidence. In 1964, the Court ruled in *Massiah* v. *United States* that the right to counsel extended to individuals subjected to police interrogation after indictment. Four weeks after *Massiah* the Court ruled that the right to counsel began while an individual was still a suspect. In *Escobedo* v. *Illinois*, it held that "when the process shifts from investigatory to accusatory . . . the accused must be permitted to consult with his lawyer." Both *Massiah* and *Escobedo* stirred a storm of protest from law enforcement officers all across the country. *Escobedo* also roused the ire of four of the nine justices. The dissent by Justices Byron R. White, Tom C. Clark, and Potter Stewart (Justice John Marshall Harlan wrote a separate dissent) said the decision was unworkable unless police cars were equipped with public defenders and reflected "a deep seated distrust of law enforcement officers everywhere." The most vocal opposition to the Court's extension of the exclusionary rule, however, came following the 1966 *Miranda* decision.

Ernesto Miranda was an uneducated, unemployed, petty criminal who was convicted of raping and kidnapping an eighteen-year-old woman at knifepoint. He was identified by the woman as her assailant and confessed to police both orally and in writing within two hours of her identification. The confession was neither coerced nor elicited by police promises. Miranda had not requested a lawyer during his interrogation nor had he refused to talk to the police. At his trial Miranda's attorney objected to admission of the confession on the grounds that it had been made without benefit of counsel. The Arizona Supreme Court upheld the conviction and ruled that since Miranda had not requested counsel he could not claim that it was denied to him.

Chief Justice Earl Warren delivered the opinion of the United States Supreme Court in *Miranda* v. *Arizona*. He stated that, even though the confession may not have been involuntary according to traditional criteria, it may not have been "truly the product of free choice." Under conditions of custodial interrogation, an individual is subject to psychological stresses, which are just as real as physical coercion. In such circumstances it is not enough to avoid purposeful deprivation of constitutional rights. The government must produce evidence against the accused "by its own independent labors." This means that the individual must be explicitly informed of what his rights are. For protection of personal rights to be fully effective, an individual must be informed of them when first subjected to police questioning and in any way deprived of his freedom of action.

To comply with the Court's ruling, most American police departments began to issue "Miranda cards" to their officers. These cards carry the warnings outlined by Chief Justice Warren in the *Miranda* case. Whenever a person is arrested, the arresting officer must read the person the list of his rights before questioning may begin. The warnings are (1) the right to remain silent; (2) the right to talk to an attorney and have him present during questioning; (3) the right to appointed counsel before questioning if one cannot be afforded; and (4) the right to exercise these rights at any time and refuse to answer any question or make any statement. After reading the warnings, the officer must ask if the person understands them as they were read. If he says he does, the officer may then ask if, with the warnings in mind, the individual wishes to make a statement. Many departments also provide officers with forms to be signed by the suspect if he is willing to waive his rights.

Since the *Miranda* decision, the courts have spent a great deal of time filling in the outline drawn by *Mapp* and *Miranda*. Many people believed that with the end of the Warren Court in 1969 the new justices appointed by Presidents Richard Nixon and Gerald Ford would back away from the strictness of the activist decisions of the mid-1960s. Some retreat was perceived in the first exclusionary case to be taken up by the Burger Court. In *Harris* v. *New York* (1971), the Court ruled that statements made to police without benefit of *Miranda* warnings, although inadmissible as direct evidence, could be used to impeach contradictory statements made under oath at trial. In the *Harris* case the trial judge had allowed the admission of an excludable statement after the defendant offered conflicting testimony. The judge advised the jury that they could not take the statement as evidence of guilt but could take it as an indication of the defendant's credibility. In upholding the trial judge's decision, Chief Justice Warren Burger wrote that every defendant could exercise his right to testify on his own behalf or to refrain from testifying. "But that privilege cannot be construed to include the right to commit perjury."

Whether *Harris* represents a retreat from *Miranda* is open to question. The *Harris* decision actually paralleled that in an earlier Supreme Court case *Walder* v. *United States* (1954), which allowed an impeachment exception to the exclusionary rule. If *Mapp* and *Miranda* were merely an effort to make protections that were available at the federal level also available at the state level, *Harris* makes sense in light of *Walder*. Moreover, the Burger Court has had numerous opportunities to reject *Miranda* but has failed to do so. In *Doyle* v. *Ohio* (1976), for example, the trial court had allowed police to testify that defendants had refused to make a statement when arrested. The judge had permitted the testimony because the defendants claimed at the trial that they had been framed. The judge reasoned that if someone were framed, he would attempt to make an exculpatory statement at the first opportunity. He accepted the police testimony as impeachment. The Supreme Court held that the admission of the police statement was contrary to *Miranda*.

Clarification of Exclusionary Rule Coverage: Search and Seizure

It is impossible to survey all the cases that have been decided on exclusionary grounds, but some of the refinements and clarifications of the rule can be discussed. The two major issues related to the exclusionary rule are the circumstances under which searches and seizures are legitimate and the conditions under which confessions are sufficiently voluntary.

In *Won Sun* v. *United States* (1963), Justice Brennan set up a two-element test for the necessity of disallowing evidence. First, the exclusionary rule has no applicability when the government learns of the evidence from an independent source; and, second, the exclusionary rule has no applicability when the connection between the lawless conduct of the police and the discovery of the challenged evidence has become so attenuated as to dissipate the taint of the discovery. The first exception is sometimes called the inevitable discovery doctrine. This doctrine allows illegally obtained evidence to be admitted if it can be proved also to have been available through legitimate means.

The inevitable discovery doctrine has been criticized as having the potential to undermine the exclusionary rule because it allows police to "test" the rule by seeing how far tolerance can be pushed. Critics suggest that the doctrine will encourage officers to use illegal shortcut methods instead of more time- and effort-consuming legal methods. The Missouri Court of Appeals has recently explained why the doctrine should be maintained in spite of the criticism: "It serves the underlying policy of the exclusionary rule by denying admission of evidence obtained by exploitation of illegal police conduct." It also avoids the undeserved and socially undesirable "exclusion of relevant evidence of great probative value." To ensure that the exception is properly administered, the court stated that it should be invoked only if the prosecution can prove clearly and convincingly that the state would have acquired the evidence through legal means regardless of illegality and that the police officers involved did not act in bad faith to accelerate the discovery of the evidence (*State* v. *Byrne*, 1979).

Several state cases fall under the attenuation doctrine. Under Justice Brennan's second exception, evidence is admissible if, despite initial police impropriety, time or circumstances change so that a new situation has arisen. For example, in *State* v. *Fortier* (Ariz., 1979), the defense moved to suppress admission of marijuana discovered after a car had been stopped without probable cause. The trial judge admitted the evidence. The officer had asked the defendant if he had a key to the trunk to determine whether he had a full set of keys. Attenuation existed because the driver went to the rear of the car on his own initiative and opened the trunk.

The exception for attenuation should not be overdrawn. The clear standard is still that illegally secured evidence will be suppressed. The seizure of narcotics paraphernalia "in plain view" was illegal and the evidence inadmissible when the officer stopped the car on the basis of intuition (*Schneider* v. *State*, Fla., 1977). Furthermore, the exclusionary rule covers indirect as well as direct products of unlawful arrests as in the Pennsylvania case, *Commonwealth* v. *Ruckinger* (1976). A man was arrested for possession of stolen property without probable cause. An hour and a half later, he was allowed to telephone his father. During the course of the conversation, he was overheard by officers to say, "Get rid of the stuff." A patrol unit dispatched to the father's house saw him driving away in his car. The officers stopped him on a highway and received consent to search the car. They discovered several stolen guns. The guns were admitted in evidence. On appeal it was ruled that the information was available only through the illegal arrest and the separate stop of the father was, therefore, also unlawful.

Both the inevitable discovery doctrine and the attenuation exception to the exclusionary rule are based on the premise that an accused is entitled to be as well off as if officers had not illegally seized evidence, but "he is not entitled to be any better off" (*Lord* v. *Kelley*, 1963). The courts attempt by these exceptions to protect society's interest in preventing criminals from escaping liability only because of inadvertent or minor technical violations by police. At the same time, however, the courts are diligent in trying to preserve personal privacy from illegal intrusion. Especially suspect are body searches.

In 1952, nine years before *Mapp* applied the exclusionary rule to the states, the Supreme Court had decided that certain invasions of personal privacy were inadmissible because they violated due process of law. In *Rochin* v. *California*, police officers were held to have engaged in "conduct that shocks the conscience." In this case, Los Angeles

County deputy sheriffs had probable cause to believe that Antonio Rochin was dealing in narcotics. Without securing an arrest warrant or a search warrant, three deputies entered his home and broke into his bedroom. When the deputies entered, Rochin swallowed two morphine capsules. The deputies beat him in the hope that he would vomit the capsules. When he did not do so, he was bound and gagged and taken to a hospital, where his stomach was pumped. The capsules were used as evidence, and Rochin was sentenced to the Los Angeles County Jail for sixty days. The United States Supreme Court unanimously overturned the conviction on the grounds that the police conduct offended "decencies of civilized conduct."

For Justice Felix Frankfurter, who wrote the majority decision, the crux of the issue in *Rochin* was the nature of the intrusion made into Rochin's body. A forced stomach pumping was egregious. Justices Hugo L. Black and William O. Douglas concurred with overturning the conviction but argued that the "does-it-shock-the-conscience" test would lead to a case-by-case approach. They contended that the important fact was that the evidence was obtained without regard for accepted procedures. Five years later, the implications of the majority view were a cause for new Court action.

Rochin was found to have been deprived of due process of law because his stomach was pumped to extract evidence. In *Briethaupt* v. *Abram* (1957), a body intrusion was found acceptable. Paul H. Briethaupt was charged with involuntary manslaughter after he was involved in a fatal traffic accident. Officers who responded to the accident call found an empty liquor bottle in his pickup truck and could smell liquor on his breath. While he was unconscious in a hospital, a physician took a blood sample. His serum alcohol count was 0.17 percent. The blood-test results were admitted as evidence, and he was convicted. He appealed on the grounds that the involuntary intrusion into his body fell under the *Rochin* "does-it-shock-the-conscience" test. The Supreme Court rejected that argument by holding that a blood test is a common procedure and neither "brutal" nor "offensive." *Briethaupt* was reaffirmed in *Schmerber* v. *California* (1966).

As a general rule, decisions by law enforcement officers to make intrusions into a person's body are subject to review on three questions: Is there probable cause to believe that evidence is to be found in the body? Is the intrusion into the body to seize the evidence reasonable under the circumstances? Is the intrusion to be carried out in a reasonable manner? Since the Court's rulings in *Briethaupt* and *Schmerber*, many states have adopted implied consent laws, which require individuals to submit to alcohol tests whenever an officer has probable cause to believe a person is driving under the influence. If the individual refuses, he loses his driving privileges as well as faces prosecution for the moving violation. In a related case, the United States Court of Appeals for the Tenth Circuit held that a threat to extract a urine sample from a suspected drug user did not taint the evidence acquired when the suspect submitted to a urinalysis. The court ruled that had the threatened use of the catheter occurred, the *Rochin* test would have made the evidence inadmissible (*Yanez* v. *Romero*, 1980).

The Louisiana Supreme Court reiterated the illegality of an actual intrusion (in contrast to a threatened intrusion). The police had good probable cause to believe that a female suspect had hidden a bottle containing Seconal in her vagina and told her she would be subjected to a pelvic examination. The court ruled that she had not consented to the examination simply because she acquiesced and that the circumstances did not require prompt action that precluded waiting for a valid court-authorized search. A female officer had custody of the suspect and could prevent her from destroying the evidence, and because the pills were known to be in a bottle, they could not have been absorbed by her body (*State* v. *Fontenot*, 1980).

If the intrusion requires a surgical procedure, as in removal of a bullet, the test of its legality rests on the risk to the suspect (or victim). If there is a grave risk to life or health, the removal cannot usually be compelled. If there is negligible risk, it may be compelled. Six points must be covered before the removal may be legal and its fruits admissible in court: (1) prosecuting authorities must present the matter to a neutral and disinterested magistrate for his decison; (2) a strong case for probable cause must be established, and a higher degree of probability may be required than for a more conventional search warrant; (3) medical testimony should be presented (preferably from more than one doctor) that removal would constitute substantially no risk to the patient; (4) the case should be one of grave public interest, such as murder or attempted muurder; (5) the magistrate may require an adversary hearing at which the defendant's counsel appears; and (6) an opportunity to appeal the order before its execution may be required.

The courts have been fairly uniform in their belief that a person does not lose his privacy rights simply because he is under arrest. This principle is illustrated by at least two other areas of attention. In a California case (*People* v. *Smith*, 1980), the issue was admissibility of evidence gathered in a booking search. The United States Supreme Court, in *United States* v. *Edwards* (1973), ruled that a search of personal possessions at booking did not require a search warrant because the search was incident to arrest. A search for weapons and to inventory possessions is legal. In the *Smith* case the defendant's purse had been legitimately examined upon initial booking. The next day it was searched again and some of its contents seized as evidence. The California Court of Appeals held that a person's possessions are not subject to police rummaging at will throughout the entire period of incarceration. The police should have sought a warrant before reexamining the property in their custody.

The other recently addressed issue involving privacy rights of arrestees is strip searches. The courts have recognized that a strip search, although "humiliating, degrading and embarrassing," is often necessary to protect the safety of officers, to maintain jail order and security, and to discover the fruits of crime. The right of police to subject a prisoner to a strip search does not, however, extend to individuals arrested for minor bailable offenses that will not involve incarceration. It is unreasonable to make misdemeanants held only for the purpose of posting preset bonds "prey of a fishing expedition for evidence of other guilt" (*People* v. *Seymour*, Ill., 1979).

Clarification of Exclusionary Rule Coverage: Confessions and Statements

The requirement that the police inform all suspects that they may remain silent and implicitly warn them that they should do so ("Anything you say can and will be used against you in court.") was seen as a disincentive to confess. Indeed, the *Miranda* decision roused some fears that any form of self-incrimination would be subject to the exclusionary rule. The courts have not gone to the feared extreme, but the volume of cases involving interpretation and clarification clearly indicates that this legal area remains in a state of flux more than a decade after *Miranda*.

The two major areas of continuing adjustment are the meaning of "in custody" and evaluation of the "voluntariness" of statements made to police. Even before the end of the Warren Court the question of the scope of the phrase "custodial police interrogation" was tested. In *Orozco* v. *Texas* (1969), statements made to police by a suspected murderer in his boarding house bedroom were held to have been improperly allowed in evidence because *Miranda* warnings had not been given. The trial court had ruled that the defendant was not subject to custodial interrogation because he was in familiar surroundings. The Supreme Court referred back to its wording in *Miranda* that the warnings had to be provided "when the individual is first subjected to police interrogation while in custody at the station *or otherwise deprived* of his freedom of action" (emphasis added). The restraint, not the location of the interrogation, is the controlling factor.

Subsequent cases have continued to examine the dimensions of custody. In *Mathis* v. *United States* (1968), the petitioner had been questioned by Internal Revenue agents while in prison for a state offense. He was not informed of his *Miranda* rights before making incriminatory statements. The trial court ruled the statements admissible because he was not in custody for the offense prosecuted in the federal court. The Supreme Court reversed the verdict on the grounds that custody is custody.

In recent court decisions the applicability of in-custody questions has been raised with regard to forms of restraint other than police custody. A Florida Court of Appeals reversed and remanded a conviction for illegal use of a credit card on *Miranda* grounds (*Peak* v. *State*, 1977). The defendant had confessed to a security guard while detained in the store security chief's office. The court ruled that the defendant was under duress and restraint so that the lack of warnings made the confession inadmissible. In a Texas case, however, an individual in prison who made inculpatory statements to a cellmate was not in custody under *Miranda*. Testimony by the cellmate and further information gathered by the police, based on his statement, were admissible in court (*McGilvery* v. *State*, 1976). The North Carolina Supreme Court upheld a lower court ruling that a defendant's statement to a police officer while he was in a hospital for treatment of a gunshot wound was admissible. At the time of the officer's questioning of the defendant, he was not actually suspected of a crime and therefore need not have been advised of his *Miranda* rights (*State* v. *Strickland*, 1976).

The other unresolved issue raised by *Miranda* is the test of voluntariness of a confession. This is, of course, the primary concern of common law tradition regarding confessions. It has assumed new significance because of the greatly restricted view of "voluntary" under *Miranda*. Chief Justice Warren's *Miranda* decision noted that the defendant's statements were not involuntary "in traditional terms." Warren's words revised the notion of voluntary statements. Even though he held that any statement "given freely and voluntarily" is admissible, the examples of voluntary statements he provides are actually examples of what he himself later termed, in the same decision, "volunteered statements" such as when a person enters a police station and states that he wishes to confess to a crime, or a person calls the police to offer a confession or other statement.

Courts also have continued to face questions about the element of coercion or compulsion in confessions and statements. In *Miranda*,

Chief Justice Warren included psychological pressure as a form of coercion. But psychological coercion is not easily identified, as the following cases indicate. Informing an individual arrested for robbery and possession of a firearm during the commission of a felony that he would receive methadone if incarcerated did not constitute a promise to provide something in exchange for a statement. The defendant's confession was, therefore, admissible because it was not induced (*De Castro* v. *State*, Fla., 1978). In another case, an interrogating officer's warning to a suspect that he had better tell the truth was not a threat. The suspect's confession subsequent to the admonishment was not, therefore, inadmissible (*State* v. *Rollwage*, Ore., 1975). Similarly, an officer's statement to a suspect that he knew the suspect was not telling the truth did not constitute a resumption of questioning after a request for counsel had been made. A statement offered before advice of counsel was received was ruled voluntary and not elicited (*State* v. *Riddick*, N.C., 1976).

As with search and seizure cases, several cases have verified that statements may be admissible despite police impropriety if the police action is attenuated. A confession made during interrogation while in police custody after full *Miranda* warnings was ruled admissible in a Mississippi case (*Thompson* v. *State*, 1977) even though the suspect had earlier been subjected to interrogation without warnings. In a Wisconsin case, statements made by a suspect when confronted with illegally obtained evidence were ruled admissible because he had received both full *Miranda* warnings and advice from counsel to say nothing. The illegal police search and seizure action was held to be attenuated because of the warnings from police and counsel; the statements were admissible even though the physical evidence was not (*Muetze* v. *State*, 1980). Similar issues have also been raised in federal courts. A district court in Ohio reversed a lower court's exclusion of statements made during an interrogation that was requested by the accused. An initial interrogation had been based on illegally obtained evidence, and statements made at that time were properly excluded. The second interrogation took place more than three weeks later and was prefaced by the appropriate warnings. The connection between the seizure and the statements was accordingly so attenuated as to make the statements admissible (*United States* v. *Cooper*, 1979).

Courts have also ruled on technical challenges to confessions and statements. Some of the technical violations of the warning procedure have been found to be insufficient to render statements inadmissible but what police may consider technical errors have sometimes been found by courts to make statements inadmissible. Even though the procedures mandated by *Miranda* are observed by police, statements may be excluded. The mere recitation of rights to an accused does not make his subsequent statements admissible. The ultimate test of admissibility of a confession is whether it was made voluntarily and with full understanding of alternatives (*State* v. *Pruitt*, N.C., 1975). The police must not only recite the warnings; they must ensure that they are understood.

The United States Supreme Court has also disregarded police claims that violations of exclusionary principles were minor or inconsequential. Just as criminals cannot use the exclusionary rule as a license for perjury (as in the *Harris* case), the police cannot use claims of technical violations of the rules to cover their own misconduct. An Illinois court had allowed statements made after receipt of *Miranda* warnings to be admitted at trial even though the original arrest was invalid. In *Brown* v. *Illinois* (1975), the High Court held that the reading of the rights does not overcome preceding misconduct.

The exclusionary rule has been binding on state officers only since 1961 and therefore has been subject to a great deal of adjustment and interpretation. The rule has been criticized because, although it has been presented as a means of inducing police conformance with the rule of law, it has little direct impact on police officers (Medalie et al., 1968; Milner, 1970; Oaks, 1970; Schlesinger, 1979; Seeburger and Wettick, 1967). It is, therefore, highly suspect as a means of achieving responsible policing.

Police criminal liability for misconduct and the exclusionary rule are direct applications of the principle of responsibility as obedience. In both of these cases one part of the government checks on another part and invokes formal legal sanctions if misbehavior is found. Police officers are held to answer for violating the will of the people as expressed through their representatives in the legislative process.

There is a seductive appeal in this approach to responsibility. It reduces the need for complex evaluation of how best to provide institutional leadership and even how best to develop personal rectitude. Neither administrators nor individual line officers have to make decisions about the police role, the departmental role, or the individual officer's role. The answers are provided by the Constitution and the criminal code. The major shortcomings of this approach will be more fully discussed at the end of the next chapter. For now it may be said that even within the context of the law as a mechanism for assuring responsible policing, there is an implicit recognition of the limits of a punitive external reactive approach. The governmentally imposed forms of legal redress are supplemented by private rights of action against miscreant police officers. Civil liability essentially rests on acceptance of the premise of legal liability as an approach to responsibility but adds responsibility to individual members of the public to responsibility to the public in general, which is the rationale of the public law forms of redress.

3 Responsibility as a Problem of Obedience II

Police Civil Liability

In the previous chapter the use of legal sanctions to control police behavior and to attempt to impose police administrative responsibility focused on criminal proceedings. This chapter will analyze civil procedure as an instrument of imposing police obedience to legal standards of proper behavior. The chapter will conclude with a general critique of the belief that litigation can provide a mechanism for securing responsible policing and responsible police administration.

The principal distinction between criminal and civil law is that the former is a branch of public law and the latter is private law. Criminal law involves actions brought by the government against individuals who commit offenses defined by legal codes to endanger society because they violate public peace, order, and good government. Such offenses are punishable by fines and imprisonment. Civil law involves actions between individuals, generally over contracts between parties or over wrongs done by one private individual to another. In civil law, personal injuries are called torts. Torts and other private conflicts are punishable by awards to the wronged party from the party doing the wrongful action.

The distinction between criminal and civil law as public and private law does not mean that the government or its agents may not be parties to civil suits. Government employees, such as police officers, are liable for the wrongs they do to individuals. In some cases the government unit that employs them may be sued for the injuries caused by the officers. A government unit may also be a plaintiff (the party claiming to have been wronged). At common law this is not possible because civil procedure is limited to private individual disputants. The right of government units to bring civil suits must, therefore, be created by statute. The discussion that follows will address civil liability, first, as a matter of common law torts and, second, as a matter of statutory right under federal law.

Police Tort Liability

The earliest cases in English law relating to law enforcement officers' legal liability concerned outrageous conduct that destroyed private property and terrorized citizens. Such actions can lead to prosecution for culpable homicide, assault, battery, and trespass, and, although involving criminal liability, are usually dealt with through civil litigation because criminal prosecution requires demonstration of a bad purpose and proof beyond a reasonable doubt. In a civil suit no motive must be proved. It must be demonstrated that the injury was the direct consequence of action (or inaction) by the officer, and the standard of proof is merely preponderance of evidence.

The major sources of police tort liability are false arrest, false imprisonment, assault and battery, trespass, defamation, malicious prosecution, and negligence. The most common civil suits against police officers allege illegal detention. A survey by the International Association of Chiefs of Police in 1976 found that suits based on false arrest and false imprisonment accounted for approximately 40 percent of police misconduct litigation (Schmidt, 1976). At common law these are considered offenses against personal freedom. The gravity of these offenses is demonstrated by the fact that the earliest formalization of legal restraints on government in England explicitly condemned them. Indeed, the most significant provision of the Magna Carta (1215) from the perspective of modern legal principles is its Chapter 39: "No freeman shall be seized or imprisoned . . . except by the legal judgement of his peers or by the law of the land." To enforce this standard, the Habeas Corpus Act was passed by the English Parliament in the seventeenth century.

The writ of habeas corpus is a judicial device to challenge the detention of an individual. It is directed at the detention. Civil actions based on false arrest and false imprisonment are intended to compensate the individual for the harm done to him by the detention. False arrest and false imprisonment are two separate torts, but as bases for litigation in police cases the two are usually joined together. To prove false imprisonment a plaintiff must show that an individual intentionally and unlawfully held him against his will. False arrest rests on a claim that the plaintiff was arrested, that is, taken into the custody of the law without proper legal justification. Since false arrest involves legal authority, a private individual may be liable for false imprisonment without a claim of false arrest, whereas a police officer sued for false arrest is, by the very case, liable for false imprisonment.

To sustain a claim of either false arrest or false imprisonment, intent must be demonstrated. In a criminal charge, intent involves malice. In a civil charge, intent goes only to intent to detain; no malice need be shown. An arrest involves custody by a legal officer and does not have to include a statement that the individual is "under arrest." The arrest has taken place if the individual has reason to believe that he has been arrested, as in *Berberian* v. *Mitchell* (R. I., 1974), when the plaintiff was led by the arm into a police squad room. Similarly, false imprisonment does not have to entail actual touching. If an officer totally restrains an individual, that is, does not allow him to proceed in any direction, without legal authority he has committed a false imprisonment. The plaintiff does not have to prove that he resisted to the point of incurring forceful restraint but must show that the detention was involuntary.

False arrest may occur when an officer makes an arrest outside his jurisdiction, when he makes a felony arrest without a warrant or probable cause, or when he makes a misdemeanor arrest without a sworn affidavit, a warrant, or witnessing the offense. An officer is not liable for false arrest when he acts upon a defective warrant, because by law he is required to execute a warrant which is valid on its face. Even if the warrant is later determined to be faulty, he cannot be liable.

An officer acting on a warrant may be liable to a false arrest suit only under special circumstances. In some circumstances, a warrant may not be fair on its face. A day warrant may not be executed at night, for example, and a warrant cannot be served outside the jurisdiction in which it was issued. In some states a police officer may not execute a warrant within the proper judicial jurisdiction if he is outside his legal jurisdiction. A warrant may not be executed after it expires. An old warrant without an expiration date may not be executed unless the officer ascertains that the conditions giving rise to the warrant still exist. An officer can be held liable if the warrant does not identify or describe the person wanted or if he fails to assure himself that the person arrested is the individual named in the warrant.

If an officer makes an arrest without a warrant he may be absolved from false arrest liability by claiming good faith and probable cause. Grounds for probable cause depend on the circumstances surrounding the arrest. Even if an after-the-fact determination is made that the arrest was erroneous, the officer is not liable. The controlling factor is whether "a man of ordinary care and prudence, knowing what the officer knows, would be led to believe or conscientiously entertain a strong suspicion that the arrested person is guilty of a crime even if there is room for doubt" (*Cole* v. *Johnson*, Cal., 1961). This means also, however, that if a group of people is arrested the officer may be liable for individual arrests if he cannot show probable cause to arrest each member of the group.

In some cases, a valid arrest may still lead to liability for false imprisonment. A plain-clothes officer who fails to identify himself as a police officer may be liable for false imprisonment even though probable cause to make the arrest exists. When an officer makes an arrest upon probable cause or makes a good faith arrest with a valid warrant but fails to release his prisoner when he finds out that the arrest was in error, he is liable. If police refuse to allow an arrested person to post an automatic bail when he wishes to do so, they are liable. If police refuse to allow access to an attorney, they may be liable. If a prisoner is not released after bond is posted or after he has served his sentence, the officer or officers ignoring the release conditions may be liable. In most of these instances, neither good faith nor probable cause will absolve the officers of liability. Mistakes of fact are valid excuses in criminal prosecutions but not in civil action.

The second leading area of suits against police officers is assault and battery. These actions may arise from the same incidents that produce false arrest and false imprisonment suits. Assault and battery are often thought of as a single charge. In fact, either may be claimed by itself. Strictly speaking, an assault is a threat or attempt to cause a person injury. The basis for the claim for legal redress is the fear or mental suffering produced by the threat. Threat in this regard must involve more than words alone. On the other hand, a verbal threat to shoot someone with an unloaded gun is grounds for suit if the person threatened has no reason to believe the gun to be unloaded. The mental anguish resulting from the false threat is the basis for the plaintiff's claims.

Battery is an actual physical attack on someone. Criminal law distinguishes between simple and aggravated battery; common law forbids any willful or in-anger touching of another person except in circumstances of self-defense, protection of personal and real property, by officials with delegated social authority to use coercive force in the line of duty (police officers, guards and attendants in mental hospitals), or in certain relationships (parents over children and, formerly, masters over servants and husbands over wives). A battery does not require prior warning, and the plaintiff need not be aware of the illicit contact at the time it occurred.

Under assault and battery intent must be proved. As in false deten-
tion cases, intent applies only to the act, not to its motive. A threat
with an unloaded gun, for example, could support a civil but not a
criminal assault charge. The difference is that in a criminal case there
must be a specific intent to cause harm, whereas in a civil case there
need only be a voluntary act that did or may cause substantial harm.
Assault and battery are also subject to the doctrine of transferred
intent. If an officer uses illegal force intended to harm one person but
instead harms another person, he is liable to the person actually
harmed.

A police officer may use whatever force is reasonably necessary to
make an arrest, to defend himself or another person, or to apprehend
a fleeing felon. Civil assault and battery cases usually turn on the issue
of the reasonableness of an officer's use of force. Two primary ques-
tions arise: Was the officer acting legally, that is, did the conditions
justify use of force? If he was acting within the law, did he use exces-
sive force? In such cases, the officer's perception of the circumstances
is the issue. Acquittal or release without prosecution does not con-
stitute grounds for suing an arresting officer. If the officer acted in
good faith or upon probable cause, he will be exonerated. Again, the
"reasonable man" test applies.

An officer will be in greater jeopardy under some circumstances. If
no arrest was made or if probable cause to make an arrest is lacking,
the officer's force is illegitimate. Also, similarly to false detention, a
plain-clothes officer may be civilly liable for using force to make a
valid arrest if he does not properly identify himself as a police officer.
The reasoning behind this view is that an individual has the right to
resist an attempt by another person to deprive him of his freedom.
Accordingly, if a disguised plain-clothes officer attempting an arrest
does not adequately identify himself, the person may reasonably flee.
If the person is injured while exercising his right to flee, the officer is
liable for the damages sustained (*Celmer* v. *Quarberg*, Wisc., 1973).

Police officers are also subject to civil suits for injury to a person's
reputation. The cause of action in such circumstances is general defa-
mation—an injury by words. Defamation through spoken words is
slander. Defamation through written words is libel. At common law,
defamation was divided into four classes: charging a person with a
felony or a misdemeanor involving moral turpitude; charging a per-
son with having socially reprehensible infectious diseases (such as
leprosy, plague, or venereal disease); charging a tradesman or profes-
sional practitioner with incompetence or malpractice or charging a
public official with official misconduct; and charging a person with
any other act or condition that leads directly to financial loss for the

person charged. Libel consists of malicious publication of false statements that tend to injure a person's reputation or to subject him to disgrace, contempt, ridicule, or hatred.

A complaint of defamation through slander or libel must prove both falsity and malice. Case law on slander and libel is very complex, but it is accepted that police officers may be held to have committed slander if they accuse an individual of illegal conduct in the presence of third parties (*Mullens* v. *Davidson*, W.Va., 1949). If the officer does not have probable cause and if he is proved to have malice, he may be subject to damage claims. The plaintiff does not have to prove intent to cause harm but only that harm resulted from the false statements. Police officers, however, enjoy the special protection of conditional privileged communication while acting within their scope of authority. If the officer has made false statements but can show probable cause and good faith, he is not liable. The law recognizes a distinction between "malice in fact" and "malice in law," but the latter does not apply to privileged communications. The distinction is that in "malice in law" malice may be inferred from the falsity of the statement itself. A police officer acting within his scope of duty is liable only for damages if he can be proved to have had malice in fact, that is, that he knew the statement to be false and sought to cause harm.

A special class of injury to reputation more commonly brought against police officers is malicious prosecution, or the initiation of legal proceedings with malicious intent. To find against an officer for malicious prosecution it must be proved that he personally initiated the legal action or that he manufactured evidence used to support the request for a warrant. The plaintiff must prove both malice and lack of probable cause. If an officer acts with malice but has probable cause and does not exceed his authority, he cannot be liable for malicious prosecution. Similarly, lack of probable cause does not of itself prove malice. Most commonly, malice is proved by showing that the officer was convicted of illegally obtaining a warrant or perjury. Without such collateral substantiation for the allegation of malice, successful litigation by the plaintiff is very difficult because of the prevailing standards for determining probable cause.

Assault, battery, slander, libel, and malicious prosecution are all torts against personal security. False arrest and false imprisonment are torts against personal freedom. Trespass is a tort against property. It consists of unauthorized entry causing damage to an individual's real property. As in the other torts, specific intent is not required. The law requires only that the entry was willful. An officer acting upon a valid warrant or upon probable cause is not normally liable for trespass. The exception would be if he caused damage to physical property. As in assault and battery, the legitimacy of using force against property (as in a forced entry) is determined with reference to the reasonable man test. If the officer has reasonable grounds to believe that forced entry is the only way to serve a warrant, to make a valid arrest, or to stop or prevent a crime he will be exonerated. The burden is on the plaintiff to prove that the officer used excessive force or acted with malice or capriciously.

Negligence

Civil law tort liability is divided into two forms of private injuries: those caused intentionally and those resulting from negligence. False arrest, false imprisonment, assault, battery, malicious prosecution, libel, slander, and trespass are intentional torts. In a negligence suit, the burden on the plaintiff is to demonstrate that the defendant carried out an inherently dangerous act without taking adequate precautions. Most negligence suits against police officers involve negligent vehicle operation, negligent use of force, or failure to protect.

Emergency vehicles are allowed to violate some traffic laws, but they do not have an absolute right to disregard all traffic laws. The operator of an emergency motor vehicle is expected to exercise due regard for the safety of the public. To be absolved from a claim of negligence an officer involved in a traffic accident must be able to show that while violating traffic laws he was acting within the scope of his duty and was in an emergency status. He must have been using warning lights, sirens, or both at the time of the accident, and this equipment must have been functioning properly and have been located so as to be visible and audible to other traffic. The operator must have slowed down at intersections or taken other steps to ensure that other people could have sufficient opportunity to respond to the warning signals. An officer not in pursuit or responding to a call may be held liable for nonmoving negligence, for example, failing to park off the roadway or parking facing the wrong way. In either case, the officer would have to claim unavoidable urgency as justification for his dangerous parking. An officer may be liable for negligence in directing traffic if his instructions cause an accident, even though he was not involved in the accident.

Negligence claims against police officers relating to use of force are most commonly made by injured bystanders. An officer may be held liable for injuries caused by stray bullets or ricochets even though the use of deadly force was justifiable. It is a longstanding rule that although use of deadly force against the suspect may have been legitimate, the officer will be adjudged liable if it is demonstrated that the time or place would cause one "to act with reasonable prudence" (*Askay* v. *Maloney*, Ore., 1919). If the bystander was negligent or if he was another police officer who failed to follow proper safety procedures, the officer doing the shooting may not be held liable. Police liability for carelessness in use of force may also arise from the use of an improper weapon. Automatic weapon fire or use of outdoor tear gas inside a dwelling may be ruled to have been inherently negligent irrespective of bystander actions.

Failure to protect is probably the most contentious basis for a negligence suit. The police officer's sworn duty to protect the public is a general obligation and not ordinarily one owed to specific individuals. Exceptions arise, however, when the officer has assumed a direct responsibility. If an officer tells a witness or complainant that he will be informed if a suspect is released from custody and the officer fails to do so, he may be liable for harm done to the person to whom he owed responsibility. If an officer witnesses a victimization and does not act or if he first intervenes but then withdraws while violence is imminent, he may be liable to the person whose injury he could have lessened. Failure to restrain someone in custody when being identified by a victim may make an officer liable. Similarly, an officer with custody of an informant or material witness who fails to protect him from a clear danger of retaliation is liable for injury to the victim. All of these examples fall under the special relationship doctrine, meaning that the officers have assumed a special obligation to protect known individuals. Officers are not, therefore, liable for unforeseeable violence to persons in custody or to witnesses who do not claim a need for protection or receive an explicit promise of special protection.

An additional basis for civil action is suit for wrongful death. Technically, a wrongful death suit is not a common law tort. Blackstone explained this anomaly by saying that ending a man's life was "one of the most atrocious species of crime" and could never be reduced to a private matter (Book 3, chap. 6). Nevertheless, both in England and in the United States statutes have authorized civil suits providing that heirs, parents, and executors may sue someone who causes an individual's death by any wrongful act, negligence, or default. This right is included in discussion of common law torts because the relevant statutes generally require that the action giving rise to the suit would have been open to tort liability if the victim had survived. Some of the police actions susceptible to these suits are shooting a misdemeanant; shooting a felon when lesser force would have sufficed to apprehend or subdue him; shooting someone in self-defense when no clear danger of bodily harm existed; negligent use of a firearm (for example, in shooting at a moving vehicle or in firing warning shots); negligent handling of a firearm (for example, accidental discharge of a gun or dropping a loaded weapon); careless operation of a motor vehicle; reckless instructions to citizens; and failure to provide obvious, necessary medical attention.

Civil Liability under Federal Law

In addition to criminal liability for police misconduct, the Civil Rights Act of 1871 provides for civil liability for every person who, under color of law, subjects, or causes to be subjected, any person within the jurisdiction to deprivation of any rights, privileges, or immunities secured by the Constitution and laws (42 U.S.C. 1983). Police civil liability also is covered by 42 U.S.C. 1985 and 42 U.S.C. 1986. These sections address conspiracies to violate civil rights. Section 1985, paragraph 3, provides legal redress for conspiracy to deny an individual equal protection of the law or equal privileges and immunities under law. Section 1986 creates additional liability by providing for damage claims against law enforcement officers who fail to prevent other people from carrying out the conspiracy alleged under section 1985.

Before the 1960s, civil action against the police under the Civil Rights Act was infrequent. The few suits that were brought rested on First Amendment grounds. Litigation on broader grounds came only when the Supreme Court, under Chief Justice Warren, greatly expanded federal oversight of police activities by extending constitutional guarantees to state jurisdictions. The leading 1983 case during the activist period was *Monroe* v. *Pape* (1961).

In the *Monroe* case, thirteen Chicago police officers broke into a black family's private home. Monroe, his wife, and children were forced to stand naked in their living room at gunpoint while the officers ransacked their house. Monroe was taken to a police station and interrogated at length about a homicide. The officers had no search warrant or arrest warrant. Monroe was released without being charged with any offense.

Monroe sued the thirteen officers and the city of Chicago, claiming gross violation of due process of law rights. The Supreme Court was called upon to settle the dimensions of 1983 liability. Among the issues presented by the case were the meaning of color of law, whether state remedies had to be sought before federal remedies, and whether the city could be a party to litigation. On the first count, the court adopted the definition provided by Justice Douglas in the 242 cases *United States* v. *Classic* (1941) and *Screws* v. *United States* (1945) that color of law means under pretense of law and clothed with legal authority. They also made a crucial distinction between 242 liability and 1983 liability based on the variant wording in the two statutes. Section 242 creates liability for an officer who *willfully* subjects someone to deprivation of rights, whereas section 1983 creates liability for an officer who subjects or causes to be subjected an individual to deprivation of rights. In *Screws*, "willfully" was interpreted to require the prosecution to prove specific intent. In *Monroe*, in contrast, the Court ruled that the plaintiff "need neither allege nor prove a specific intent."

On the question of whether redress had first to be sought in state court, the Supreme Court ruled that the federal remedy is supplementary to the state and the state remedy need not be first sought and refused before the federal one is involved.

The only point of contention on which the plaintiffs lost was the right to sue the city. Even though the Court had long before recognized corporations as persons under the Fourteenth Amendment (*Santa Clara County* v. *Southern Pacific Railroad*, 1886), "person" in section 1983 was ruled to apply only to human beings. Recovery was made from all thirteen officers but not from the city of Chicago.

The major breakthroughs of *Monroe* were that willfulness was not to be considered an element in a 1983 suit and that color of law was broadly construed. The two principal limitations made on 1983 suits were that complaints under the section had to be specific, not general, and that municipal corporations employing police officers could not be made co-defendants in suits against officers.

The definition of color of law accepted in *Monroe* has allowed suits against police on grounds that would have been problematical under a narrower interpretation. Since color of law means clothed with state power, a civil rights violation cannot be reduced to a common tort suit by claiming that a defendant officer was acting outside state law. Police officers who take unauthorized action or action in excess of their authority are liable. Moreover, they are liable even if the action in question "was proscribed by state law" (*Marshall* v. *Sawyer*, 1962). In another case, an officer who was off duty shot and killed two people and paralyzed another. He was held to be acting under color of law because his department required him to carry his service weapon at all times. The U.S. District Court for Ohio ruled that whether an officer is "on or off duty, or in or out of uniform is not controlling" (*Stengel* v. *Belcher*, 1975). To show that a defendant is acting under color of law it is necessary to prove only that he is a police officer and that some connection between his peace officer status and the complained-of action exists.

Other forms of police liability and immunity under section 1983 are determined by state law. The connection between common law tort liability and the Civil Rights Act's coverage is close. Section 1983 covers only those torts that also violate federally guaranteed rights. The primary question in linking a tort claim to a 1983 claim is whether the tort under consideration is one that amounts to deprivation of due process of law. If such a connection seems evident, the facts underlying an acceptable state tort claim may provide the basis for a 1983 claim (*Somers* v. *Strader*, 1977).

Some federal cases have arisen through police actions directly contrary to due process of law provisions. The best example is, of course, *Monroe* v. *Pape*, based on an illegal search and seizure. Still, the significance of state law and common law tort liability cannot be overstressed in evaluating federal liability. In *Stringer* v. *Dilger* (1963), for example, the plaintiff was able to recover damages because he had been denied the right to post bail in spite of a Colorado statute allowing him to do so. Plaintiffs have won suits involving deprivations of civil rights before the rights were made binding on the states. Assault and battery issues, for example, were cited in cases based on freedom from coerced confessions through prolonged interrogation (*Refoule* v. *Ellis*, 1947) and freedom from self-incrimination through physical coercion (*Hardwick* v. *Hurley*, 1961). The issues involved in assault and battery have also been directly addressed in civil rights cases. Undue or excessive force in making an arrest has been held to violate due process of law (*Morgan* v. *Labiak*, 1966). The test of whether the amount of force used to make an arrest is excessive has been specified in *Hausman* v. *Tredinnick* (1977): the officer's conduct is illicit if he uses force far exceeding that which is reasonable and necessary under the circumstances to make the arrest and also violates generally accepted standards of decency. Under this construction it is apparently not sufficient to prove merely that the force was more than minimally necessary. The force must take a form that violates standards of decency. A police officer is liable for any assault and battery even of a minor nature if no arrest is made (*Nugent* v. *Sheppard*, 1970).

Closely related to assault and battery is wrongful death. Wrongful death actions are often based on police use of deadly force. Federal law has been held to bar a party from bringing suit under section 1983 on behalf of another party (*United States* v. *City of Philadelphia*, 1979), but the heirs or guardians of an individual wrongfully slain by police may sue for deprivation of life without due process of law (*Glover* v. *City of New York*, 1975). The limitation on this cause of action is that it is permissible only if state law in the state where the case arose has enacted a wrongful death civil liability statute.

Civil rights cases also arise under circumstances of false arrest and false imprisonment. In 1949, the Civil Rights Act of 1871 was held to protect individuals from illegal detentions and from fraudulent trials and convictions (*McShane* v. *Moldvan*). Again, the connection between common law and federal rules is highly significant because the defense of good faith and probable cause available to the officers in the common law action for false arrest and imprisonment is also available to them in the action under 1983 (*Pierson* v. *Ray*, 1967). Furthermore, as in state litigation, the United States Supreme Court has ruled that in judging police decisions on probable cause, the circumstances the court must consider "are those of the moment" (*Dixon* v. *United States*, 1961). More recently the Court has relaxed its standards somewhat by recognizing that a "brief stop of a suspicious individual . . . may be most reasonable" even though the officer "lacks the precise level of information necessary for probable cause to arrest" (*Adams* v. *Williams*, 1972). This has been interpreted to mean that liability for unlawful arrests under 1983 depends on the more subjective test of reasonable good faith belief in the legality of action than on the objective test of probable cause (*Diamond* v. *Marland*, 1975). An officer may be liable under 1983 for a false arrest when he lacks reasonable grounds even if the incident is relatively minor. For example, in *Richardson* v. *Newark* (1978), a police officer was held liable for illegally stopping a motorist for speeding even though he only gave him a ticket and did not take him into custody.

Malicious prosecution is actionable under the Civil Rights Act (*Nesmith* v. *Alford*, 1963), but honest mistakes about law or about the facts of a particular case are valid defenses. An officer cannot be held liable for enforcing an unconstitutional law unless he can be shown to have known or to be reasonably expected to have known that it was unconstitutional (*Pierson* v. *Ray*). Similarly, a bad motive must be shown to underlie initiation of prosecution when probable cause is absent (*Whirl* v. *Kern*, 1968). If the bad intent is not shown, it is to be presumed that the officer simply made a mistake about law or facts.

In view of the foregoing, federal civil liability is limited in scope. There are many situations in which the police cannot be held liable for harm to individuals. A federal district court has stated that there are many individual rights which are not granted by the Constitution. "These include the right to be secure from intentional and unintentional harm to person, reputation and property. The fact that such rights are violated by policemen does not spell out federal constitutional violations" (*Johnson* v. *Hacket*, 1968). Accordingly defamation is not actionable under the Civil Rights Act because no federal right is involved (*Paul* v. *Davis*, 1976).

There is no 1983 liability for failure to provide criminal suspects their *Miranda* warnings (*Thornton* v. *Buchmann*, 1968). The contentious issue of police discretion is not a suitable basis for federal civil rights litigation unless selectivity in enforcement of laws or in providing services is based upon "unjustified standards such as race, religion, or other arbitrary classification" (*Oyler* v. *Boles*, 1962). There is no civil rights liability for "mere negligence" (*Mullins* v. *River Rouge*, 1972).

Enforcement of Police Civil Liability

Civil liability is enforced through the awarding of damages to aggrieved individuals and through court orders to police departments to refrain from illicit practices. Damages awards may be assessed against the officers directly involved in the tortious conduct or in certain circumstances against their superior officers or their corporate employers.

Civil Damages Awards

Damages awards are assessed primarily on compensatory grounds on the basis of the plaintiff's pain and suffering, both physical and mental. Physical damage includes both direct injury and subsequent illnesses or physical conditions that result from the tortious conduct. Mental damage includes fright, humiliation, harm to reputation, and alienation of friends or family. Special compensatory damages are awarded to reimburse expenses resulting from the injury, such as medical expenses, financial losses because of inability to earn wages or because of harm to business or property, and legal expenses incurred as a result of bringing suit.

In addition, punitive damages in the form of monetary awards intended to punish the officers found to have caused harm to plaintiffs may be awarded. Punitive damages are based on the conduct of the defendants, which may involve reckless disregard for the interest of the plaintiff, gross negligence, malice, or bad faith. The availability of punitive damages varies by state. In some, they are possible only if malice is proved. In others, they are possible only if substantial physical injury has occurred. The United States Supreme Court has stated that in civil rights cases punitive damages should be awarded only if there is malicious deprivation of constitutional rights (*Carey* v. *Piphus*,

1978). In *Carey*, the Court stated, however, that even if no compensatory damages are involved (because the plaintiff suffered no actual injury), courts may award nominal damages. These are damages in a small amount, such as $100, which are intended to demonstrate that constitutional rights cannot be violated with impunity even if no physical or emotional injury was done. Successful plaintiffs in false arrest suits are entitled to have the arrest expunged from police records (*Bilick* v. *Dudley*, 1973).

There is a dynamic relationship between civil liability enforcement and state law just as there is between definitions of tort liability and statutory liability. In cases based on use of deadly force, an officer will be exonerated if statutory provisions allow deadly force in the given circumstances (*Wiley* v. *Memphis Police Department*, 1977). In at least one state it has also been ruled that the advice of a police legal adviser is a valid defense to false arrest and false imprisonment charges (*Toomey* v. *City of Fort Lauderdale*, Fla., 1975).

The protections afforded to police officers by statute or good faith do not always apply, however. In several cases departmental policies have been held to increase the risks of police liability because they represent self-imposed standards of care. As a result, plaintiffs have won cases in which state statutes apparently protected the defendant officers. In *Dillenbeck* v. *City of Los Angeles* (Cal., 1968) and in *Delong* v. *City of Denver* (Colo., 1974), violations of departmental rules on responding to emergency calls were determined to be evidence of failure to exercise due care. Similarly, in *Grundt* v. *City of Los Angeles* (Cal., 1970), use of deadly force in conformance with state law but contrary to administrative policy led to damage awards.

Liability of Superior Officers

The superior officers of policemen sued in civil cases can be named as co-defendants only if they personally participated in the tortious conduct by directing or approving of the misconduct or being present at the incident with knowledge of what was happening but taking no action to stop it (*Hampton* v. *Chicago*, 1972, and *Richardson* v. *Snow*, 1972). A superior officer is equally liable with his subordinates if he knows of their conduct and consents to it (*Alvarez* v. *Wilson*, 1977) or condones it (*Smith* v. *Ambrogio*, 1978), as indicated by his actions or inaction.

Chiefs of police or other superior officers may also be subject to civil liability if their negligence causes or contributes to the misconduct. Some examples of such negligence are failure to screen out applicants for employment who have known mental disabilities or histories of prior violence; failure to train employees properly; failure to investigate complaints against officers who subsequently inflict damages; failure to dismiss or discipline officers known to have committed misconduct and who subsequently commit the same illicit action; failure to retract policies that have a natural consequence of denial of rights; and failure to supervise or direct officers.

Employer Liability

Monroe v. *Pape* opened the federal courts to a flood of suits against police officers on civil rights grounds. It also limited the scope of such suits by ruling that the employers of defendant police officers could not be named as co-defendants. This position rested partially on the venerable principle of sovereign immunity as defined by the United States Supreme Court: "There can be no legal right as against the authority that makes the law on which the right depends" (*Kawananakoa* v. *Polybank*, 1907). It also rested in part on the assumption that Congress did not intend, as a matter of federal law, to impose vicarious liability on municipalities for violations of federal civil rights by their employees (*Moor* v. *Alameda County*, 1973).

The doctrine of sovereign immunity, however, stands in opposition to the equally venerable principle of respondeat superior. This principle holds that a master is responsible for the wrongful acts of his servant. Although the notion of master and servant is medieval, respondeat superior generally means that an employer is liable for torts committed by his employees when they are acting within the scope of their employment. This does not mean that the employer is guilty of wrongdoing, but, rather, imposes liability on the party better able to sustain the losses incurred by a damages award.

The exclusion of suits against cities when police officers are named in tort or civil rights violations was widely criticized. The American Bar Association's *Standards Relating to the Urban Police Function* stated that, "to strengthen the effectiveness of the tort remedy for improper police activities," government immunity should be eliminated and tort liability and costs attendant to the defense of a tort action against an officer acting within his scope of employment "should be borne by the government subdivision" employing him (1973: Standard 5.5). Kenneth Culp Davis (1974), an administrative law expert, asserted that shifting the burden of tort liability from the police officer to the city would have four beneficial effects: (1) Officers will be more diligent because they will not have to fear litigation if they make reasonable choices that later turn out to have been wrong. (2) Officers will be more justly treated by the system which they serve. (3) Parties injured by police actions will receive a higher quality of justice. (4) Cities will be more diligent in providing oversight of police activity.

In 1961, the California Supreme Court ruled that sovereign immunity was "an anachronism, without rational basis," which had persisted "only by the force of inertia" (*Muskopf* v. *Corning Hospital District*). By 1975, courts in the District of Columbia and nineteen states had abolished government immunity for torts, and in approximately ten states legislative action against immunity had been taken (Davis, 1975:97). Finally, in 1978, the United States Supreme Court decided that cities could be sued for their employees' violations of section 1983 (*Monell* v. *Department of Social Services*). Subsequently, a lower federal court extended *Monell* to cover county liability (*Gill* v. *Monroe County Department of Services*, 1978). The Supreme Court has continued to allow state immunity from 1983 suits, however (*Quern* v. *Jordan*, 1979).

Cities and counties are now liable for damages caused by their employees in a majority of the states and in federal courts. There is, however, no blanket liability—the government unit must be shown to have had a direct role in the tortious conduct. Respondeat superior does not apply; the government unit is not liable just because it employs the officers who commit a civil rights violation. Liability arises only when the officers acted in conformance with official policy, ordinance, or custom (*Monell* v. *Department of Social Services*). This interpretation extends to unarticulated policy that is manifested as a recurring pattern of civil rights violations known to officials who do not take steps to end it (*Smith* v. *Ambrogio*, 1978). These judicial steps open the way to suits against cities, which are generally considered to be more likely sources of money damages than are police officers. It remains to be seen whether police responsibility will be enforceable through civil liability even with liability extended to their employers.

The Limits of Legal Liability

The real world of policing is such that it is impossible to control police behavior by imposing a legal obligation to act only according to law. The highly complex and fluid nature of police work requires a great deal of personal initiative and discretion. To demand that the police enforce all laws at all times is unrealistic because neither resources nor public support allows total enforcement. More important, the police in American society are expected to be more than law enforcers.

For these reasons, the legal mandate of discretionless police behavior is so far out of line with reality as to require no further attention. Instead, the perspective of responsibility as a problem of obedience must rest upon legal controls on police misbehavior. The legal code cannot stand by itself. The police make the provisions of the criminal code real by their enforcement. Similarly, legal controls on the police are real only insofar as they are applied to actual behavioral patterns. It is an entirely false hope to maintain that, because the law says the police have no discretion, they will exercise no discretion. There are three forms of legal liability which may be seen as directed at controlling police behavior in order to secure socially responsible police. Nevertheless, legal liability through the exclusionary rule, criminal prosecution, and civil suits is seriously deficient. Each is directed at punishing or redressing irresponsibility, not at developing responsibility.

The Exclusionary Rule

The exclusionary rule has been subjected to great criticism. Among its primary defects are the relationship between exclusion and social good and the relationship between judicial decisions and police policy and police behavior. Public debate on the rule has primarily focused on the first count.

The exclusionary rule is supposed to deter police violations of citizens' rights on the theory that judicially imposed rules of conduct would formalize and standardize police procedures. Instead, the rule seems to immunize criminals from prosecution. Justice Benjamin Cardozo made this point in the *Defore* case when he said it is unreasonable to allow criminals to go free because officers make mistakes. As it stands, the rule protects criminals by blocking the prosecutor's use of evidence. It has no impact on illegal intrusion or coercion. The defense attorney's motive is not to protect his client's privacy rights. The inculpatory evidence has already been exposed. He wants to win an acquittal for his client in spite of inculpatory evidence. Coerced confessions have long been banned at common law because they are inherently unreliable, but the post-*Miranda* rule on confessions makes technical procedure more important than reliability and precludes only good evidence.

The fact that the rule immunizes criminals was borne out by an extensive study by James E. Spiotto (1973) of motions to suppress evidence in Chicago superior courts over the twenty-year period 1950-71. He discovered that defendants with no previous criminal record were granted their suppression motions 72 percent of the time. Defendants with previous sentences of five years or more were granted 100 percent of the suppression motions.

Some applications of the exclusionary rule have been bizarre. In one case, an FBI agent had spent three and one-half hours negotiating on the telephone the peaceful surrender of an armed, emotionally disturbed man, barricaded in a motel room, who was wanted for shooting his wife and daughter. A federal court ruled that the man's inculpatory statements about the shootings while on the phone with the agent were inadmissible. The basis for this decision was that, because the motel was surrounded by law enforcement officers, the suspect was in custody and should have been given *Miranda* warnings (*United States* v. *Mesa*, 1980). In *Coolidge* v. *New Hampshire* (1971), a conviction for the brutal murder of a fourteen-year-old girl was overturned by the U.S. Supreme Court because evidence against the killer was acquired by police officers acting on a defective warrant. An even more bizarre ruling concerned a kidnapping suspect who had received full *Miranda* warnings and had been advised by his attorney to remain silent. He told police where he had buried the body of his ten-year-old victim when an officer said that the parents of the girl deserved the right to give her a Christian funeral. The Supreme Court ruled that the police statement was an interrogation that tricked the defendant into an unadvised confession (*Brewer* v. *Williams*, 1977). The Supreme Court did allow a conviction to stand in a related case (*Rhode Island* v. *Innis*, 1980), in which one officer had said to another that he hoped a missing shotgun used in an armed robbery would not be found by students at a nearby school for handicapped children. The suspect then divulged the location of the gun. The Court ruled that the officer's remark was not an interrogation. Despite the *Innis* decision, there are many more examples of criminals escaping punishment because of technical violations of procedure than there are of judicial restraint in evaluating the overall issues in a case.

The rule is also seriously defective as a vehicle for assuring administrative responsibility. There is little ground to support the assumption that suppression of evidence and testimony will cause police to alter their behavior. For a case to wind its way through the appellate process and determine the propriety of a search and seizure or confession takes years. When the case is settled, the officer involved may never learn that he committed an error. He may not even remember the case. Neither judges nor prosecutors can be expected to provide police departments with detailed information on judicial decisions. Police legal advisers often have a great deal of trouble trying to relate specific court decisions to police policy.

A more important limitation on judicial rules as a guide to police administrative responsibility is the different perspectives of judges and police officers on the administration of justice. Police see the world as a hostile, often dangerous, place with which they can cope by becoming acutely aware of subtle indications of criminal and deviant behavior. The judge assumes the trial to be the center of crime control; the police officer assumes his own ability to apprehend offenders, to prevent disruption, and to protect himself and his authority to be most important. For the police officer, his own abilities are paramount; for the judge, the law is paramount.

A clash between judicial and police views on proper police procedure is inevitable. The law and the courts say a man on trial is innocent until proved guilty; the police believe that if a man is on trial, he is probably guilty or he would not have been arrested and indicted. At a trial, a defendant is usually calm, clean, and deferential. The judicial assumption seems realistic to the judge, the lawyers, and even the jury. At the time people are arrested the police often find them "dirty, angry, rowdy, obscene, dazed, savage, or bloodied" (Wilson, 1975:36). As Sir Robert Mark, former commissioner of the London Metropolitan Police, says, lawyers and police have different meanings in mind when they talk of the ends of the administration of justice: "The lawyer is speaking of 'fair play according to the rules': the policeman is speaking of establishment of the truth, with which criminal justice is not necessarily concerned" (1970:86).

Judicial emphasis on the importance of procedures at trial creates another defect because the exclusionary rule touches only the law enforcement role, and it presumes that when police use their law enforcement powers they are uniformly concerned about securing a conviction. Arrests can be made for a variety of reasons other than criminal prosecution. They can be made to create a false image of vigorous enforcement, to punish individuals who demonstrate contempt or disrespect for the police, or to punish persons suspected of criminal activity against whom a valid case cannot be made. Furthermore, since the primary overall mission of the police is to protect peace and order in society, an officer has done his job when he gets weapons, dope, gambling equipment, and other illicit goods off the streets even if no prosecution follows because the evidence is inadmissible.

The United States Supreme Court has noted that, if the purpose of the exclusionary rule is to deter illegitimate police behavior, it would make sense to suppress illegally obtained evidence only if the officer knew he was acting unconstitutionally (*United States* v. *Peltier*, 1975). Still, good evidence continues to be kept out of criminal prosecutions simply because an officer committed a procedural error. A former attorney general of England and Wales has criticized the general Anglo-Saxon "sentimental and sporting attitude in dealing with the criminal," which debases a judge from a scientist seeking the truth to an umpire seeing to it that "each side observes the rules of the game" (Shawcross, 1965:227). The exclusionary rule carries this attitude to its extreme.

An Australian jurist has criticized the American judicial system's "quixotic exclusion of the truth, on the highest moral grounds" for producing "popular ridicule" of our criminal justice system (Sholl, 1968:145). Empirical studies have found the rule to have little effect on police practices (Medalie et al., 1968; Milner, 1970; Oaks, 1970; Schlesinger, 1979; Seeburger and Wettick, 1967; Wald, 1967). Even Chief Justice Burger of the United States Supreme Court has said that, judged by practical consequences, the rule has not been a notable success. Worse, it exposes the public to a spectacle "repugnant to all decent people: the frustration of justice" (1964:12).

The exclusionary rule does not have a positive effect on police policy making or police officers' street behavior. It alienates the police from the judiciary. It arouses the hostility of the public when it results in obviously guilty people going free. Its emphasis on technical procedure to the neglect of good judgment is so obvious that the United States Congress reinstituted the common law rule on confessions. The Omnibus Crime Control and Safe Streets Act of 1968 provides that the test of admissibility of confessions is "voluntariness," and failure to give *Miranda* warnings is only one factor to be considered (18 U.S.C. 3501).

Criminal and Civil Liability

Criminal and civil liability have the advantage over the exclusionary rule of applying sanctions directly to the officer involved. Criminal liability is the more severe of the alternatives and would appear to be the more potent source of control over police behavior. Yet it has not been a workable mechanism of assuring police administrative responsibility.

Criminal prosecutions are brought against police officers for only the most serious violations of trust. Criminal violations directly related to routine police procedures such as trespass, excessive force, perjury in cases against common criminals, and illicit search and seizures are highly unlikely. Even corrupt practices such as extortion, accepting bribes, larceny, and misappropriation of property are more often settled by forced resignation than by prosecution. The reasons criminal prosecution is unworkable relate to the various people involved in making a criminal case. The district attorney is dependent on the police. He cannot win cases without effective police cooperation and therefore will be extremely hesitant to jeopardize his relationship with the department. When the only witnesses to police misconduct are other officers, they are usually hesitant to "rat" on a fellow officer. Police administrators prefer to protect the department's image by quietly disposing of cases internally rather than in a public trial. The people who frequently lodge complaints against officers are not credible. They are suspected or known criminals, whose credibility is low both because of their personal reputation and because they are perceived to be attempting to divert attention from their own criminality by charging the arresting officer with impropriety. Finally, jurors are often indisposed to find police officers guilty of a criminal offense unless it is particularly unsettling and a particularly good case has been made.

All of these problems are magnified when the charge against the officer arises from zealousness in acquiring evidence or testimony. An officer who takes forceful action to seize contraband or physical evidence against a violent offender may violate the Fourth Amendment. But the prosecutor may be unable to convince a jury that he acted criminally. A 1979 survey of police, prosecutors, and defense attorneys found prosecutors more opposed to prosecution of officers who violate the Fourth Amendment than were police officers. Respondents were presented with six alternatives: to prosecute in all cases; only when the violation was excessive; only when the violation was intentional; when the violation was either excessive or intentional; when the violation was both excessive and intentional; and in no case. The last alternative, "in no case," was chosen by 47.3 percent of the police but by 57.1 percent of the prosecutors. Even 26.3 percent of the defense attorneys believed a police officer should be prosecuted in no case (Hirschel, 1979).

The exclusionary rule fails as a mechanism for achieving police responsibility in large part because it does not directly touch the offending officer. Criminal liability for police irresponsible behavior goes too much to the other extreme. It punishes the officer harshly but does nothing to redress the harm done to the person whose rights were violated. Civil liability, therefore, would appear to be a better alternative. It provides for compensation to the victim, has a direct impact on the offending officer, and can involve the superior and employers of the defendant officers.

In a seminal article, Caleb Foote said that the only way to enforce police legal liability is to place enforcement in the hands of injured persons, "who are offered a selfish motive" (1955:516). The tort alternative offers such a motive and could also be used to mitigate the weaknesses of the exclusionary rule. With a viable tort alternative, suppression of evidence could be limited to serious or blatant violations of individual rights. Reliable evidence would be admissible, but aggrieved individuals would receive some redress. More important, it would provide a means of compensating victims of illegal police practices who did not commit an offense, evidence of which could be excluded. The obverse of this last point is that victims of technical violations who do not deserve compensation would not receive any. The possibility of assessment of civil damages against superior officers and government units should motivate police administrators and political overseers to provide training, rules, counseling, and selection procedures that minimize the risks of tortious conduct.

In spite of the apparent advantages of civil liability, there are obstacles to its effective use as a mechanism for providing police administrative responsibility. Two primary limiting factors are the relationship between the police and local governments and people who bring suits against the police. Even if a plaintiff wins a suit against an officer, he may find his award to be uncollectible. Police officers do not usually have the income or property to pay large damages or large settlements. Moreover, as agents of the government, the police can usually expect to be protected by their government employer. To this end, various states have passed legislation to blunt the possibility of police officers facing damages awards. In Illinois and Connecticut, for example, officers are entitled to indemnification for recoveries made against them. In Kentucky, police officers, like sheriffs in most states, are bonded. A form of malpractice insurance is available to peace officers in many states.

In California and Hawaii, statutes provide for defense fees in both criminal and civil suits. The California Government Code (section 995.8) allows cities and counties to pay for officers' defenses if three circumstances apply: the litigation arises from action within the officer's scope of employment; it is in the public interest to provide the defense; and the officer is believed to have acted in good faith without malice in the apparent interest of his employer. The Hawaiian statute allows cities and counties to employ legal counsel in criminal cases against police officers and to authorize corporation counsels and county attorneys to act as defense attorneys in civil actions against officers (Hawaii Statutes, section 52-3, Police officers, counsel for).

The only limitation is that the police commission of the officer's juris-
diction must first consult with its corporation counsel or county at-
torney to determine that the officer was acting within his scope of
duty. Even in those states that have statutory provisions similar to
those of California and Hawaii, however, the employer will not indem-
nify officers for punitive damages assessments.

The second major difficulty with civil liability is that juries seldom
have much sympathy for the people who bring such suits. In 1886 the
United States Supreme Court ruled, in *Kerr* v. *Illinois*, that damages in
trespass and false imprisonment actions depend on the "moral aspects
of the case." For the most part, criminals and social deviants, who are
most often subjected to police torts, do not possess a minimum level of
respectability to impart strong moral aspects to their suits.

The discussion of the advantages and limitations of police legal
liability leads to the conclusion that responsibility cannot be viewed
solely, or even primarily, as a problem of obedience. Judicial oversight
of the police is reactive, negative, and individualistic. It is not positive
or institutional. It does little to build responsibility. It only addresses
specific acts of irresponsibility, and even then it touches upon a limited
range of irresponsible behaviors. Contemptuous conduct toward the
public, laxity in pursuit of social welfare, inattention to high stan-
dards of comportment, carelessness short of negligence, and high-
handed treatment of citizens are all serious breaches of responsibility,
but they are not amenable to judicial action.

Criminal cases are infrequently initiated against police officers.
They are extremely difficult to prosecute successfully. Civil cases are
expensive and take years to settle. Plaintiffs usually are disreputable
except in negligence cases. The exclusionary rule protects only crimi-
nals. It has been bitterly attacked by police, politicians, and even the
chief justice of the United States Supreme Court. A foreign observer
was moved to ask: "What is the real value to a decent law abiding
American citizen of being less in danger of possible abuse of power by
the police, but in greater danger of fraud, theft, violence or death
from criminals" (Scholl, 1968:146).

None of the three forms of legal liability can ensure that police
administration and police behavior are loyal to the values and desires
of American society. Suppression of evidence, conviction of officers,
and damage awards against officers and their employers do not pro-
vide the basis for police operational guidance. The judges and lawyers
who direct the judicial process have a different perspective on the
administration of justice and on the roles of the various occupational
groups. Nor are these judges and lawyers paragons of virtue. One
legal scholar has referred to criminal lawyers as participants in a

"confidence game" (Blumberg, 1967). Another lawyer, in an article discussing professional responsibility of the criminal defense lawyer, states that an attorney is acting properly to cross-examine an adverse witness in such a way as to discredit him even though he is known to be telling the truth, put his client on the stand when he is known to be intending to commit perjury, and give his client legal advice that will induce him to perjure himself (Freedman, 1970).

An alternative is necessary that accepts the formal legal system as a source of legitimate guidance but is based on systematic and conscientious efforts to integrate legally mandated procedures with real-world police problems. An effort to develop such an alternative is bureaucratization of the police. Instead of responsibility as obedience, it emphasizes responsibility as accountability. The police organization articulates the norms of proper police procedure and behavior. The officers are required to account to the organizational hierarchy for deviation from the norms. The organizational hierarchy then evaluates the procedures and behaviors in light of the rationale of the norms. This approach differs from reliance on pure obedience because it is more flexible and is adapted to the dynamics of police field work rather than rooted in generalized prescriptions and proscriptions developed by cloistered legislators and jurists. The next chapter evaluates this perspective on responsible administration.

4 Responsibility as Accountability
The Police Bureaucracy

The police are agents of the law. The law sets out the basic tasks of policing. But the police are not just ministerial agents of the law. They frequently confront situations in which they must attempt to relate the general purpose of the law to specific conditions— to supply meaning to the law in the process of enforcing it. To do so they must have discretion in choosing their course of action.

Left on their own, individual police officers may vigorously enforce one law while ignoring others, thus distorting or nullifying the intent of carefully considered and carefully worded public policy. Therefore, the police must have sufficient power to perform their duties, but that power must be controlled. To deal with the simultaneous needs for discretion and for control of discretion, responsibility can be treated as a problem of accountability. Responsibility, according to this view, can be accomplished by establishing formal administrative structures for authoritative interpretation of the law into guidelines for application in the real world. What this means is that the elected representatives of the people establish police departments and provide them a broad mandate. The departments then review the actions of individual police officers in light of the broad mandate. In doing so they act as the vehicle for confining and structuring discretion.

Bureaucratization of the Police

Development of administrative organizations capable of providing guidance and discipline seems a viable method to achieve administrative responsibility. This view reduces the control of police behavior to a problem of technology. The design of organizational structures rather than the working of statutes becomes the paramount concern.

In response to the widespread corruption in many, if not most, American police departments in the 1920s and 1930s, an intense effort was made to bureaucratize the law enforcement establishment. It was believed that the introduction of military discipline could eliminate both the political and venal corruption that seemed to flourish under the prevailing system. The leading aspiration of reformers of the police systems seemed to be to replace "the tragicomic figure of the flatfoot cop on the take" with cadres of personally incorruptible operatives "working under the command of bureaucrats in uniform" (Bittner, 1978:43).

The tremendous faith vested in the drive for bureaucratization seemed reasonable in theory. Max Weber had asserted that bureaucratic organization is unsurpassed for controlling both the human beings within an organization and the organization itself. He identified such an organization as having a clearly defined hierarchy of offices; each office with a clearly defined sphere of competence and candidates selected on the basis of technical qualifications; employment in such offices constituting a career; promotion through the hierarchy dependent on the judgment of superiors; and the officials subject to strict and systematic discipline and control in the conduct of their duties.

Police departments seem eminently suited to conformance with the ideal bureaucracy described by Weber. The force is organized on the military model with insignia and titles of rank to distinguish among hierarchical levels. Key subunits of the organization are grouped to carry out three main functions: administration, services, and operations. Personnel within the organization specialize in subordinate subcategories of the primary functions such as investigation and forensic sciences. The time-honored path of promotion is through the ranks. Entry into the organization is usually possible only at the very bottom or the very top, but the latter is infrequent. Not only are officers expected to make police service a lifelong career, but, because of the virtual exclusiveness of bottom-level entry, they are expected to remain in the same department in which they start.

Frederick C. Mosher has hailed hierarchy as an important safeguard to administrative responsibility because it forces important decisions to the higher levels of the organization (1982:232). Ideally, organizational hierarchy is conceived to rest upon the premise that individuals have differential capacities to exercise discretion and to make reliable value judgments. Consequently, individuals should be

able to exercise broad discretion or to make significant decisions in-
volving value choices only after they have demonstrated an ability to
make lesser decisions. Thus, in theory, the range of discretion declines
as the hierarchical ladder is descended.

In such an organizational structure, decisions about policy are made
at the top of the police hierarchy and then transmitted downward.
Since nearly everyone is tied into the central communications center,
messages can be dispersed throughout the force with only a minimum
of distortion.

The Mechanics of Accountability

Internal Review

The significant change from reliance on the law to reliance on orga-
nizational accountability involves more than the creation of a formal
hierarchy and specifically assigned areas of discretion. When bureau-
cratic police departments were established, however, there was a
failure to distinguish between the form and the substance of bureau-
cracy. Weber had cautioned that simply structuring an agency along
bureaucratic lines does not guarantee an effective bureaucracy.
There is always a potential for individual members to pursue their
own interests or those of some special group. To minimize that poten-
tial, a system of sanctions must exist to compel obedience by establish-
ing patterns of responsibility. Roles must be identified, conduct to be
avoided specified, and accountability delineated. Procedures for
checking and reporting on performance and taking corrective action
must be designed. To be fully effective the system of sanctions must
reside within the organization.

The courts and special external tribunals cannot provide the day-
to-day guidance of administrative behavior which is essential for be-
havioral control in the field. Invocation of criminal and civil law is
uneconomical for dealing with petty or minor transgressions and es-
pecially for dealing with conduct that is undesirable or unethical but is
neither illegal nor tortious. Sanction mechanisms can be effective only
if they reinforce command capabilities, which external mechanisms
are not likely to do.

The National Commission on the Causes and Prevention of Violence
noted that external control tends to be sporadic and inconsistent and
that second-guessing by outsiders tends to destroy morale and encour-
age immobility. The commission maintained that internal investiga-
tion and review of administrative behavior are more effective control

mechanisms (Paulsen et al., 1970:386). Police officials concur that an individual department is capable of keeping its own house in order. They claim that only professional policemen can be effective judges of whether officers are carrying out their duties and responsibilities in the best interest of law and public safety. No general adjudicatory body and no special lay tribunal could successfully combine negative sanctions with positive guidance.

Jerry Wilson, former chief of the Metropolitan Police Department in Washington, D.C., maintains that reliance on external mechanisms of control leads to an ambiguous and ambivalent system. Since such a system is not geared to a systematic approach to structuring behavior, it cannot provide thoroughgoing guidance. The police agency itself can establish clear-cut guidelines, and if it does so, officers will learn to comply (Wilson and Alprin, 1971:494).

To be effective, an internal investigatory unit must focus on two general operational goals: gathering intelligence about agency functioning and inquiring into specific reported cases of official misconduct. In both instances, the aim is to identify potential or actual gaps in organizational preparation to serve the public. This does not mean that such a unit is simply a spy network within the organization. Its overall, systemic goal is to inform the departmental chief executive not only about cases of misconduct but also about the causes of misconduct. It, therefore, has a positive as well as a negative role.

There is, then, agreement among knowledgeable groups and individuals upon the necessity and utility of internal review of police conduct. There is general agreement on the functions of internal investigation as identified by the California Commission on Peace Officer Standards and Training. These functions are protection of the public interest, protection of the integrity and reputation of the police department, and protection of accused employees from unjust accusations (1971:3–53). Agreement on utility and functions does not, however, provide guidance on how an internal investigatory system should be structured or operated.

Internal Investigatory Units

The first issue the head of a department or the external overseers of the department may face in setting up an internal inspectorate or disciplinary system is whether to create a separate, specialized unit. In theory, one of the attributes of the chain of command is that management levels can function as an inspectorate and disciplinary system. For a manager to fulfill his management functions he must monitor the activities of his subordinates, discipline those who contravene the rules, and report problems in policy execution to his superiors.

In small police departments it would be impossible to provide for a full-time, special internal affairs unit. There are alternatives to exclusive review by immediate superiors, however, even while keeping investigations within the department. In Western Australia, for example, although using an immediate superior to investigate a complaint against an officer is not prohibited, it is generally avoided (Harding, 1972:211). In the United Kingdom, according to the Police Act of 1964, complaints against officers must be investigated by an officer of a higher rank and from a different division. Additionally, a chief officer of police may request that an investigation be made by a member of a different force, and he may be compelled to do so by the home secretary. Although from 1969 to 1974, an average of eighty-nine investigations were conducted by officers from outside the department (Russell, 1977:9), the secretary has never used his power to compel one.

An extreme example of keeping an investigation a police matter yet removing it from the chain of command occurred in South Australia. As in all Australian states, there is no separate internal investigatory unit. A new police commissioner, appointed in mid-1972, was faced with allegations that vice squad officers were implicated in a drowning death. To contend with public apprehension about a cover-up he had Scotland Yard send two detectives to investigate the case at a cost of A$20,000 (Harding, 1975:130–31).

Most large police departments have special, internal investigatory units. The New York City Police Department provides a good example of how a well-developed, internal investigatory system in a large department can be organized. The Internal Affairs Division (IAD), directed by the Chief Inspector's Investigation Unit, is responsible for investigation of possible criminal or departmental violations by police officers. The division acts upon complaints by command officers, requests from the district attorney's offices, direct complaints by citizens, and directives from the commissioner's office for special or routine random checks on various units. It also acts in cases that come to its attention from special agents (officially known as field associates) within the department.

In addition to the central IAD, there are field internal affairs divisions within each bureau of the department (for example, patrol, detective, personnel). These units are responsible for investigating less serious charges than the central unit and serve as a more direct link between field personnel and the central mechanisms. The premise underlying maintenance of these smaller, localized units is that their proximity can provide a deterrent to misconduct through peer-group pressure to encourage conformity with expected standards. As a check on the reverse process, co-optation of IAD personnel by the local personnel, the central IAD monitors their investigations by conducting parallel investigations in some cases and by auditing others. In addition to these permanent, specialized units, the department organizes special ad hoc teams to investigate especially important cases.

Two other units are responsible for internal disciplinary investigations. The Public Morals Section, also under the chief inspector, has primary responsibility for notifying licensing agencies about police action involving gambling, vice, and alcoholic beverages. It also records and distributes to appropriate investigatory units complaints made against officers in these areas. The Civilian Complaint Review Board (CCRB), established in 1953, is empowered to investigate and review allegations against police officers for use of unnecessary or excessive force, abuse of authority, discourteous behavior, and ethnic slurs. From June to November 1966, the CCRB was staffed and operated by civilians. Then a referendum ended outside civilian control, and the board has since been staffed by civilian employees of the police department, including two deputy commissioners. Although they may have worked their way up through the department, these commissioners are considered civilians because they are not uniformed police or detectives.

Internal Adjudicatory Processes

Just as the organization of internal investigatory units may vary among departments, so may their jurisdictions and procedures. The New York system divides jurisdiction among the several units. Other departments follow different procedures.

The handling of complaints by citizens is an important aspect of administrative responsibility to the public. In Los Angeles, complaints may be filed at police stations, with police commissioners, elected city officials, or the district attorney. All complaints are then routed to the IAD, which may refer them to the offending officer's precinct for investigation or, if the alleged misconduct is severe or of political significance, will itself investigate. The New York City Police Department specifies that complaints against officers may be made at any time and at any precinct station, the Office of the Civilian Complaint Review Board, or the Office of the Commissioner or of any deputy commissioner. Complaints may be filed by interested persons or groups in writing, in person, or by telephone, whether or not the complainant offers his name (New York City Police Department, Charges and Trials, Section 5.0).

Impartial acceptance of all complaints is necessary to instill public confidence in the internal justice system. The National Commission on the Causes and Prevention of Violence asserted that an increased volume of complaints could be an indication that a department is winning public faith in its integrity (Paulsen et al., 1970:384). The Task Force on the Police of the President's Commission on Law Enforcement and Administration of Justice praised the Oakland, California, department for actively informing the public about its complaint receipt and investigation procedures (1967:195). Such open disclosure has been recommended as a standard by the National Advisory Commission on Criminal Justice Standards and Goals (1973:477).

The procedure for handling complaints is different in different systems. Robert Carr, former British home secretary, contended that the procedure followed in England and Wales set a standard higher than that in any other country in the world (Public Law, 1973:232). All police departments in the United Kingdom are required to maintain an official Complaints Register in which citizen complaints are recorded. When a complaint has been received and recorded, the deputy chief constable appoints an officer to investigate. The investigating officer then informs the accused officer, in writing, that a complaint has been received and gives the details of the complaint and notification that it will be investigated. The accused officer enters a plea and is provided the opportunity to make a statement, which may be used against him in subsequent disciplinary proceedings. The complainant is also asked to make an official on-the-record statement.

The investigating officer's report is then submitted to the deputy chief constable. Unless the complaint is of a nature that would lead to dismissal, the officer remains on normal duty; however, the chief officer of police has unchallengeable discretion to suspend him at two-thirds pay during the investigation, with full pay retroactive if there is no subsequent dismissal, reduction in rank, or suspension without pay. If the complaint is of a criminal nature and seems, after investigation, to be justified, the report is sent to the director of public prosecutions for action. If the complaint is of a noncriminal nature, the deputy chief constable decides whether to dismiss the complaint, admonish the officer, or invoke disciplinary proceedings.

If the officer has pleaded not guilty to a noncriminal allegation that appears founded, a trial is convened. For nonserious charges, the chief constable or his direct subordinate sits as judge and prosecutor. For serious charges, since 1976, a tribunal may be required by the Police Complaints Board. A tribunal consists of the chief constable as chairman and two lay members of the board. In both cases, the defendant is entitled to be informed of all statements obtained by the investigator even if they are not to be used as evidence. He also has the right to assistance and representation by a serving police officer. The standard of proof is less than in criminal cases before a court and generally amounts to satisfactory proof. When tribunals are held, verdicts are by majority decision with punishment determined by the chairman in consultation with the other members (Police Act 1976, section 49).

Outside of the United Kingdom, lay members do not serve on disciplinary tribunals. Even in Britain inclusion of lay members did not come easily. The original House of Commons motion to establish an independent public voice in inquiries into citizens' complaints was made in July 1969. In his annual report for 1969, the chief inspector of constabulary rejected the idea on the grounds that the attempt to increase public confidence would instead undermine police morale. The Police Act of 1976 establishing such tribunals was passed, after a stormy battle in Parliament, seven years after it was proposed.

In spite of the American rejection of lay participation in police internal discipline, concern has been evinced that the adjudicatory process be acceptable to the public. In addition to its recommendation that the complaint receipt process be open, the National Advisory Commission on Criminal Justice Standards and Goals recommended that the adjudicatory process also be open. It held that all persons who file a complaint should be notified of its final outcome and that statistical summaries of the complaints and outcomes be distributed within the department and to the public (1973:477). The Oakland, California, Kansas City, Kansas, and Kansas City, Missouri, police departments were singled out for praise because they notify complainants in person about their complaints' outcomes, a practice the commission felt fosters better understanding and acceptance by the public (478).

Overall, the Los Angeles Police Department's internal discipline system is probably the most highly regarded by American police professionals. Even that system, however, is not conducive to promotion of public faith through openness. Its investigatory system is similar to that in New York. Its Board of Rights' hearings only incidentally involve the original complainant. The department assumes the role of prosecutor, and the complainant becomes merely a witness in the case presented against the officer. The complainant may bring counsel to the hearing, but his attorney may not examine or cross-examine other witnesses or in any way act as an advocate for his client.

No matter what the results of the investigation or the hearing are, the complainant receives only a terse notification that action has or has not been taken. If the complaint was substantiated by the investigation and upheld by the board, the complainant is not informed of what the "appropriate action" taken actually was. When the complaint is not substantiated, the complainant is not told why and is denied access to the report of the investigation (American Civil Liberties Union of Southern California, 1969:20). In a 1980 survey of internal investigatory practices in large American police departments, only the Kansas City, Missouri, Police Department allowed complainants and their attorneys to examine internal affairs investigation records (Krajick, 1980). (The Kansas City department is unusual in that it also has an Office of Civilian Complaints that acts as an official liaison between the internal affairs division and complainants.) The general picture still is one of secrecy.

Such closed procedures may alienate the public and have no compensatory value of securing support from within the department. O. W. Wilson asserted that it is necessary not only to show the public that miscreant officers are punished but also to show the police that establishment of innocence is as important to the reviewers as establishment of guilt (1963:121). Most current rules of proceedings would not seem to engender great faith on the part of rank-and-file officers, however.

Many departments do not provide the opportunity for an administrative trial. Those that have hearing boards follow diverse approaches. Hearings may be held before one superior officer, before a panel of three, five, or seven officers of different ranks (but never a lower rank than the accused), or before a panel of executive rank officials. Right to counsel may or may not exist. Subpoena power is not afforded. Right to confront witnesses is not always provided; in many departments the complainant's only involvement is the initial complaint and testimony to the investigators. The Milwaukee Police Department's *Rules Manual* states, for example, that Board of Inquiry hearings are free from "unnecessary technical rules of evidence" (Wisconsin State Committee, 1972:59). Observation of Philadelphia Police Board of Inquiry hearings found much of the questioning to be immaterial and irrelevant with little effort made by the hearing officer to control improper questioning (Lohman and Misner, 1966:Section III, 198).

The Buffalo commissioner has been accused of subverting the formal hearing process by convoking an informal hearing in which the accused officer could explain his behavior and extenuating circumstances before the formal hearing. After the officer's presentation, the commissioner would advise the officer of what the penalty would be if he pleaded guilty (which would preempt the formal hearing). Officers knew that he would be lenient if there were mitigating circumstances and a guilty plea were made but that he would not be lenient if there were a guilty verdict. Most officers settled for a guilty plea. Control over discipline thus remained in the commissioner's hands, the public disclosure that would follow formal hearings was avoided, and subordinates supported the commissioner because they knew he might show leniency (Halpern, 1974:571).

In Philadelphia, procedures are molded to fit the desires of the officers. The Board of Inquiry hearings have three-member panels, one captain, one lieutenant, and one officer of the same rank as the accused, chosen from a list of ten named by the Fraternal Order of Police, which provides free legal counsel for the officer. The Disciplinary Code provides a clear penalty schedule so that penalties cannot be arbitrary or inconsistent. Citizen complainants have no independent rights at the hearings (no counsel, no cross-examination, no objections). A survey of Philadelphia patrolmen found that a near majority (42 percent) thought that patrolmen were frequently found guilty and penalized severely and that an overwhelming majority (70 percent) thought that patrolmen would not get a fair and impartial trial at departmental hearings (Savitz, 1970:698).

The Dysfunctions of Police Bureaucratization

The police do, and must, exercise great discretion in executing their duties. But this discretion must be controlled. The primary mechanism for providing that control has been based on the principle of check. Actions of individual police are subject to direction by officials above them in the hierarchy and to review by both higher officials and special internal investigatory and adjudicatory units. These higher officials and special units are to guard against arbitrariness and abuse of authority.

Those arrangements seem a good compromise. Nevertheless, there is a lingering question whether bureaucratization has really effected responsibility. In spite of the optimistic expectations of those police executives and other public officials who led the police reform efforts of the 1930s to 1950s, the image of the modern urban police department as a model Weberian bureaucracy is severely vitiated when departments in actual operation are examined. In the Weberian scheme, bureaucratic officials receive specialized training and, by constant practice, learn more and more about their jobs as defined by their employers, and they are responsible for the objective discharge of their duties according to preestablished rules on an impersonal basis (Weber, 1973:15). This view of bureaucratic practice clearly precludes discretionary or innovative activity by low-level members of the organization. It also ignores the power of the informal organization, the web of unprogrammed relations and group norms that arise from the shared experiences of everyday work.

For the police officer in the field the bureaucratic ideal is inapplicable. At the operations level the police officer is relatively autonomous. As was illustrated in chapter 1, the very essence of police work is individual discretionary action in a fluid and often hostile environment. Patrol officers and detectives perform the major portion of their duties in isolation without supervision. Their training experience and their primary job orientation emphasize independent behavior and decision making. The view that initiative and discretion are intrinsic elements of the police occupation collides head-on with the principles of monocratic bureaucracy upon which the police department is organized (Allen, 1982:91).

Individual police officers may be put into action by a dispatch from the communications center, a direct citizen request, or an observed violation. No matter how an officer is activated, once in action he is on his own except in unusual circumstances. As long ago as 1936, Marshall Dimock observed that, although in principle higher officials are granted more room for discretion than lower officials, discretionary power is not in direct ratio to rank. He specifically identified the police as lower-level officials whose discretionary power is extensive (51). James Q. Wilson maintains that in police departments discretion is greatest at the lowest level (1975:7).

Subunit specialization, also highly regarded as a means of ensuring efficiency and bureaucratic-hierarchized authority, has been less than fully functional in that regard. When low-level members of an organization have significant autonomy, the homogeneity of the meaning and role of the entire department and the relationship of subunits to the overall organizational role may be difficult to maintain. Arrangements for direction and control must be peculiar to each subunit. Structural contingencies and constraints affect the distribution of power within various units. A mechanism of control or direction that is successful in one unit or department may not be similarly efficacious in another.

The organizational units in a police department have different work roles, control structures, task environments, and clientele. They are, therefore, variously amenable to control through formal structures. Larry L. Tifft, for example, in a large-scale 1970 observational survey of a large Illinois municipal police department found significant differences among the various functional units. Officers assigned to patrol, traffic, and general detective units operated with little direct supervision. They were spatially dispersed and had little need for interaction with their sergeants. The sergeants had little reward power with regard to assignments and the like, and the men under them did not depend on them for expert guidance, so the sergeants were in a very weak leadership position. The vice and tactical squads needed field coordination of efforts and, consequently, had a low ratio of men to sergeants. In both these units, the sergeants had reward power because they controlled work-team assignments and unit tenure. They also had a measure of expert power and were relied upon in field operations for superior knowledge or experience. Detectives in specialized units such as burglary, homicide, and sex assault also relied on sergeants for expert knowledge and were subject to reward power through work-group assignments. The general imposition of uniform levels of superordination, therefore, is not sufficient to maintain uniform levels of control. The variations in the work patterns largely determine the degree of supervisors' control (1978: 97–104).

Beyond these differences in orientation and internal control, subunit variability may have a more directly debilitating impact on the overall organization. Jerome H. Skolnick found in his study of the Oakland Police Department that even though various subunits directed their operations toward "efficient" law enforcement, the overall effect was not necessarily departmental law enforcement efficiency. The use of informers by the different units is an especially illuminating example of focusing on narrow responsibilities. Skolnick found that burglary and narcotics detectives frequently, even routinely, keep relevant information from each other and avoid learning about their informants' involvement in the other detectives' areas (1975:129). Burglary detectives are especially prone to use dopers as informants, and narcotics detectives know that often their informers commit burglaries, but they do not share this information with their fellow officers in the other units.

Deficiencies of Police Bureaucratization

Lack of Direction from Chiefs of Police. The negative impact of bureaucratic structures on responsibility can be overemphasized. The defects of excessive structure may be ameliorated by effective departmental direction. One of the primary benefits of bureaucracy is deemed to be the ability of the uppermost levels of the hierarchy to make their decisions the basis of organizational performance. As stated in chapter 1, the administrative process could be viewed as directed organizational goal achievement. If the officials in administrative positions take seriously that goal-oriented role they can more effectively deal with the structural problems of bureaucracy. But officials in formal leadership roles are often reluctant to assume a directive function. This failure to see administration in its broad context, moreover, includes not just the internal administrative level of the department but also the external overseers of the department. Without direction, accountability is empty. Being accountable to an organization adrift does not amount to responsibility.

The top administrative official in any bureaucratic organization is the link between the personnel and the elected officials who are the stewards of public power. Ideally, he influences the character and quality of administration by incorporating his own preferences in the more important policies formulated by those above him and carried out by those under his direction. He also selects his subordinates and determines personnel relationships. He serves not only as a director but as an exemplar and legitimizer.

The American Bar Association Project on Standards for Criminal Justice (1973:15) and the *Handbook for Local Government* on police chief selection (Kelly, 1975:6) both point out the significant role of police administrators in local government. But there is a tremendous disparity between the perceived requirements for effective police leadership and the actual conditions. One of the primary sources of this disparity is widespread adherence to the principle of exclusive internal promotion. A 1975 survey of 1,665 United States chiefs of police by the International Association of Chiefs of Police found that a variety of procedures are used for selecting a police chief. Nevertheless, nearly three-fourths (72 percent) of the responding chiefs indicated they had advanced through the department they headed (Police Chief Executive Committee of IACP, 1976:App. D-1, H, M).

The view that a chief should be a policeman who has worked his way up through the ranks is one of the most crucial blockages to effective leadership in law enforcement. Climbing through the ranks cannot provide adequate training for administrative competence. Directing a modern police department is a complex and demanding job that bears little resemblance to writing tickets or performing investigations. The chief must know how to manage the department and how to provide policy guidance. He must assume responsibility for budgetary matters, for public education, for liaison with political officeholders, and much more.

Promotion through the ranks can only incidentally prepare an officer for the challenges of top-level administration. In fact, long experience at street level may actually be detrimental to leadership by narrowing vision. The chief who has risen through the ranks is thoroughly imbued with the occupational and organizational culture. Insofar as he exercises authority over the personnel under his formal command, it may be more because he reflects their interests than because he is exercising his legal responsibility for direction of the department. When the position is achieved as a reward for long service, the person need have no other qualification for the job. In fact, Charles R. Gain, chief of police in San Francisco, maintains that such is the general circumstance. He further notes that most chiefs are so grateful that they have finally made it to the top that they are careful not to jeopardize their position and, therefore, assume a "holding operation" (quoted in Grosman, 1975:13).

Data on the demands and backgrounds of chiefs highlight the deleteriousness of the current system. Although departmental experience is emphasized in choosing a chief, the chiefs surveyed by the International Association of Chiefs of Police reported that less than one-fourth of their time (24 percent) is spent participating in field operations. The rest of their time is devoted to internal management and interaction with other agencies and officials or the public (8 percent, 11 percent, and 14 percent, respectively) (Police Chief Executive Committee of the IACP, 1976:App. D-1, 6). Because tenure in the department is the primary key to promotion, top police officials have a very low degree of formal education; less than one-seventh of the chiefs (14.2 percent) had received at least a baccalaureate degree (Table 4-1).

There are good reasons for the low level of educational attainment. An International City Management Association survey of police departments in cities of over one hundred thousand population found that only 36 percent granted pay increases for education beyond high school. Even more significantly, in spite of the clear need for greater professional and technical training at higher levels in the organization, pay incentives are far less likely at the higher grades. Of the 36 percent of the cities providing pay incentives for education, the distribution doing so for the various grades was as follows: patrolman 100 percent, sergeant 91 percent, lieutenant 85 percent, captain 76 percent, and chief 52 percent (Frankel and Allard, 1972:3).

The muddle at the top of the police agency is not solely a function of the nature of the chief of police role. Responsibility through

Table 4-1. Educational Levels of U.S. Chiefs of Police

Highest Educational Level Achieved	Percent
Law degree	2.5
Master's degree	1.8
Bachelor's degree	9.9
Associate degree	10.8
Some college	37.3
High school graduate	23.6
High school equivalent	9.6
Less than high school diploma	4.5

Source: Police Chief Executive Committee of the IACP, 1976:App. D-1, 5.

accountability requires more than a hierarchy. The failure of direction extends also to the external overseers of the police agencies.

Lack of Direction from External Superiors. The Task Force on the Police of the President's Commission on Law Enforcement and Administration of Justice noted that there is a strong formal commitment to local control of law enforcement in this country (1967:30). The essence of the commitment to control is summed up by Charles R. Gain: "A police department must realize that it is subordinate to the public, the law, the politically elected city council, and the city manager. While there are limitations governing the nature, method, and degree of its accountability, the police constantly must maintain a philosophy of public service" (Gain and Galvin, 1973:14).

As the president's commission pointed out, however, the means of exerting control, not the commitment to control, is where problems lie. Although Gain identifies several sources of legitimate control over police departments, there is no clear way to determine the relative degrees of responsibility among them. In line with the general American diversity in forms of local government arrangements, the International Association of Chiefs of Police reports that a variety of offices and institutions are immediately superior to the chief (Table 4-2). Nor are the superior-subordinate relationships among these various offices and institutions uniform.

The most common arrangement is for the bureaucratic head of the police department to be immediately subordinate to the municipal chief executive (either city manager or mayor). Gain and Galvin (1973) identify five key areas of police management to which a city

Table 4-2. Immediate Superiors of Chiefs of Police

Immediate Superior	Percent
Mayor	31.0
City manager	31.9
Director of public safety	10.4
City council	17.9
Police commission	7.1
Electorate	0.9

Source: Police Chief Executive Committee of the IACP, 1976:App. D-1, K.

manager or mayor should give special attention. Foremost among them is helping to clarify departmental goals and establish priorities among those goals. Even though it is an accepted principle that policy making and policy execution are intertwined, the two are conceptually distinct. Although there are legal and other limitations on how much the chief executive can involve himself in the latter and how much the police executive can involve himself in the former, there is still broad leeway in establishing a philosophy and style of policing. Second, the chief executive should encourage the police chief to fulfill his leadership role, both within the police department and as a member of the municipal administration leadership team. Third, the chief executive should ensure that there is an aggressive and sincere police-community relations program. Finally, the police administrator should be required to develop a system of performance evaluation and be forced to commit the department to efficient and effective operations. In sum, the chief executive should do all he can to ensure that he has a chief of police rather than a chief policeman.

In the great majority of cases, such an active role is rarely fulfilled by the chief executive. Although most mayors and city managers take responsibility for the hardware and technology of law enforcement, they avoid involvement in substantive concerns. When the chief executive and the police administrator communicate with each other they generally confine their attention to routine matters such as labor relations or funding or to crisis situations.

There are several reasons for the lack of effective interaction. Although the chief executive may recognize that he has a significant responsibility in public safety, he is also aware of pitfalls. The public expects him to take action in law enforcement crises whether or not he has formal authority. At the same time there has been significant pressure to protect the criminal justice system from untoward influence. Furthermore, crime and public safety can be highly emotional issues that are not amenable to rational assuagement. It, therefore, becomes politically prudent to avoid imbroglios over police policy.

Many municipal chief executives have actively aided in perpetuating the myth that police are discretionless functionaries enforcing the letter of the law. If the police are merely ministerial agents of the law, any effort to influence their actions would be an effort to manipulate the law. At the same time, chief executives have long labored to insulate the bureaucracies from partisan political pressure as a means of enhancing their own control over administration. Insulation has, however, contributed to agency autonomy. Professional city managers tend to be highly mobile, whereas the police chief often has long tenure and has built up a supporting clientele that enables him to challenge the manager over policy direction and thereby increase his autonomy. As a result, the chief executive abdicates responsibility for police policy and may even make noninterference in police department affairs an operational priority.

Leadership and control by the legislative body has similarly been lacking. There is a general position that the city council or board of supervisors acts as a board of directors with regard to the local administration. The council has primary responsibility for determination of broad policy, appropriations, establishment of the framework of organization, general control of personnel policy, and control and oversight of administrative procedure.

According to optimistic accounts, the city manager movement and the professionalization of local administration have been accompanied by a clarification of responsibility whereby petty legislative interference in administration is reduced and executive responsibility consolidated (Appleby, 1952:119). In fact, as was pointed out with regard to the pattern of relationships between chief executives and police administrators, apparently clear areas of responsibility are often more conducive to independent action than to consolidated responsibility and clear areas of direct accountability. Administrative organizations receive only intermittent and uncoordinated direction and control from the legislature. At the local level as at the national, legislators do not find their basic function to be initiation of substantive legislation.

Popular education and integration of conflicting interests and viewpoints have assumed legislative primacy (Friedrich, 1950:297). Legislative intervention in the administrative process thus tends to be highly particularistic, often motivated by partisan jealousies or reflecting fear of rather than confidence in the administrative apparatus.

Although legislative investigations can provide information about the needs and qualities of the bureaucracy and may be productive in bringing to light cases of injustice or malfeasance, they do not provide a constructive basis for direction. In short, local legislative bodies have all of the handicaps of local chief executives in assuming leadership and control over the police bureaucracy. Unfortunately, they have none of the positive qualities.

The failure of external leadership involves more than political issues and the structural impediments that have been a concomitant of urban reform. Cultural values that support a presumed separation of politics and administration encourage political officials to see policing as a technical problem.

The "Retreat to Technology." Max Weber warned that the bureaucrat's expert knowledge could reverse the master-servant relationship formally ascribed to political masters and administrative servants. The city manager generalist or the elected mayor can easily feel that he is at a disadvantage in dealing with police executives. These officials usually lack knowledge of police work. They are aware of the political power of the police and the political liabilities of identification with crime-related policies. Furthermore, although the political culture places a high value on civilian control, there is a venerable American faith in technology that reinforces these feelings of incompetence.

The faith in technology leads to a belief that fundamental societal problems can be treated administratively—that the key problem is finding the experts and letting them work out the solutions. Such faith is eminently seductive. It easily can give rise to what Philip Selznick calls "the retreat to technology," a process that is guaranteed to preclude an adequate definition of institutional mission. Selznick maintains that when military and diplomatic personnel attempt to identify a sphere of purely military decisions, they withdraw within boundaries that mark known principles and known rules of application of principles. Both sides, consequently, establish a rationale for avoidance of responsibilities for decisions that cut across the boundaries (1957:74–76).

Harold Laski long ago warned that there is no illusion so fatal to good government as allowing individuals to make their expert insight the measure of social need (1930:106). Nevertheless, that is precisely what the retreat to technology represents. Once the police have been acknowledged as experts in all matters of law enforcement, the public and its political institutions have avoided involvement by deferring judgment on questions dealing with the police.

A bureaucratic head should be required to give his expert opinion on the wisdom, dangers, and likely or possible consequences of proposed policies. For the chief executive to allow the bureaucratic perspective to dictate the course of action is an abject abdication of responsibility. Although such abdication may be premised on the belief that treatment of problems in a technical manner is correct, a likely consequence is to support or enhance the power position of the bureaucracy.

A striking example of how far the retreat to technology has eroded joint responsibility for police policy is provided by an exchange between Mayor John V. Lindsay of New York and Norman Frank, the Police Benevolent Association counsel, in December 1967. Even though Lindsay had clear statutory responsibility for fixing public policy in all areas of city government and publicly asserted that responsibility, Frank attacked him for intentionally undermining the police. The point of contention was that City Hall was actively calling policy in all areas of departmental activity in the face of objections within the department. Frank particularly deplored the fact that "the people who are interfering at the highest levels have no background in law enforcement" (Ruchelman, 1974:42).

The Dysfunctions of Punishment-Centered Internal Affairs Systems

Departmental Consequences. The internal affairs system has also fallen short of expectations. There are significant differences of opinion over the efficacy of specific internal review systems. In Chicago, for instance, the Citizens' Committee, appointed by Mayor Richard Daley to look into police-community relations, reported in May 1967 that internal investigations were thorough and efficient and assured punishment of guilty officers. In December 1967, however, the *Chicago Daily News* reported that an officer, Jack Muller, had uncovered a police theft ring and informed the Internal Investigation Division (IID) but to no avail. Muller was quoted as saying the IID was like "a great big washing machine: everything you put in comes out clean" (Knoohuizen, 1974:13).

Such conflict involving individual departments is to be expected and does not necessarily indicate major problems. There are, however, valid reasons for questioning the efficacy of internal affairs systems as currently operated. Just as overreliance on the bureaucratic model has had a deleterious impact on leadership by equating hierarchy with direction and command with control, it may have had a deleterious impact on leadership by equating repression with correction. One of the major shortcomings of American police (and of police in other common law countries as well) is the dependence placed on the internal justice system to provide responsibility.

According to Alvin W. Gouldner, such a situation is not surprising. Building upon Arthur O. Lovejoy's assertion that every theory generates a set of sentiments, "a metaphysical pathos of ideas," he asserts that Weber's theory of bureaucracy carries with it a structure of sentiments engendering pessimism and fatalism. Since adoption of the theory carries with it adoption of its *Weltanschauung*, bureaucratic organization becomes "punishment centered" (1955:24).

When the punishment-centeredness described by Gouldner is recognized as a potential concomitant of bureaucratic organization a light is shown on the failure of that form of organization to deliver what it ostensibly promised. An important element in establishing responsibility in the police system is a reorientation from negative (punishment-centered) and repressive structures to positive and corrective structures.

The number of rules is not the problem confronting police departments. William A. Westley noted in his study of a suburban Chicago department that the rules were so extensive and minutely detailed that no one could obey all of them all the time (1970:24, 27). Since everyone was open to potential disciplinary action, such action lost much of its significance. The threat of punishment was more likely to accomplish paranoia than responsibility. Indeed, an article on internal affairs divisions was subtitled "Fear, Loathing and Mystery" (Krajick, 1980). A pervasive fear of punishment for honest mistakes and a belief that even the most minor transgression must be hidden exists in many departments. When negative sanctions are the primary focus of internal behavior control, officers will concentrate on avoiding doing bad rather than on doing good. In the process, fear of the former can effectively suppress desire for the latter.

Superiors know that there are too many rules and do not expect all of them to be observed. They are put in the position of either looking ridiculous for stressing the need to comply fully with all the rules or of looking tyrannical for enforcing a Draconian regimen. Consequently, they commonly tolerate wholesale disregard of the rules and actively encourage surreptitious minor violations by punishing only blatant, repetitive, or serious infractions. Jack J. Preiss and Howard J. Ehrlich found that Nebraska State Police recruits gradually lost anxiety about formal rules and learned local norms (1966:19). Similarly, in England, Maurene E. Cain found that inspectors were not expected to look for violations and were expected to take action against their men only when catching them flagrante delicto (1971:90).

Since everyone seems to be violating some rules much of the time, individual officers must be discreet and depend on peer acquiescence. The informal structure of the department resulting from spontaneous personal interaction rests not just on behavior patterns not covered by the formal rules but on active contravention of the formal rules. Being repressive rather than supportive, the hierarchy cannot be depended upon to provide the confidence necessary for an individual to function in a hostile environment. Each officer must develop a supporting network to afford him protection both in the field and in the station house.

Superior officers cannot rely on the information that comes up through the hierarchy because it will be highly edited. They have the alternative of maintaining an extensive internal spy system. Such a system has inherent deficiencies. It must be large enough to monitor the whole department. As it acquires and processes the information it gathers, it has the potential to become a power center independent of the administrative level of the department. An effective mechanism for oversight of the spy system becomes necessary. The direct costs of operating a complex spy system are great, but there is also a significant indirect cost. Conversion of the disciplinary system into a spy network virtually eliminates its legitimacy for the rank-and-file officers.

The reliance on the rules and punishment leads, according to Fritz J. Roethlisberger, to a vicious cycle. The unintended dysfunctional consequences of the traditional control methods tend to encourage continued usage of them. The inefficacy of the rules leads to more rules to take care of the inefficacy. The long-run effect is a continuous process of reactive rulemaking (1964:54). Discipline is, therefore, relied on to bolster a failure of direction. Conformity to rules and formalized procedures is substituted for understanding and rational determination of behavior in complex circumstances.

Public Relations Consequences. It is not only with regard to departmental personnel that internal affairs divisions as tools of command orientation have been dysfunctional. The internal affairs division can act as a communication channel. It can, therefore, be used as a feedback channel from the public presumed to be served by a particular police department and thereby create a symbolic tie between the department and the citizenry. Because administrative responsibility in a democracy is related to responsiveness to public desires, the failure to mobilize internal affairs as a vehicle of police-public interface indicates a gap in the efforts to effect responsibility.

A major question for police policy makers is how well the various internal investigatory systems fulfill their task of making police action responsible. The key issues are the organizational consequences of the complaint investigation and adjudication system and the impact of those consequences on the administrative process and public policy. Unfortunately, there is very mixed opinion on this issue.

In Chicago, a Citizens' Committee to Study Police Community Relations reported to the mayor that the Internal Investigation Division functioned as desired. The committee found that citizens' complaints received serious and thorough investigation followed by punishment of the guilty (1967:31). It even held that a cover-up would be almost impossible because of the sophisticated monitoring of each investigation. An Australian commentator on the investigation of public complaints in England and Wales came to the same conclusions (Harding, 1972:204–105).

Such optimism may be somewhat overexuberant, however. The Citizens' Committee noted that some aggrieved citizens failed to avail themsevles of the complaint-remedy system. Even in England, with the system that sets a higher standard than any other country in the world, there is a basis for disquiet. Ken Russell's study of complaint investigation in England found a sizable number of potential complainants who failed to make use of the grievance procedures. Although he could not estimate the number of individuals, he was able to identify six basic reasons for refraining from invoking the complaint process. People failed to complain because they were: advised by an expert that it was not practical; apathetic; apprehensive of retaliation; fatalistic, believing nothing would be done; public-spirited; or unaware of how to do it (1977:52–53).

There are also structural elements that deter complaints. The typical complaint consists of an assertion that a policeman committed a transgression unwitnessed except by the complainant alone or with other police officers who are not disinterested. The officer denies the charges. The departmental superiors have no means of corroborating either account. Most often the complainant is lower in the social status hierarchy than the policeman and, therefore, less believable. Even when the complainant is not lower in the social hierarchy and his veracity is less in doubt, the consequences of frequently disbelieving subordinates would be detrimental to departmental morale.

The complaints, moreover, frequently involve some form of misbehavior which, although contrary to good manners or prevailing police practice, is not illegal or clearly against departmental policy. When exercising discipline, superior officers have to be attentive not only to making the employee more tractable in the future but also to the effect on other employees as well as the public. The public is a diffuse, nontangible conception, whereas the officer and the force are concrete and identifiable. The superior may, therefore, be forced to uphold an officer's conduct which he finds reprehensible or foolish. He is compelled to maintain that if an action were not illegal or illicit in departmental terms, it is nonculpable. The superior is, perforce, constrained, by circumstances largely beyond his control, to accept both the officer's version of the incident and the permissibility of his actions, unless there is good reason to believe that he has fabricated the story or has, in fact, violated the law or departmental policy.

Individual officers can take steps to preempt effective complaint processing. One of the most common is to arrest potential complainants. (For New York City see Bittner, 1970:81; for Philadelphia see President's Commission on Law Enforcement and Administration of Justice, 1967:195, and Hudson, 1970:191–92; for Washington, D.C., see Paulsen et al., 1970:405, n. 126). This tactic of accusing the accuser can be a ploy to gain a bargaining chip. Police can drop charges in exchange for withdrawal of the complaint in a process of implicit reciprocal exculpation. Arrest can also be used indirectly to discredit the veracity of the complainant. Short of arresting the complainant, the officer can note in his report of the original incident that the complainant was drunk, on dope, or deranged. During the progress of the investigation, it can be established and written into the record that the complainant had a criminal record.

Russell, in his examination of complaint procedures in two English cities, found a striking relationship between the discrediting circumstances surrounding an incident and the probability of the complaint being substantiated. He constructed an index of discredibility based on the incident report considering arrest, criminal record, mental illness, under the influence of alcohol, and under the influence of drugs as discrediting elements. He found that 80 percent of the substantiated cases involved individuals with a zero on the index and that there were no substantiated charges against an officer when the complainant had a two or more on the index. Among charges substantiated, of those made by individuals with a zero on the index, 40 percent were substantiated; of those made by individuals with a one on the index, only 10 percent were substantiated. Significantly, the effect of discredibility was intensified when complainants were grouped by class. Complainants with working-class status had only 63 percent as great a rate of substantiation as middle-class complainants with no discrediting elements; they had only 38 percent as great a success rate with one discrediting element (1977:70).

The police apparently have the power to screen off a large number of complaints. In addition, there is some opinion that board of rights hearings are only marginally concerned with providing redress for citizens. Rather, the operational goal of internal affairs departments seems to be enforcement of internal discipline. The Los Angeles Police Department claims, however, that although the board of rights hearings are restricted, they still serve to protect citizens from police malpractice and that even though such hearings are closed, they are in no way prejudiced in favor of police officers.

Los Angeles, like other cities, does not release details of trial board proceedings. Nevertheless, the American Civil Liberties Union of Southern California was able to secure a court order for access to departmental files for the three-year period 1965–67. During those years, 42.4 percent of the charges brought to department trial were sustained. Comparison of charges of neglect of duty, which are predominantly internally generated, with charges for excessive force, which are primarily citizen-generated, showed a tremendous difference in rate of sustainment: 80.6 percent for neglect of duty versus 7.8 percent for excessive force (Table 4-3).

Los Angeles is not unique in regard to complaint disposition. In New York thre is a very similar pattern when charges for departmental infractions are compared with citizens' (Civilian Complaint Review Board) complaints for the cohort of officers appointed to the department in 1957 (Table 4-4). The Los Angeles and New York rates of substantiation of citizens' complaints compare favorably with the rates in London and the rest of England and Wales and are far above the rate for Western Australia (Table 4-5). Furthermore, even a low percentage is an improvement over previous periods. Spencer Coxe, former executive director of the Philadelphia chapter of the ACLU, claimed that in the sixteen years before the establishment of the Philadelphia Police Advisory Board, the ACLU knew of "not one instance of the Police Department's disciplining a member of the force because of a wrong done a civilian, on the complaint of a civilian" (1961:140). During the life of the advisory board, 1958–66, however, 330 officers were disciplined by the Police Board of Inquiry for civilian-initiated complaints (Hudson, 1972:430).

Distinguishing Form and Substance in Police Bureaucracy

Judging by outward appearance, the modern urban police force closely approximates Max Weber's ideal monocratic bureaucracy. In theory, therefore, if Weber is to be believed, police departments should be capable of attaining a high degree of efficiency (1952:24). The facts of the actual police role and mode of operation bring such a conclusion into serious doubt.

Table 4-3. Los Angeles Police Department Board of Rights Hearings,
          1965–1967

	All Complaints				
Year	Received	Sustained	Percent Sustained		
1965	979	445	45.4		
1966	953	415	43.5		
1967	1,016	391	38.5		
Total	2,948	1,251	42.4		

	Excessive Force			Percentage of Total Sustained Cases
Year	Received	Sustained	Percent Sustained	
1965	231	12	5.2	2.4
1966	301	16	5.3	3.8
1967	369	42	11.4	10.7
Total	901	70	7.8	

	Neglect of Duty			Percentage of Total Sustained Cases
Year	Received	Sustained	Percent Sustained	
1965	326	265	81.2	59.9
1966	288	232	80.6	55.9
1967	241	192	79.9	49.1
Total	855	689	80.6	

Source: American Civil Liberties Union of Southern California, 1969:22.

Like all formal organizations, police departments need to be given
direction and purpose. In spite of the organizational system used,
which should facilitate command from the center, the nature of police
work involving personal initiative, personal judgment, and indepen-
dent action encourages autonomy at the lowest levels. Nevertheless,
administrators, city managers, police commissioners, and elected pol-
iticians seem to have accepted the proposition that the departments
are, in fact, ideal bureaucracies and that individual officers are minis-
terial agents who merely carry out the law.

Table 4-4. Disposition of Complaints against New York City Police
Officers Who Joined the Department in 1957

Type of Complaint	Distribution (percent)	Sustained (percent)
Criminal	9.5	64.5
Departmental	65.1	83.3
Civilian	25.3	16.8
Overall	99.9*	56.7

*Error due to rounding
Source: Cohen, 1970:25.

This fundamental misunderstanding about police operations and
police organization has led to an abdication of leadership. Acceptance
of the myth of ministerial policemen has fostered a belief that a chief
policeman should head a department. The result has been a tradition
of choosing a chief from among the longest tenured members of an
agency. Although such a chief may favor reform, he is a product of the
system. Even when he learns of policies with which he disagrees, he
may refrain from taking action.

The problems extend to levels above the chiefs. The belief that
police activity is a technological issue has placed heavy burdens on
those political officeholders who attempt to play an active role in
police policy. Both the police and the public are wary of politicians'
influence over police departments. In reformed departments politi-
cians are seen as corruptors. In unreformed departments, even
though the police owe their positions to the politicians, the latter are
suspect because they can upset the internal balance of the department
by creating dissensus and factions.

The public seems to endorse the position that policy making for the
police should be left to the experts. In a 1969 survey of middle-class
Detroit, for example, a near majority (42 percent) of the 624 re-
spondents thought that the mayor exercised the most influence in
police policy making. Asked who they thought should be most influ-
ential, however, the majority (61 percent) named the police commis-
sioner. The mayor was named last out of five possible choices (Table
4-6).

Table 4-5. Comparison of Citizens' Complaints against Police Officers Upheld by Police Internal Reviews

Jurisdiction	Percent Sustained
1. New York City	16.8
2. England and Wales*	11.4
3. London	7.2
4. Los Angeles	5.6
5. Western Australia	1.7

*Exclusive of London Metropolitan Police.
Sources: (1) Cohen, 1970:20; (2) Regan, 1971:403–5; (3) Russell, 1977:61; (4) ACLU, 1969:22; (5) Harding, 1972:212.

At the same time the potential for direction is undercut by the myths of ministeriality and the technological nature of policing, the potential for effecting administrative responsibility through an internal review system is undercut by making the system punishment-centered. Many officers see internal affairs as mysterious, arbitrary, and cruel. In fact, secrecy is so common that an IACP survey of seventeen large departments found that only a little over one-half of their of-

Table 4-6. Public Opinion on Police Policy-Making Responsibility in Detroit

Who Exercises the Most Influence in Police Policy Making		Who Should Exercise the Most Influence in Police Policy Making
(percent identifying)		(percent identifying)
42	Mayor	4
17	Common council	8
23	Police commissioner	61
12	Police associaton	8
6	Citizens of Detroit	19

Source: Goldner and Koenig, 1972.

ficers understood how internal affairs operated or what would happen to them if they were investigated (Pederson, 1977). Not surprisingly, many officers lack faith in internal affairs departments to vindicate them when they are unjustly accused of misconduct. Citizens, similarly, often see such divisions as part of the police department and not interested in the public. Neither the police nor the public is able to see them as neutral fact-finders concerned with fair and open treatment of accused officers and aggrieved citizens.

It would be too extreme to conclude that responsibility as accountability is improbable. It does appear, however, that the current administration of the traditional police organization is confronted with contradictions that stem from the nature of police work and from assumptions about administrative processes in the police bureaucracy. In short, accountability has been no more successful in ensuring responsibility than has obedience. Thus several observers have concluded that perhaps it is not possible to enforce responsibility from outside the personnel who are police officers.

5 Responsibility as a Problem of Representativeness

I: Equal Employment Opportunity

In the bureaucratic model of police organization the primary mechanism for securing responsibility is for the departmental hierarchy to make rules which departmental personnel are to follow. The rules are to be based on the expert knowledge that superior officers have gained during performance of progressively more broadly focused jobs within the department. When individual officers break the rules they are to be disciplined either through the chain of command or through specially designed administrative control procedures. Responsibility is treated as a problem of accountability. The system is almost totally depersonalized. The rules are applicable to all and are enforced impersonally by departmental authority figures who act through their professional positions, not as individuals.

In the bureaucratic model personnel administration is seen as a technical matter. The emphasis on efficiency and predictability results in application of these criteria to the hiring and management of human resources. Attention is focused on achieving a good fit between personnel and structures and procedures. There are two major reasons for this focus. First, police work involves human services. Even though computers, telecommunication and forensic sciences equipment, and other sophisticated hardware are now common in police departments, most police work is still person-to-person. Second, police work is labor-intensive. Not only are most police duties person-centered but personnel costs account for the major portion of operating budgets (Table 5-1). Given these two factors, it follows that the same rational processes are applied to personnel management as are applied to structural design.

Table 5-1. Personnel Expenditures as Percentage of Total Police
Department Expenditures

Population Group	Percentage
1,000,000	93
500,000–999,999	85
250,000–499,999	86
100,000–249,999	86
50,000– 99,999	86
25,000– 49,999	85
10,000– 24,999	84
Geographic Region	
Northeast	90
North Central	89
South	83
West	86
Metropolitan Status	
Central	88
Suburban	86
Independent	83
Form of Government	
Mayor-Council	89
Council-Manager	85
Commission	88

Source: National Criminal Justice Information and Statistics Service, 1980:40.

For most of the past century, police personnel administration has
emphasized a mechanical approach to recruitment, predominantly
the civil service merit system. Traditionally, entry into police work has
been based on paper-and-pencil aptitude or achievement tests supple-
mented with physical examinations and sometimes agility tests and
oral examinations. An entering recruit serves a probationary period.
After successfully completing probation, an officer can be removed
from the police force only for serious violations of departmental rules
or the law and then only after complex hearing and review
procedures.

There have been three basic challenges to the principles of the traditional civil service personnel system in police administration. First, it has been alleged that there is little if any relationship between the test scores and actual police performance (Cohen and Chaiken, 1972) since the basis of the system is protection of the civil service from political influences (Carter, 1978:1; Sayre, 1948). It has also been alleged that an independent civil service commission undercuts executives by depriving them of flexibility in assignment of personnel and denying discipline and reward capabilities (Wilson and McLaren, 1977:246; Shafritz, 1978:36–37). Finally, it has been alleged that the traditional system is geared to preservation of white, Anglo-Saxon, middle-class dominance of the civil service (Rosenbloom, 1971:72; Congressional Research Service, 1976). These criticisms bridge the concerns of the preceding chapter (accountability) and the present one (representativeness). The criticism that police executives do not have control of personnel and that job skills are not reflected in traditional testing fit the concerns of bureaucratization. Imperative control over personnel and efficiency are the essential putative benefits of bureaucracy. The criticism that the traditional approach has served the interest of a specific segment of the population is at the heart of the issue of representativeness.

The increased concern with compatibility between personnel policies and police work is an advance over simple faith in organizational structure and rules. Such concern recognizes that holding individuals to account for misconduct cannot override the need for qualified individuals. If the personnel are not capable of appropriate conduct, little good will be achieved by punishing them for inappropriate conduct. Of itself the effort to get better qualified police officers does not have a significant impact on responsibility. Accountability remains the dominant approach to responsibility.

An alternative approach to responsibility is to combine the effort to secure technically qualified personnel with an effort to secure a work force demographically representative of the community served. The premise is that a democratic government must be representative and that representativeness may be both active (as in the case of elected officials) and passive (as in the case of civil servants). As expressed through the equal employment opportunity (EEO) mandate, this premise is joined with the assumptions that all demographic groups in society share the desire to provide public service and that if artificial barriers to entry into the public service which limit access by certain groups are removed, the composition of the public service will mirror the composition of the general public. As public policy, EEO is prescribed as a vehicle for achieving responsible administration by building commitment to serve the whole public because of affinity between the civil service and the community.

This chapter will discuss the nature of the EEO mandate and its impact on police personnel administration. It will, first, present an overview of the legal dimensions of EEO. Second, it will outline the enforcement mechanisms for the mandate. Finally, it will analyze the impact of EEO on the various aspects of police personnel administration. The following chapter will address the logical extension of the passive representation version of responsibility beyond EEO; it will deal with affirmative action to achieve representativeness.

The Equal Opportunity Mandate

Development before 1964

The most significant single step in the drive for equal employment opportunity was passage of the Civil Rights Act of 1964. Title VII of the act banned discrimination in employment on the basis of race, color, sex, and national origin. The roots of the legal effort to combat discrimination actually lie in federal legislation enacted a century earlier. The Civil Rights Acts of 1866 and 1871 and the Fourteenth Amendment to the United States Constitution (1868) remain active sources of litigation in discrimination cases involving police departments. Each became applicable to employment discrimination cases only after 1964, but the extent to which they have been invoked since that time attests to their significance.

The Civil Rights Act of 1866 (42 U.S.C. 1981, commonly referred to as Section 1981) states: "All persons within the jurisdiction of the United States shall have the same right in every State and Territory to make and enforce contracts . . . as is enjoyed by white citizens." Litigation of discrimination charges falls under this statute on the grounds that employment constitutes a form of contract. The exact boundaries of Section 1981 are not clear, however. In *Brown* v. *General Services Administration* (1976), it was held that the statute does not apply to federal government employment but that it does apply to both the public and private sectors. It has been applied to municipal police departments in several cases, most notably *Washington* v. *Davis* (1976) and *United States* v. *City of Chicago* (1977).

The Civil Rights Act of 1871 (Section 1983) applies explicitly and nearly exclusively to government units and agencies. Again, the federal government is excluded from coverage. It provides that

any person who under color of any state or territorial law "sub-
jects, or causes to be subjected" any person "to the deprivation of any
rights, privileges, or immunities secured by the Constitution and
laws shall be liable to the party injured." This statute is relevant
because the Civil Rights Act of 1964 made equal employment oppor-
tunity a protected legal right. Until 1978 the act was held not to
be applicable in the public sector to units of government. The
Supreme Court had held in *Monroe* v. *Pape* (1961) that munici-
palities were not persons under Section 1983 and in *Moor* v. *Alameda*
(1973) that counties were not. In 1978, however, the Court reversed
itself and held that local government bodies could be sued directly
(*Monell* v. *Department of Social Services of the City of New York*).
This section has been less liberally construed in employment
cases than has Section 1981. It was an available cause of action
before the Civil Rights Act of 1964 was extended to state and
local government in 1972. It is of less importance to police per-
sonnel administration today than during the period from 1964
to 1972.

As the legal basis for equal employment opportunity developed be-
fore 1964 a number of statutes and executive orders were directly
addressed to the problem of discrimination in personnel policy. The
Classification Act of 1923 required the federal government to follow
the principle of equal compensation for equal work irrespective of sex.
The Fair Labor Standards Act of 1938 was amended by the Equal Pay
Act of 1963 and prescribed equal pay for equal work irrespective of
sex for workers engaged in interstate commerce and forbade unions
to cause or attempt to cause employers to discriminate in rates of
compensation on the basis of sex. Executive Order 8802, issued by
President Franklin D. Roosevelt in 1941, banned defense contractors
from discriminating in employment practices on the basis of race,
creed, color, or national origin. In 1961, President John F. Kennedy
extended the nondiscrimination requirement to all federal contrac-
tors through Executive Order 11141, banning age discrimination by
government contractors.

Clear but halting steps were taken toward ensuring non-
discrimination in employment in public policy before 1964. Only
since 1964, however, has the depth of commitment to the principle
of equal employment opportunity been articulated. And only since
1972, when the employment practices provisions of the Civil Rights
Act of 1964 became applicable to state and local government, has
police personnel administration been markedly affected by that
commitment.

The Civil Rights Act of 1964 and After

The single most important piece of legislation pertaining to equal employment opportunity in American history is Title VII of the Civil Rights Act of 1964, enacted on 2 July 1964. Section 703(a) makes it an unlawful employment practice for an employer "(1) To fail or refuse to hire or to discharge any individual, or otherwise to discriminate against any individual with respect to his compensation, terms, conditions, or privileges of employment . . . or . . . (2) To limit, segregate, or classify his employees in any way which would deprive or tend to deprive any individual of employment opportunities or otherwise adversely affect his status as an employee, because of such individual's race, color, religion, sex, or national origin." Title VII also created the Equal Employment Opportunity Commission (EEOC) to enforce the nondiscrimination mandate.

When a complaint is made alleging employment discrimination contrary to Title VII, the commission is required to notify the employer within ten days and then to begin an investigation of the charge but not to make the charge public. If a reasonable cause to believe that the charge is true is found, the commission is to attempt informal action to reconcile the parties and eliminate the unlawful practice. These negotiations are not to be made public and may not be introduced as evidence in subsequent legal proceedings. If no conciliation agreement is reached, the commission may bring a civil action against the employer. When the commission determines that prompt judicial action is necessary to preclude further violations of Title VII, action may be brought to secure a temporary restraining order from a federal district court. If there is no finding of reasonable cause to believe that unlawful employment activity has occurred, or if the commission fails to act after 180 days, the party bringing the original charge may personally bring suit. In such a case, the court may appoint counsel for the complainant without cost.

If the court finds that the employer has violated the law, it may prohibit continuation of the illegal practice and take other action to remedy past illegality. Remedial action can include reinstatement or hiring of aggrieved parties, with or without back pay, or other similar forms of relief. Back pay may not, however, be accruable for more than two years before the filing of the charge with the commission, and amounts earned in other employment during this period by the person discriminated against reduce the back pay allowable. The prevailing party in a suit under Title VII is eligible, within the discretion of the court, to receive reasonable attorney's fees from the losing party. Of course, the findings of the court on all matters are subject to appeal.

As originally enacted, Title VII applied to private sector employers, labor unions, and employment agencies. The federal government, corporations owned by the United States, Indian tribes, agencies of the District of Columbia, tax-exempt private membership clubs, religious corporations, associations, and societies employing individuals to carry on a religious purpose, and state and local governments and their agents were exempt from coverage. In 1972, Title VII was amended by the Equal Employment Opportunity Act. Most significant about this amendment for police administration was the extension of coverage of Title VII to state and local governments.

Title VII of the Equal Employment Opportunity Act of 1972 is not the only public policy element that bears on the process of police personnel administration. The act revived interest in the nineteenth-century civil rights acts. It reinforced earlier statements of the essential place of nondiscrimination in employment practices. The 1972 act has been the major focus of litigation in the area of employment discrimination, but it has also affirmed the primacy of equality of treatment in a fashion unparalleled since the post-Civil War period.

Several other public policy steps that followed the 1964 act and extended the scope of the nondiscrimination mandate have had an impact on police personnel administration. Some of these apply to state and local government units and agencies in general, for example, the Equal Pay Act of 1963, which precludes wage discrimination on the basis of sex, and the Age Discrimination in Employment Act of 1967 were both extended to cover state and local governments by the Fair Labor Standards Amendments of 1974. Nevertheless, because of the complex issues related to federalism and social welfare policies of the national government, there has been much greater effort to induce conformance with federal objectives through control of financial aid than through direct legislative mandate.

The State and Local Fiscal Assistance Act of 1972 provides for sharing of federal income tax revenues with state and local government units. Section 122(a) of the act, as amended in 1976, states that no person shall "be excluded from participation in, be denied the benefits of, or be subjected to discrimination under any program or activity" funded under the act on the basis of race, color, national origin, sex, age, handicap, or religion. The section authorizes the attorney general to initiate civil suits against grant recipients determined to have engaged in a discriminatory practice or pattern; it further empowers the federal courts to order suspension, termination, or repayment of revenue-sharing funds. The recipient may escape liability under this section if it can be shown in a clear and convincing manner that the program or activity involving discrimination is not funded in whole or in part with revenue-sharing money. Police departments have been subjected to withholding of funds in *United States* v. *City of Chicago* (1977) and *Officers for Justice* v. *Civil Service Commission* (1978), and the section was cited in a case providing for an internal employment practices review board in *United States* v. *City of Buffalo* (1979).

Predating the Revenue Sharing Act but not actually applied to employment practices until afterward is Title VI of the Civil Rights Act of 1964. This title bars discrimination based on race, color, and national origin in federally funded or supported programs. It has been the subject of far less litigation than Title VII, in part because of uncertainty about the meaning of "program." It was not until 1974 that Executive Order 11764 established enforcement procedures and not until 1977, in *Guardians Association of the New York City Police Department* v. *Civil Service Commission*, that a U.S. district court held that a police department expending federal funds was a program under the law.

In the area of federal government contracts, the broadest effort to require nondiscriminatory employment practices has been Executive Order 11246 issued by President Lyndon B. Johnson on 24 September 1965. The order (as amended by Executive Order 11375 [1967]) requires all government contracting agencies to include in every government contract the promise that the contractor will not discriminate and will take action to ensure that "applicants are employed, and that employees are treated fairly during employment, without regard to their race, color, religion, sex or national origin." In general, the order is enforced by the Office of Federal Contract Compliance Programs (OFCCP). It does, however, include the provision that the secretary of labor may delegate to any officer, agency, or employee in the executive branch of the government any function or duty imposed on him by the order. In the criminal justice area the Department of Labor delegated responsibility for enforcement of the order to the Law Enforcement Assistance Administration's Office of Civil Rights Compliance.

In addition to the OFCCP directive developed as a result of Executive Order 11246, the LEAA Office of Civil Rights Compliance has been given responsibility for oversight of discrimination by contractors by the Crime Control Act of 1973. This act provides that the EEOC shall bring suit against state and local governments that engage in patterns or practices of discrimination in employment. All federal funds available under the act will be cut off forty-five days after the filing of such a suit unless a federal court blocks suspension. In almost all the actions initiated under this section, the courts have in fact blocked the mandatory cut-off. But, in *United States* v. *Commonwealth of*

Virginia (1980) the Fourth Circuit Court of Appeals overturned the district court's stay of the suspension order in a case involving alleged employment discrimination by the Virginia State Police. The potency of the cut-off power is illustrated by the fact that the Commonwealth of Virginia dropped the discriminatory standards when the stay order was vacated.

The LEAA issued its *Equal Employment Opportunity Program Development Manual* in 1973. The *Manual* stipulates that an LEAA grant recipient must include in grant applications a document stating that it will provide mechanisms for equal employment opportunity enforcement; present an equal employment opportunity program or plan; eliminate minimum height and weight requirements that cannot be shown to be bona fide occupational qualifications; anticipate that the statutory exemption of bona fide occupational requirements will be narrowly construed; and validate all selection instruments that have the consequence of disproportionately eliminating minorities and women.

In 1977, the LEAA attempted to counter criticisms that its Office of Civil Rights Compliance was ineffective by issuing a set of procedures for dealing with charges of discrimination. A report of preliminary findings on each complaint investigation must be presented within 150 days of the initiation of the investigation (or within 175 days when an on-sight investigation is necessary). If the grant recipient is found to be using a personnel system, pattern, or practice that discriminates, it has thirty days to bring itself into compliance. At the end of thirty days, the administrator of the LEAA has fourteen days to determine if compliance has been achieved. If it has not, he is to begin administrative procedures cutting off funds.

Even before the dismemberment of the LEAA in 1980, it was apparent that it was not meeting the standards set out by the OFCCP. The United States Commission on Civil Rights found that the agency admitted that it had "no specific knowledge as to the scope of compliance with the height guidelines" (1975:319). A study of the agency's performance with regard to funding formulas, composition of state planning agencies, site selection, service delivery by recipients, educational programs, and employment practices concluded that "in these areas LEAA's record has been dismal" (Salas and Lewis, 1979:396). In October 1977, the Department of Labor withdrew its designation of the Office of Civil Rights Compliance as the criminal justice monitor of Executive Order 11246, leaving the office largely to compile compliance data only for internal use. It may be drawn upon to support Justice Department and Equal Opportunity Commission actions, but given its record these agencies rely on their own efforts.

Since 1964 personnel practices have been an important focus of public policy. Prohibition of discrimination has extended from race, color, creed, national origin, religion, and sex to include age, handicap, Vietnam veterans, marital status, and political beliefs and affiliation (Table 5-2). Not all of the statutes that prohibit these forms of discrimination apply to police personnel practices. Those that do impose various overseers of employment policy. The Equal Employment Opportunity Commission, the Department of Justice, the Department of Labor, and various agencies under them may require reports and information or may bring suit for violations of constitutional amendments, federal statutes, departmental guidelines, and commission rules and regulations. It is small wonder that the equal employment opportunity mandate has had a broad impact on police personnel practices.

Enforcing the Mandate

Mechanisms

For the police service the equal employment opportunity mandate has defined two dominant goals of personnel administration. As always, one goal is to secure the best employees for police departments. Operational efficiency in a rather narrow, technical sense is the controlling factor. Because of the importance of the human factor in police service delivery, a second goal is to provide a model human resources management system in line with the equal employment opportunity ideal. Combating racism, sexism, and other invidious forms of discrimination is the controlling factor. In line with the passive representation version of responsibility, police personnel policy has come to be concerned in filling the ranks not only with people who have the right skills and abilities but also with those who are representative of their communities. This is not to say that group membership is the determinant of suitability for police work; rather, group membership defined by race, national origin, and sex cannot be held to preclude employment in the police service.

Effective personnel administration is clearly dependent on developing policies and following procedures to match jobs and skills. It has been largely as a result of the EEO mandate, however, that effort has been expended to ensure that meaningful matching of individual qualifications with job requirements actually does enter into the various decisional points of the personnel cycle. The various laws, orders, and guidelines that constitute the mandate assume that employers

Table 5-2. Legal Standards Relating to Equal Employment Opportunity
in Police Personnel Administration

Protective Measures	*Purposes*
Amendments V, XIII, XIV	State basic rights
Section 1981	Assure equal rights to make and enforce contracts
Section 1983	Protect civil rights from deprivation under color of law
Section 1985	Provide civil penalty for conspiracy to deprive of civil rights
Civil Rights Act of 1968	Provide criminal penalty for conspiracy to deprive of civil rights
Prohibitive Measures	*Forbid Discrimination by*
Title VII; Discrimination in Employment Act; Equal Pay Act	Employers
Title VI; Revenue Sharing Act; Comprehensive Employment and Training Act	Government grantees
Executive Order 11246; Vocational Rehabilitation Act; Vietnam Era Veterans Readjustment Act; Crime Control Act	Government contractors

seek and desire the most productive employees. The presumption of
the law is essentially that if selection, promotion, and transfer policies
lead to underrepresentation of qualified members of protected classes
or overconcentration of members of protected classes in discrete jobs
or areas, the decisional criteria are not based on concern with produc-
tivity or efficiency but with unlawful discrimination.

The EEO mandate has been difficult to implement because so many
different agencies have been charged with monitoring of employment
practices. Before 1978, the Equal Employment Opportunity Commis-
sion (under Title VII), the Department of Labor (under Executive
Order 11246), the Civil Service Commission (under Title VII, Section
717, and the Intergovernmental-Personnel Act), the Department of
Treasury (under the State and Local Fiscal Assistance Act), the De-
partment of Justice (under various statutes), and other agencies by
delegation all had responsibility for applying the principles of equal
opportunity to employers. Not surprisingly, the result was lack of clear
guidelines for employers to follow in attempting to fulfill their non-

discrimination obligations. The requirements set out by one agency often conflicted with those set out by other agencies. To resolve this situation, the agencies concerned with civilian compliance with the EEO mandate developed *Uniform Guidelines on Employee Selection Procedures*, which became effective 25 September 1978.

Although the *Uniform Guidelines* title specifies employee selection procedures, "selection" is very broadly construed. The *Guidelines* are applicable to selection procedures which are the basis of employment decisions. "Employment decisions" under the *Guidelines* "include but are not limited to hiring, promotion, demotion, membership, referral, retention. . . . Other selection decisions such as selection for training or transfer, may also be considered employment decisions if they lead to any of the decisions listed above." The *Guidelines*, therefore, cover nearly the full range of concerns of human resources management. They may thus be viewed in conjunction with various judicial decisions as forming the basis for identifying the mechanism for enforcement of the EEO mandate.

The impact of the statutory mandate must be viewed from two perspectives. First, from the perspective of the enforcement mechanism, how have the general proscriptions of the laws been converted into specific prescriptions to accomplish the goals of the laws? Second, from the perspective of the police personnel process, how have the administrative and judicial interpretations of the laws, which constitute the enforcement mechanism, affected personnel decisional criteria? Inquiry into the first matter logically precedes the second because only against the background of the enforcement mechanisms can the impact on police personnel administration be placed in its proper context, a context of complex interweaving of public policy, transcendent cultural values, administrative processes, and legal norms.

Procedures and Available Remedies

To carry out the EEO mandate, the designated agencies of the government and the courts have had to put its terms into operation. The laws specify broadly that discrimination on the basis of race, color, creed, religion, national origin, sex, handicap, and age is forbidden. They specify who may not discriminate—employers and contractors with more than fifteen employees, labor unions, and employment agencies. They identify exemptions from coverage. Title VII does not apply, for example, to aliens employed outside the United States or to religious corporations (including schools), and it allows discrimination on the generally proscribed grounds where religion, sex, or national origin is a "bona fide occupational qualification reasonably necessary to the normal operation" of an enterprise. The administrative-judicial system has to fit the generalized statement to real world cases.

Most of the antidiscrimination measures stipulate procedures for processing complaints. The procedural provisions of Title VII have been outlined earlier in this chapter, and, in general, they apply to the other laws and executive orders. The appropriate agency is required to investigate the charge, and when it finds evidence of a violation it must first attempt to secure voluntary compliance with the law. When conciliation fails, the case is turned over to the Justice Department for litigation in the federal courts, or, if action arises under Executive Order 11246, the Revenue Sharing Act, the Crime Control Act, or the other measures involving grants and contracts, funds to the grantee or contractor are terminated.

Under most of the acts and orders, the enforcement agency is expected to prevent violations and to uncover uncomplained-of violations as well as to undertake efforts at remedial action when conciliation fails and there is an ultimate determination that unlawful discrimination did occur. They vary, however, in explicitly defining the sanctions to be invoked (Table 5-3). The Vocational Rehabilitation Act (banning discrimination on the basis of handicap) and the Vietnam Era Veterans Readjustment Act state only that violations will result in such action "as the facts and circumstances warrant" consistent with the terms of the contract, law, and applicable regulations. The Age Discrimination in Employment Act and the Equal Pay Act, in contrast, specifically provide for back pay, attorneys' fees, and monetary damage awards equal to the amount of back pay under certain conditions. The Age Discrimination Act also provides for reemployment, reinstatement, and promotion of aggrieved parties. Both acts contain criminal penalties: $10,000 fine for willful violation of the Equal Pay Act and $500 fine for impeding enforcement of the Age Discrimination Act.

The greatest breadth of discretion in applying remedies is illustrated by Title VII and by Executive Order 11246. The Executive Order explicitly states that the appropriate contracting agency may "cancel, terminate, suspend . . . any contract" and may forbid "further contracts, or extensions or other modifications of existing contracts with any noncomplying contractor." It also provides that in cases in which there is "substantial or material violation" recommendation shall be made to the Equal Employment Opportunity Commission or the Department of Justice that Title VII proceedings be instituted.

Table 5-3. Remedies Available under Antidiscrimination Measures

Measure	Remedies Available
Age Discrimination Act	Back pay; reemployment, reinstatement, promotion; damages equal to lost pay; attorneys' fees
Equal Pay Act	Back pay; damages equal to lost pay; attorneys' fees
Vocational Rehabilitation Act	Appropriate administrative action
Vietnam Era Veterans Readjustment Act	Appropriate administrative action
Civil Rights Acts of 1866 and 1871	Compensatory and punitive damages; attorneys' fees*
Crime Control Act	Suspension, termination of grants
Revenue Sharing Act	Suspension, termination, repayment of grants
Title VI	Suspension, termination of funding
Title VII	Equitable relief, attorneys' fees
Executive Order 11246	Cancellation, suspension, termination of contracts; debarment from future contracts; action under Title VII

*Attorneys' fees collectable under the Civil Rights Attorneys' Fees Award Act of 1976.

Such proceedings may in turn lead to court-ordered appropriate action, "which may include, but is not limited to, reinstatement or hiring of employees, with or without back pay, or any other equitable relief as the court deems appropriate."

The essential concern of the district courts in hearing discrimination cases under Title VII is much broader than stopping unlawful patterns and practices. In *Louisiana v. United States* (1965), the Supreme Court stated that the federal courts have "not merely the power but the duty to render a decree which will so far as possible eliminate the discriminatory effects of the past as well as bar like discrimination in the future." The broad power to order whatever equitable relief is necessary is predicated on the belief that ingenuity is often required to deal with employment discrimination. The purpose of the broad grant of power, according to the Supreme Court, is to permit the Court to "fashion the most complete relief possible" to "make whole those who have been victims of unlawful discrimination" (*Albermarle Paper Co.* v. *Moody*, 1975).

To reinforce the court's power it may issue temporary injunctions to stop questionable practices before they are proved to be unlawful. An injunction may be issued if there is a clear showing of probable success by the plaintiff on the merits of the case and of possible irreparable injury from delay. An injunction may also be issued if sufficiently serious questions for litigation are raised on the merits of the case and there is a balance of hardships tipping toward the plaintiff. In either case, the important factor is protection of individuals and groups from further harm while the need for remedial steps is ascertained.

To fulfill their obligations under the law, federal courts have forced employers to cease discriminatory practices. They have also supervised conciliation agreements between employers and the Equal Employment Opportunity Commission. They have negotiated consent decrees to establish voluntary efforts to redress previous discrimination and to handle future discrimination complaints without litigation. For example, in a case involving the Buffalo Police Department (*United States* v. *City of Buffalo*, 1979), in which the Police Commissioners Investigative Unit was given responsibility for receiving and investigating discrimination complaints against the department and a review panel (consisting of one minority male member of the department chosen by minority members of the department, one female member of the department chosen by female members of the department, and three other individuals designated by the department) was created to rule on the merits of the complaints. District courts have also used their power of equitable relief to modify provisions of collective bargaining agreements which are held to be "practical impediments" to overcoming discrimination (as in *Equal Employment Opportunity Commission* v. *American Telephone and Telegraph*, 1977). The back-pay remedy and recovery of legal fees have been considered valuable in discrimination cases because such awards "provide a spur to speed up the elimination of discriminatory practices and they give full compensation to the injured parties" (*Stryker* v. *Register Publishing Co.*, 1976).

Identifying Discrimination

The decisions that have to be made about case processing and available sanctions are closely tied to the legal structures, even though discretion clearly exists. The legislation left open questions that require extensive administrative and judicial filling in. These questions

are the definition of discrimination and how to prove that it has oc-
curred. Title VII merely says that it is an unlawful employment prac-
tice "to discriminate"; Executive Order 11246 says contractors "will
not discriminate"; the Safe Streets Act and the Revenue Sharing Act
say that no person shall "be subjected to discrimination." Unless an
employer actually tells applicants they will not be hired or tells current
employees they will not be trained, promoted, or transferred because
of their minority group status, sex, or religion, discrimination is not
easily proved. Each of the legal standards seems on its face to be
concerned with protecting individuals from discrimination because of
non-job-related factors. In any individual case it may not be obvious
that failure to be hired, promoted, or whatever was the result of
discrimination.

   The Supreme Court in *International Brotherhood of Teamsters* v. *United
States* (1977) states that there are two forms of illegal discrimination.
One form is disparate treatment such as blatantly treating someone
differently because of his race, sex, or other prohibited factor. In the
Teamsters case, the trial court heard testimony that a trucking com-
pany, T.I.M.E.-D.C. (co-petitioner in the case), was explicitly discrimi-
natory in hiring line drivers. Feliberto Trujillo testified that a person-
nel officer told him when he applied for a line driver position that he
had a strike against him: "You're a Chicano." Similarly, a black man,
George Taylor, was told, "I don't think the company is ready for this
now." The other form of illicit discrimination is disparate impact,
which consists of maintaining standards or following practices that
have an adverse impact (fall more harshly) on one group but "cannot
be justified by business necessity." In cases where this concept is at
issue seemingly innocent criteria may be functionally equivalent to
racist or sexist criteria by being unrelated to productivity or service
quality.

   In any Title VII case the initial burden lies with the complainant to
show that a prima facie case of discrimination exists. To do so he must
demonstrate four facts, according to the Supreme Court ruling in
McDonnell Douglas Corp. v. *Green* (1973): that he belongs to a racial
minority (or other protected class); that he applied for and was
qualified for the job for which the employer was seeking employees;
that, despite his qualifications, he was rejected; and that, after his
rejection, the position remained open and the employer continued to
seek applicants from persons of applicant's qualifications. Once a
prima facie case has been established, the burden shifts to the em-
ployer to demonstrate a legitimate nondiscriminatory reason for re-
jecting the complainant.

The *McDonnell Douglas* Court also indicated that, since the company presented an argument that its refusal to rehire Green was not racially motivated, "statistics as to petitioner's employment policy and practice may ... demonstrate by competent evidence that the presumptively valid reasons for his rejection were in fact a cover up for a racially discriminatory decision." The administrative implication is clear. The police department must be prepared to demonstrate the legitimacy of its policies in general and cannot expect, even in an apparently obvious case of nondiscriminatory intent, that logic and right prevail. Prudence dictates that rebuttal evidence for discrimination be acquired and available for use in court *before* any litigation begins.

To counter charges of discrimination, the department must be sure that it has data to back up any claim that the person was rejected on job-related grounds. It must also be able to justify the use of the data. The *Uniform Guidelines* specify standards for validation studies which must be met in order for the studies to be acceptable. In *Association Against Discrimination* v. *City of Bridgeport* (1978), a concurrent criterion validity study was held to be insufficient because it was based on perfunctory data that were not the result of a detailed list of critical work elements and analysis of their relative importance. In *United States* v. *City of Chicago* (1977), a similar validation study was rejected because it was based on data chosen on the basis of availability rather than on the significance of the data for job performance. Also rejected on general grounds was use of promotability evaluations for new recruits because only one-third of the officers involved would have realistic expectation of promotion in a reasonable time period and their promotability would change over time. Even when there is a high correlation between initial selection criteria and a later performance measure, the department will have to show that the latter is itself a reasonable factor. In *Guardians Association of the New York City Police Department* v. *Civil Service Commission* (1977) and in *United States* v. *Commonwealth of Virginia* (1980), it was demonstrated that there was a high positive correlation between scores on entry-level tests and success in police academy training. The courts held that it was further necessary to prove that success in the academy correlated with on-the-job performance.

The courts have also held that indications of discrimination cannot be based only on applicants for hire or promotion. The agency involved may have a reputation as discriminatory or it may follow standards perceived as preemptory for minorities. Statistical elements are, therefore, also brought to bear to determine the question of the relevant labor pool. In the *Teamsters* case, the United States Supreme

Court held that over time nondiscriminatory labor practices lead to a work force representative of the community from which it is drawn. The question of how to define the labor pool is accordingly of great significance. For police departments in cities with residency requirements that is relatively easy. For others it is most often the Standard Metropolitan Statistical Area but may sometimes be the entire state. The determination of the appropriate area is most often made by analysis of the current department work force, but if the department has had a history of discrimination it may be done by analysis of the general municipal work force.

For hiring of specialized personnel requiring certification or pre-employment training, the courts (in opposition to the Equal Employment Opportunity Commission) have held that the racial composition of relevant positions is to be compared to the racial composition of qualified individuals, not to the total population (*EEOC* v. *United Virginia Bank/Seaboard National*, 1980; *EEOC* v. *Radiator Specialty Co.*, 1980). Similarly, in *Hill* v. *Western Electric Co.* (1980), the court held that when special experiential qualifications are germane to a position into which promotions are sought, only those with the necessary experience rather than all employees in the grade from which promotions are sought form the relevant pool. In a police case, *Bridgeport Guardians* v. *Bridgeport Police Department* (1977), favorable statistical comparison of upper-level officers with lower-level officers countered claims of discrimination even though the higher grades were grossly out of proportion with the racial composition of the community.

Measures to Avoid Sanctions

There are obviously many conflicting signals on equal employment practices. The courts do not all agree; the EEOC and OFCCP may not agree with the courts. Standards change over time and from place to place. The exact dimensions of discrimination tolerance are not settled. The question of bottom line or competent differential impact to guide enforcement is unclear. The appropriate labor pool for comparison in determining substantial adverse impact is open to disagreement. Still, there are some general practices that police departments can follow that will minimize the uncertainty of external intervention in employment decisions. Three are especially relevant.

The first rule is that once the department has determined a set of reasonable, valid criteria and procedures it must stick to them. In 1954 in *United States ex rel Accardi* v. *Shaughnessy*, the Supreme Court said an agency must "scrupulously observe rules, regulations or pro-

cedures which it has established." Adherence to the rules will not
protect the department if the rules are in opposition to the law, but
even the *Guidelines* recognize that enforcement agencies should give
due consideration to "the general posture of the employer" with re-
spect to equal employment opportunity for the job or group of jobs in
question (Section 4.E). Adherence to the rules without favor can be an
indication of faithful regard for avoiding discrimination.

Second, the importance of good record keeping cannot be mini-
mized. Title VII requires employers to "make and keep such records
relevant to the determinations of whether unlawful employment prac-
tices have been or are being committed" as the EEOC may prescribe.
Under that authority the *Uniform Guidelines* require employers to
"maintain and have available for inspection records or other informa-
tion which will disclose the impact which its tests and other selection
procedures have upon employment opportunities of persons by iden-
tifiable race, sex or ethnic group" (blacks, American Indians, Asians,
Hispanics, and whites other than Hispanics). The police department
has to be able to protect itself by keeping careful records of every
aspect of its interactions with employees and applicants.

To avoid the pitfalls that lead to findings of unlawful employment
practices in spite of good-faith efforts to comply with the law, pro-
cedures must be standardized, objective, and centrally reviewed. The
chief is ultimately responsible, and he has to be kept apprised of all
procedures and their consequences. Recruitment has to be carried
out in a manner that provides realistic probability that women and
minorities will be aware of openings. The method of recruitment must
be able to withstand criticism of subtle preclusion of female and mi-
nority applicants. Records are valuable in proving that recruitment
efforts are not directed at all-male or all-white schools or clubs. Bro-
chures showing women and minority police officers working together
should be kept on file along with an indication of their distribution.
Evidence should be maintained to show that recruitment literature
includes the phrase "An Equal Employment Employer." The depart-
ment should have a policy of accepting applications for employment at
all times even when no vacancy exists, so as not to appear to rely on
inside recruitment.

Selection procedures must be validated, of course, but they must
also be openly articulated to avoid charges of subterfuge. The writ-
ten, standardized, validated criteria have to be clearly enough articu-
lated that even if there is no charge of adverse impact there will be
protection from charges of individual disparate treatment by provid-
ing data to justify rejections of applicants. The department is not
obligated to post promotion openings, but if there is a differential

promotion rate between white males and protected classes, the failure to post will have to be proved not to be a discriminatory factor. Again, it is advisable to accept applications for promotion at all times or to announce openings when they occur in such a manner that everyone, irrespective of race or sex, has a reasonable chance to become aware of and compete for the vacant position. There must also be good documentation of decisions to dismiss or demote officers. The record must show a clear example of unsatisfactory performance and sincere efforts by superiors to resolve problems without formal sanction or with the least severe sanction available. To avoid charges of harassment, the record should also show that credit for satisfactory performance was given. Reductions in force must similarly be backed up with documentation to demonstrate that layoff decisions were nondiscriminatory.

Third, given the importance of statistics in settling the issue of substantial adverse impact, good statistical analysis and support has to be available to the department. Several statistical tests are available which can be applied to employment decisions to rate degree of differential effects (Haworth and Haworth, 1980, discuss these techniques and their application). Guidelines for determining the characteristics of the labor pool can be found in EEOC, *Job Patterns for Minorities and Women in Private Industry*; State Employment Security Division, U.S. Bureau of the Census, *Manpower Reports* by state, county, and SMSA; and Department of Labor, *Handbook of Labor Statistics*, all annual publications. The department and its legal counsel must be able to draw upon experts who can handle statistics in the EEOC context. According to Joan G. Haworth and Charles T. Haworth, the best choice is "a professionally trained applied social scientist with a strong administrative and statistical background" (1980:265). The expert cannot rely solely on statistical expertise because, although the courts give deference to statistics, statistical significance is not always judicial significance. In two important police-relevant cases, *Vulcan Society of New York* v. *Civil Service Commission of New York City* (1973) and *Kirkland* v. *New York State Department of Correctional Services* (1975), New York district courts held that employment practices had adverse impact, even though there was no showing of statistically significant differences. To make the department's case, the expert, has to be familiar with employment practices, law, and job and labor force analysis.

Equal employment opportunity fits well into the premise of representativeness as a vehicle for achieving responsible police. Ironically, however, in place of a passive approach to assuring passive representativeness, there has been extensive effort to develop active approaches. The drive for representative police service has in many cases shifted from breaking down barriers to entry to promoting entry of previously excluded groups. In effect, equal employment opportunity has been extended to include efforts to produce a self-fulfilling prophecy. Under the EEO mandate, statistical evidence that police departments have an imbalance in personnel based on demographic characteristics could be used to imply discrimination. The courts believe that if there is no discrimination there will be no imbalance. This reasoning has been altered to conclude that if there is an imbalance there is discrimination. Affirmative action programs have accordingly been developed to create the desired balance and to speed up achievement of representative police service.

6 Responsibility as a Problem of Representativeness

II: Affirmative Action

The issue of the demographic composition of police departments has been addressed on several occasions. The President's Commission on Law Enforcement and Administration of Justice (1967) and the National Advisory Commission on Criminal Justice Standards and Goals (1973) both called for an increase in the proportion of minority officers in American police departments. Both reports correctly perceived that police departments throughout the country underemploy minorities. In 1960, only 3.5 percent of police service employees (officers and staff) were nonwhite. A decade later, an International City Management Association survey of 588 municipal police departments found about 9 percent of the sworn officers to be members of minority groups (1970:443). When the Equal Employment Opportunity Act of 1972 made Title VII applicable to state and local governments and their agencies, the general picture had changed little. The Equal Employment Opportunity Commission estimated that, although minorities comprised 18 percent of the state and local government work force, they made up only 10 percent of police department employees: 6.3 percent black, 2.3 percent Hispanic, 2.0 percent Asian, and 0.5 percent other (1974:49). (See Table 6-1 for comparative figures for other public sector functional areas.) The IACP/Police Foundation survey of police personnel practices in 493 agencies found that minorities accounted for 8 percent of total employment—7.5 percent of sworn personnel and 10.2 percent of nonsworn personnel (Eisenberg, Kent, and Wall, 1973:35).

Enforcement of the Equal Employment Opportunity mandate has shifted primary emphasis on eliminating barriers to an open merit

Table 6-1. Minority Proportion of State and Local Government Employment by Function in 1972 (percent)

Function	Black	Spanish-speaking	Others
Hospitals and sanitoriums	24.3	4.3	1.9
Financial administration	7.7	2.5	1.3
Streets and highways	7.5	3.1	1.1
Sanitation and sewage	32.8	5.6	0.4
Health	14.4	2.2	1.3
Public welfare	19.1	3.4	1.2
Natural resources/Parks and recreation	10.5	4.0	1.4
Housing	29.6	4.3	0.7
Corrections	14.5	2.8	1.4
Employment security	13.1	3.5	2.1
Community development	11.1	2.7	1.4
Utilities and transportation	17.2	4.4	1.1
Police protection	6.3	2.3	0.7
Fire protection	3.0	1.5	0.6
Other	13.5	4.0	1.6
Total	13.7	3.3	1.3

Source: Equal Employment Opportunity Commission, 1974:5.

system to concern with adverse impact. This change symbolizes an essential change in basic philosophy in which representativeness has assumed preeminence. Affirmative action programs have been ordered as mechanisms for elimination or reduction of patterns of underemployment of women and minorities even in situations where there is little, if any, proof that the underemployment results from discrimination. This approach to equal opportunity makes sense only if it is viewed as evidence of a faith in numerical representation as a means for securing responsibility.

The police have received special attention in operationalizing this approach to responsibility. In this chapter, the concept of affirmative action and its divergence from equal opportunity will be analyzed. The implications of the two processes by which affirmative action programs have been imposed on police departments will be discussed, and the transformation of affirmative action from a means to achieve equal opportunity into a means to make police departments representative will be demonstrated.

Equal Access or Equal Results?

The traditional civil service reformers and the EEO proponents of the 1960s and 1970s had different concepts of equality. Under the earlier concept, equal opportunity means simply that everyone should be allowed to compete. Hidden behind the rhetoric of openness was the reality of bias and prejudice. Everyone who took a test would be evaluated by the same criteria. The fact that societal circumstances facilitated preparation for the examination by one group (WASPs) but hindered preparation by other groups was glossed over, if addressed at all.

The later reformers believe that equal opportunity means little when rampant inequality exists because of social conventions. The game may be played by the rules without being fair. If one team comes to the game trained and equipped for top performance and the other is not only less well prepared but ignorant of many of the technical aspects of adequate performance, it matters little that the rules may be applied impartially. Equal opportunity in its later guise emphasizes consequences rather than access. It focuses on the question of how groups end up after competing. Equal opportunity is recast as equal results. This attitude is summed up by the Supreme Court's statement in the *Teamsters* case that over time nondiscriminatory labor practices lead to a work force representative of the community from which it is drawn. In other words, the degree of equality of opportunity may be surmised by the degree of demographic similarity between a department's work force and its labor pool.

This perspective on equal employment opportunity forces consideration of the question: How can the effects of past discrimination be overridden? If the EEO mandate is taken to require merely that employment practices cease being discriminatory, the cumulative effect of long-entrenched biases will be perpetuation of basically nonrepresentative departments. The answer to this question which has been worked out is that direct efforts must be made to integrate departments at a faster rate than would occur simply from true equal opportunity. The mechanism for this accelerated integration is affirmative action.

The term "affirmative action" appears in Title VII, section 706g, which states that if a court finds that an employer has intentionally engaged in or is engaging in an unlawful employment practice, the court may enjoin the practice "and order such affirmative action as may be appropriate." This section would seem to provide the court with the power to force employers found guilty of discrimination to undo their past practices. The section specifically mentions equitable relief. In practice, this power has been expanded to provide not only for redress of past discrimination but to preclude future discrimination. That seems to be reasonable since the intent of the law is to end discrimination. The paradox is the idea that equitable relief can be provided to individuals who never suffered harm.

Additionally, the idea of affirmative action has been expanded to require agencies that do not have demographically representative work forces to take steps toward becoming representative. The pervasiveness of the acceptance of this position cannot be underestimated. The courts have held that past discriminatory practices may be indicative of continuing discrimination even without direct evidence of continuing discrimination. Similarly, the existence of an affirmative action plan may be held to be indicative of good-faith efforts to eliminate discrimination even though evidence of adverse impact may exist. The courts have explicitly stated that they are not bound by administrative procedures established to carry out the EEO mandate, but they have further held that those procedures will be given great deference. The *Uniform Guidelines on Employee Selection Procedures* include the provision that federal enforcement agencies will "consider the general posture of the user with regard to equal employment opportunity" when reviewing compliance with EEO standards. The evidence the *Guidelines* accept for verification of "general posture" is whether the agency has adopted and made progress on an affirmative action program (Section 4E). Furthermore, Executive Order 11246, the Rehabilitation Act of 1973, and the Vietnam Era Veteran's Readjustment Act of 1972 specifically require government contractors to develop affirmative action programs.

Affirmative Action Policy

As an administrative procedure, the National Civil Service League (NCSL) (1973:vi) defines affirmative action as a comprehensive effort to identify all barriers in the personnel management system that limit the ability of applicants and employees to reach their full employment potential, without regard to race, sex, religion, national origin, or other extraneous factors; eliminate all such barriers in a timely and coordinated manner; and undertake whatever special programs are needed to accelerate the process. To implement the plan, the head of an agency must make a firm commitment to EEO and designate an affirmative action coordinator. Implementation has to cover the full range of the personnel cycle from outreach recruitment through training programs for line personnel and supervisors to internal complaint resolution devices.

The National Civil Service League's outline of affirmative action essentially relies on the equal access concept. It implies that elimination of barriers to equal access is the thrust of affirmative action. The main point of controversy over affirmative action has arisen over the third point in the NCSL outline—the special programs to accelerate the process. On its face, this point would seem to be a technical process. In fact, affirmative action has been interpreted to involve much more.

Proponents of affirmative action assume that the current configuration of an agency's work force has an impact on its future ability to recruit and retain minorities and women. An agency's reputation as a discriminatory employer that has practiced overt discrimination in the past is presumed to have a chilling effect on current recruitment and retention efforts. A simple change from discrimination to non-discrimination rather than to active recruitment will not undo the consequences of past practices and will perpetuate those consequences. The *Uniform Guidelines on Employee Selection* accordingly require that employers analyze their work forces "to determine whether percentages of sex, race or ethnic groups in individual job classifications are substantially similar to the percentages of those groups available in the relevant job market who possess the basic job-related qualifications" (Section 17.2). If substantial disparities exist, affirmative action is called for.

The *Guidelines* claim that they do not impose an obligation on employers. For most government employers, they need not. Government contractors and grantees are obliged by law to develop affirmative action programs. Under the Law Enforcement Assistance Administration's 1973 guidelines, for example, a grant recipient is required to develop a program for women and minorities if it has fifty or more employees; it has received grants or subgrants of $25,000 or more; and its service population is at least 3 percent minorities. A grant recipient must develop a plan for women only if the first two points apply but the service population is less than 3 percent. More to the point, failure to develop an affirmative action program by an agency with an unrepresentative work force may be taken by enforcement agencies as evidence of bad faith. At the same time, Section 713 of Title VII protects employers from liability and punishment for unlawful practices that have been undertaken in accord with written interpretations and opinions of the Equal Employment Opportunity Commission. Clearly, the force of circumstances impels establishment of a plan even if an agency is not explicitly required by law to do so.

Problems arise under the assertion in the *Uniform Guidelines* that following an analysis of the demographic similarity of an agency's work force and labor pool, goals and timetables should be established for redressing disparities. The *Guidelines* maintain that selection under such plans should be based on the ability of applicants to do the work. Nevertheless, the goals and timetables and steps to achieve them "may be race, color, sex or ethnic conscious" (Section 17.1). That is, the number or proportion of target groups to be attracted by the affirmative action program may be an integral part of the program's design.

The problem is that Title VII provides that it may not be interpreted to require anyone "to grant preferential treatment to any individual or to any group . . . on account of an imbalance which may exist with respect to the total number or percentage of persons of any race, color, religion, sex or national origin employed by an employer" (Section 703j). This wording seems clear, and it is backed up by legislative history. The act's sponsor, Senator Hubert Humphrey, said flatly that "the title would prohibit preferential treatment for any particular group" (110 *Congressional Record*, 1964:11848). The EEOC has, nevertheless, aggregated unto itself the power to recast the meaning of this section.

According to the commission's interpretive policy statement, *Affirmative Action Appropriate under Title VII of the Civil Rights Act of 1964, as Amended* (1979), the intent of Title VII is "to improve the economic and social conditions of minorities and women" (Section 1.6). So long as an affirmative action program is directed at that purpose, it is justified in the opinion of the EEOC. Two very elementary problems arise from the apparent conflicts over the propriety of race- and sex-conscious affirmative action. One is how far the courts should go in imposing quotas or similar relief instead of more traditional forms of equitable relief such as injunctions and back pay. The second is how far the courts should go in allowing employers to set voluntary quotas.

Implementing Affirmative Action

Court-ordered Affirmative Action

Court-ordered affirmative action has covered a range of approaches and has varied in specificity. At one extreme, a district court ordered merely that an employer "educate and sensitize supervisors, superintendents and managers as to the nature of racial and national origin discrimination and as to Title VII requirements that the terms and conditions of employment be equal for all employees and that work rules be uniformly applied to all employees" (*Equal Employment Opportunity Commission* v. *Murphy Motor Freight Lines*, 1980). At the other extreme, another district court ordered that blacks be given absolute preference in hiring until their proportion in the department equaled their employment in the community (*Boston Chapter, NAACP* v. *Beecher*, 1974). Between the extremes have been orders that new recruit groups hired by police departments be composed of 50 percent minorities (*United States* v. *City of Buffalo*, 1979) or 40 percent minorities (*United States* v. *State of New York*, 1979) until the department's demographic profile is approximately equal to that of the community. Quotas have also been ordered without long-term goals (for example, *U.S.* v. *City of Buffalo* and *U.S.* v. *State of New York* required that 25 and 10 percent, respectively, of new hirees be women). Quotas have also been ordered both without long-term goals and with a termination date (for example, *Arnold* v. *Ballard*, 1976, ordered that one in three persons hired by the police department for three years had to be black).

Goals versus Quotas

The major issue has not been the form that quota orders take but the basic justification of quotas. Strong sentiment has been expressed against quotas. Nearly a century ago Justice Harlan, in one of the most notable dissents in a Supreme Court case, criticized his fellow justices for sanctioning the separate but equal doctrine. He stated that our legal system and the Constitution are color-blind, that race and color distinctions should be given no legal recognition (*Plessy* v. *Ferguson*, 1896). Associate Justice of the California Supreme Court Stanley Mosk expanded upon that principle in *Price* v. *Civil Service Commission of Sacramento County* (1980). He stated that affirmative action programs should be concerned only with preparing the underprivileged to compete for jobs on an equal basis. The attempt to redress underrepresentation rather than discrimination, he believed, had led to a drive to eliminate discrimination by creating discrimination. The proponents of hiring quotas are construing "equality of all persons regardless of race" to mean "preference for persons of some races over others."

Proponents of quotas counter the reverse discrimination charges on several grounds. One is that minority preference is necessary to achieve social justice. The mandate Title VII provides the courts is not only to stop discrimination but "to eliminate discriminatory effects of the past" (*Louisiana* v. *United States*, 1965). The pervasive effects of the past will not be eradicated simply by adopting fair employment practices. If an equal society is a legitimate goal, then affirmative action steps which bring that equality closer are rational aspects of public policy. A second ground is that Title VII is not color-blind. To enforce it, the government must require employers to keep detailed records of the racial and sexual composition of their work forces. Compliance with the EEO mandate can be proved only by identifying the effects of employment practices on discrete groups. Requirements actively to seek out minority applicants presume that specific groups will be identified and targeted.

A third argument is that affirmative action is not contrary to the merit principle. The two would be in conflict only if affirmative action leads to hiring and promoting unqualified individuals. Proponents of affirmative action claim that their concern is with securing qualified personnel who are minorities and women, not with securing minorities and women simply to fill quotas. The *Uniform Guidelines* emphasize that affirmative action is meant "to assure that positions in the public service are genuinely and equally accessible to qualified persons" (Section 17.1). Affirmative action should not require the selection of "the unqualified, or the unneeded" (Section 17.4). Finally, a case is advanced that quotas for nonwhites, even if they exclude whites, are not discriminatory. In his partial dissent from the *Bakke* decision voiding an affirmative action program at the University of California, Davis, Medical School, Justice Brennan took this position. He said that exclusion of some whites was not the form of discrimination the law seeks to overcome. The exclusion of whites is not based on racial prejudice. It does not mean that whites are stamped as inferior or as second-class citizens (*Regents of the University of California* v. *Bakke*, 1978).

The consequence of this dispute has been a gingerly approach to the use of quotas by the courts. In one case, the Second Circuit of the Court of Appeals held that the nonpreferential treatment section of Title VII was intended to bar preferential quotas to change imbalances in employment which result from factors other than unlawful discrimination but was not intended to prohibit the use of hiring goals to overcome the effects of past discrimination (*United States* v. *Wood, Wire and Metal Lathers International Union, Local 46*, 1973). In another case (*Rios* v. *Enterprize Association Steamfitters Local 638*, 1974), the same court denied that hiring goals were quotas because goals do not have the connotation of permanence that quotas have. Once attained, goals dissolve. The distinction seems to turn on the Supreme Court's decision in *Swann* v. *Charlotte-Mecklenberg Board of Education* (1971), in which it was held that mathematical ratios are forbidden if they are permanent or inflexible but that they are appropriate and useful as starting points to redress past violations of the EEO mandate.

Definitional disputes aside, the courts have not been overbearing in imposing quotas or goals to redress discrimination. Even in the context of proven racial discrimination of a long duration (as in the fact that the Alabama Department of Public Safety had never hired a black state trooper in its thirty-seven-year history), the general opinion seems to be that temporary, carefully circumscribed use of racial criteria in hiring should be ordered only when a court determines that such action is the only "rational, non-arbitrary means of eradicating past evils" (*NAACP* v. *Allen*, 1974). In *Kirkland* v. *New York State Department of Correctional Services* (1975), a twofold test for determining the need for imposition of temporary hiring goals was articulated. It was the opinion of the court that racial quotas are repugnant to the basic tenets of our society but that they may be necessary if there has been a clear-cut, long-term pattern of egregious discrimination and the effects of reverse discrimination will not be concentrated on a relatively small, ascertainable group of nonminority persons.

The exact meaning of "egregious" is open to question, but a review of cases involving police departments indicates that quotas are most likely to be imposed if there has been longstanding overt discrimination, as in the cases of the Mississippi Highway Safety Patrol and the Alabama State Police, or if the court feels itself to have been provoked. Because the days of open discrimination are probably past, the latter circumstance is most likely to be at issue in the future, especially in police cases. The appearance of discrimination in the administration of justice has a deleterious impact on public confidence in government; therefore the imposition of quotas for police departments with long-term patterns of discrimination serves an important public interest.

Punitive Court Orders

Several cases illustrate how the courts can be provoked into imposing quotas. Two police cases, *Bridgeport Guardians* v. *Bridgeport Police Department* (1977) and *Guardians Association of the New York City Police Department* v. *New York Civil Service Commission* (1980), are especially illuminating. In *Bridgeport Guardians* the police department was ordered to hire 102 minority individuals (blacks and Hispanics) before hiring any more white officers. In screening the minority candidates, the department was allowed to use only a medical examination and a physical agility test. This rigidity was imposed because the department had shown itself to have maintained a particularly intransigent attitude toward racial integration.

In 1973 an interim hiring quota had been imposed while a validated entry-level examination was being developed. The court had been hesitant to apply even the limited quota but did so because the department was not a private employer and the court believed that the visibility of the black patrolmen in the community would be of benefit to the public at a time when "racial divisiveness is plaguing law enforcement." The court was content to impose the limited interim quota in spite of the public advantage of getting minorities into uniform and onto the streets because it appeared that good-faith efforts were being undertaken to achieve voluntary compliance with EEO.

A coalition of community minority groups was formed in 1973 to provide assistance to minorities who sought access to civil service jobs, especially in the police and fire departments. To show the city's interest in cooperating with the coalition, the city personnel director supplied an outline of the general subjects to be covered by an upcoming police entry test. The city also altered its filing procedures for the test. Instead of requiring applicants to file at the city hall, they could file with the Association for Bridgeport Community Development (ABCD). The coalition provided training sessions open to all races and groups for three hours a night, three to four nights per week, for two months before the examination. The questions on the actual test bore no resemblance to the questions anticipated by those who had attended the training sessions based on the personnel director's information. The city claimed the applications processed by the ABCD had never been received. The court's acceptance of good faith had clearly been misplaced, and the court had little recourse but to use its full authority to compel compliance. That full authority was the imposition of the rigid quota and the disallowal of the city's own testing system.

In *Guardians Association of the New York City Police Department*, the court also found its patience tested. The New York City Civil Service Commission had been found guilty of using unvalidated tests in 1968 and 1970 and had continued to use them after 1972. The city was held to have violated Title VII in six different cases involving women and minorities. The city persisted in designing and administering tests that discriminated. In the case that finally provoked the court, the city gave an entry-level examination on 30 June 1979 that had not been professionally designed and did not conform to the *Uniform Guidelines*. The New York labor pool at the time the test was administered was 34.9 percent black and Hispanic, while the NYPD was 8.9 percent black and 3.8 percent Hispanic. Although 30.9 percent of those who took the test were black or Hispanic, only 15.4 percent of those who passed were black or Hispanic; 46 percent of the whites passed compared to 17 percent of the blacks and 20.5 percent of the Hispanics. There was clear evidence of adverse impact caused by the design of the test. The examination measured constructs or abstract ideas rather than the potential to perform the duties of a police officer. It was essentially an aptitude or IQ test, precisely the type of test on which minorities do least well. When selection is based on rank order scores on such a test, whites will be disproportionately represented because they tend to cluster in the upper ranks while minorities cluster in the lower ranks. The court found no reason to believe that the relative rankings on the unvalidated test actually reflected potential to do the job. It held that since the city had previously been found to have used discriminatory tests "it would have been expected that defendants in structuring any new examinations would be especially careful to follow requisite guidelines and procedures." The city did not do so, and the court ruled that "this studied adherence to discriminatory procedures must at this point be deemed conscious and deliberate." The result was an order that 50 percent of entry-level officers must be blacks and Hispanics.

The courts have also been willing to order affirmative action to redress discriminatory practices related to matters other than selection. It is generally recognized that affirmative action as active preparation of minorities and women for equal competition does not stop with recruitment and selection. Once minorities and women are in the department, affirmative action programs concentrate on developing careers for them. An effort must be made to provide them upward mobility through career counseling and information about promotional criteria and availability. Specialized training may be necessary. The courts have held, however, that an employer is under no obligation to provide upward mobility assistance for minorities and women which it does not provide for white males (*Morita v. Southern California Permanente Medical Group*, 1976). Again, however, egregious discrimination can provoke the courts.

Court-ordered affirmative action has been imposed in cases of blatant discrimination in assignments that preclude promotion and in cases in which less drastic forms of censure are not heeded. As an example of the first, the Pittsburgh Police Department was ordered to promote women to each detective grade until each grade is 10 percent women before promoting any men to those grades (*Commonwealth of Pennsylvania* v. *Flaherty*, 1980). An example of the second is *United States* v. *San Diego County* (1979). The *San Diego* case is similar to the *Guardians Association* and *Bridgeport Guardians* cases except that it is based on promotional rather than hiring criteria. The county of San Diego had entered a consent decree in May 1977 to take affirmative steps to increase employment of minorities and women. The Sheriff's Department's contribution to that effort was found to be almost totally ineffective. In September of 1977, Sheriff John Duffy promoted twelve white males and three white females to the rank of sergeant. In February 1978, the District Court for Southern California denied a request for a preliminary injunction to void the promotions. It did, however, direct the sheriff to take more constructive action to fulfill the county's agreement, and it directed the department to develop an acceptable procedure for promotion to sheriff sergeant. Nevertheless, in April 1978, six more white males were promoted to sergeant. This time the court admonished the department, nullified the promotions, and again directed the sheriff to establish an acceptable promotional system. Finally, in February 1979, when the court learned that twenty-three promotions were to be made, involving at least nineteen white males, it took direct action.

The court ascertained that since 1972 fifty-two individuals had been promoted to sergeant. Of those, forty-nine were white males and three were white females. No blacks or Mexican-Americans had been promoted to that rank. In fact, there had never been a black sheriff sergeant and only one Mexican-American sergeant. Furthermore, the 1979 examination had a clearly adverse impact on minorities because the relative pass rates for whites were 46.6 percent, for blacks 23.1 percent, and for Hispanics 35 percent (the combined black/Hispanic rate was 30.3 percent). The group of proposed new sergeants would not have included any blacks or women; it would have included nineteen whites, one Mexican-American, one Asian, and one Native American. There was, in short, ample evidence of discriminatory effects. There was no evidence that the promotional examination had been validated in accordance with the *Uniform Guidelines*. A pattern of resistance to the court's efforts to induce the department to comply with EEO standards was clear.

The court recognized that affirmative numerical relief should be imposed only with great caution. But it was convinced by the response of the department to other forms of relief that "it would be shirking its duty to fashion an effective remedy were it not to order such relief here." The county and the sheriff were ordered to promote three blacks, six Mexican-Americans, and two women to the rank of sergeant.

The Bridgeport, New York City, Pittsburgh, and San Diego cases involving quotas do not contradict the assertion that the courts have, for the most part, been hesitant to use the power to order quotas. They have been mindful that quotas can be disruptive and perhaps counterproductive. In *Blake* v. *City of Los Angeles* (1979), it was recognized that imposition of a quota could place a burden on the police department that would harm efficient police protection for the city. A 25 percent quota for hiring women (the necessary figure in the case) would have been unfruitful because, even after an intense, good-faith recruitment drive by the city, only forty-five females applied when four hundred positions were open. In *United States* v. *San Diego County*, the court recognized that nullification of promotions would be "extremely disruptive and demoralizing to the individuals involved" and held off imposing quotas until it had been tested three times. In *Bridgeport Guardians*, although a quota was set for hiring, none was set for promotion. The imposition of promotional quotas was rejected because it would discriminate against white officers who had joined the department with the expectation of advancement. Although the hiring quota might keep some whites out of the department, they were not individually identifiable as victims of reverse discrimination. But a promotional quota would hit identifiable members of the department: "The impact of the quota on these men would be harsh and can only exacerbate rather than diminish racial attitudes." The general opinion of the courts seems to be that "preferential numerical relief . . . remains an extraordinary remedy" to be avoided except in the face of "recalcitrance in voluntarily taking steps to correct racial and sexual imbalances within the Police Department" (*United States* v. *City of Chicago*, 1977).

Voluntary Programs

Court-ordered programs are not the only or even the most common sources of affirmative action plans. The 1979 opinion by the Equal Employment Opportunity Commission, *Affirmative Action Appropriate under Title VII of the Civil Rights Act of 1964, as Amended*, emphasizes that "Congress strongly encouraged employers . . . to act on a voluntary basis" to end discriminatory practices (Section 1608.1.b). The commission stated that "voluntary affirmative action to improve opportunities for minorities and women must be encouraged and protected in order to carry out the Congressional intent embodied in Title VII" (Section 1608.1.c). The procedures for enforcing Title VII include provisions to assure that voluntary compliance will be sought before litigation begins. The EEOC opinion further ensures that no one will be subject to suit or punishment for undertaking a voluntary affirmative action program which is in line with commission policy. Clearly, there is a sound basis for concluding that the obligation to undertake affirmative action is felt to be directed primarily at voluntary efforts.

The legitimacy of affirmative action as a voluntary step by an employer to break down artificial barriers to equal access is not at issue. Employers in both the public and private sectors may publicize their intentions to be equal opportunity employers. They may undertake analyses to determine the distribution of women and minorities within their organizations. Aggressive minority recruitment efforts may be made. Joint recruitment efforts may be made by several departments such as the Northern Virginia Police Minority Recruitment Office operated by police agencies in Alexandria, Arlington, and Fairfax counties. These practices do not generate conflict within the police profession. Contention has occurred, however, over the development of explicit numerical goals and timetables to redress under-representation.

Affirmative Action or Reverse Discrimination

In a number of court cases, plaintiffs have raised the question of reverse discrimination. The term denotes either a reversal of the putatively most common form of employment discrimination (white against black or male against female) or the reverse of discrimination (preference). Preferential treatment has been justified to overcome the effects of past discrimination and to serve legitimate state interests.

The first justification has entered into the two most publicized cases involving voluntary imposition of goals and timetables. In the private sector, the leading case was *United Steelworkers of America* v. *Weber* (1979). The Steelworkers Union and Kaiser Aluminum had entered into a collective bargaining agreement in 1974, which included an affirmative action plan to redress racial imbalances in Kaiser's craft worker work force. The plan called for Kaiser to train production workers for craft positions rather than hiring them from outside the company. Trainees were to be chosen on the basis of seniority. The reverse discrimination issue arose because the selection process was to be color-conscious. Blacks had not been hired in proportion to their representation in the labor pool and would be negatively affected by the selection criteria. The union-company agreement provided that 50 percent of the workers chosen for the in-plant training program would be black until the black representation in craft jobs was roughly equal to that in the population. A white male worker, who was not chosen for advanced training while blacks with less seniority were admitted to the program, brought suit alleging disparate treatment.

The district court and the Fifth Circuit of the Court of Appeals agreed that white employees of Kaiser Aluminum had been discriminated against on the basis of race. The Supreme Court, however, ruled that the plan was not unlawful. It took a position similar to that of the EEOC. The Court held that the prohibition against racial discrimination in Title VII had to be placed in the context of the Civil Rights Act, which sought to end discrimination against minorities. In that context the effort of the plan to redress the clear and acknowledged pattern of past discrimination was found to be reasonable. Furthermore, the Kaiser plan did not unnecessarily infringe on the interests of white workers and did not present an absolute barrier to white access to the training program. Both aspects of the *Kirkland* test (egregious past discrimination and no concentrated effect on a small group of nonminority persons) were satisfied, and the quotas were not permanent. Perhaps most significant, the Court also was able to find support for its position in Title VII.

Section 703j of Title VII states that the title cannot be used to *require* employers to grant preferential treatment. The Court's interpretation of the section was that if Congress had meant to preclude race-conscience affirmative action, it would have said "require or permit." Since only requiring preferential treatment was forbidden, voluntary plans in traditionally segregated occupations are permissible.

Similar reasoning has been applied in the public sector. The Seattle Civil Service Commission had conducted a work-force utilization analysis and a review of selection procedures. It found that minorities were afforded little chance for selection except into the lowest un-skilled positions. Once employed, they were likely to remain concentrated in those positions. The Supreme Court of the state of Washington held that the city's plan was intended to eliminate the continuing effects of past discrimination; that it did not place an undue burden on white employees because no one was displaced from a job and there were no clearly identifiable victims of reverse discrimination; that the plan did not call for hiring unqualified personnel; and that the plan did not create an absolute preference (*Maehren* v. *City of Seattle*, 1979, and *Lindsay* v. *City of Seattle*, 1976).

These cases do not mean that all voluntary plans will be accepted. In the other case that received widespread publicity, the decision went the other way. In *Regents of the University of California* v. *Bakke* (1978), the United States Supreme Court struck down a preferential admission program for minorities at the University of California, Davis, Medical School. In this case, victims of reverse discrimination were clearly identifiable, and the claim of the university to be redressing past discrimination was rejected. The university alleged that its program was intended to deal with the cumulative effects of societal discrimination in the medical profession. The Court held that the claim failed to carry the case because there was no showing of past discrimination by the university. It held that the good-faith effort to counter past societal discrimination could be channeled through a program that considers race as one criterion among several, but race alone cannot suffice to justify preference.

In a similar, more recent case (*Harmon* v. *San Diego County*, 1980), the United States District Court for the District of Southern California struck down a public affirmative action program because it involved an absolute bar to white males. The claim that a preferential treatment program is justified on the grounds of remedying past discrimination cannot be expected to be upheld without proof of past discrimination directly attributable to the agency concerned. A program instituted on those grounds will not be approved unless it also meets the *Kirkland* test's other condition—no identifiable victims of reverse discrimination.

Reverse Discrimination and the Public Interest

Cases have also arisen under the justification that preferential treatment serves a legitimate government interest. It is in this area that major police reverse discrimination cases are found and that the extremely complex interweaving of social factors which confront police administrators is most apparent.

The issue of legitimate government interest may be raised from several perspectives. One ground for its consideration is illustrated by *Doores* v. *McNamara* (1979). The Kansas City Police Department instituted a voluntary affirmative action program in 1974. At that time the city was approximately 22.9 percent minority, but the department was only about 5 percent minority. To reduce the disparity between the demographic composition of the city and that of the department, an effort was launched to bring the minority component of the department up to 15–16 percent. In 1977 a former Kansas City police officer seeking reemployment brought suit against the department under Section 1983 claiming reverse discrimination. He charged that since there was no court order or consent decree requiring preferential hiring for minorities, the program was clearly unlawful. The department countered that since no quota was involved and no absolute preference was granted to minority applicants, the program was a good-faith effort to promote the spirit of the equal employment mandate.

The court upheld the department. Its decision was based largely on the testimony of Patrick V. Murphy, a former chief administrator of several major urban police departments and the director of the Police Foundation (a privately funded foundation dedicated to police research and policy analysis). Based on his testimony, the court determined that a minority representation in the department approximately equal to the minority percentage of the population was a legitimate public goal. Its conclusion was based on the assumptions that adequate minority representation serves to foster better community relations between the police and the public; that the absence of minority police officers in areas with large minority concentrations tends to heighten hostility toward the police, which leads to increased violence by and against officers in those areas; and that metropolitan police forces that more closely correspond to their communities are, overall, more effective. What is perhaps most informative about this decision is that although sophisticated statistical data are required to rebut charges of discrimination against protected classes, "expert testimony" unsubstantiated by any objective data can rebut charges of reverse discrimination.

The most significant case involving voluntary affirmative action has been *Detroit Police Officers Association* v. *Young* (1978). Through several trials and appeals, this case has highlighted the many difficulties confronting police departments in their struggles to deal with the equal employment opportunity mandate. From 1968 to 1980 the mayor, city council, and police executives were caught up in a public debate over the responsibilities of the police department as a government entity that aroused social, political, legal, and administrative conflicts.

In the summer of 1967 rioting in the black areas of Detroit resulted in at least forty deaths and thousands of injuries. Nearly thirteen thousand federal paratroopers and Michigan National Guardsmen were mobilized to quell the disturbances, which lasted a full week. One response to the riots was appointment of a police advisory council to evaluate the police department's relationship with the black community. The council found that a major complaint was the absence of black officers. In 1950, when the city of Detroit was 16 percent black, the department was 1 percent black. By 1960 the city had become 29 percent black, but the police were still 98 percent white. By 1968 the department's black proportion had increased only to 4.5 percent. A special committee of psychologists and personnel administrators (the Vickery Committee) was charged with developing recruitment and selection guidelines for opening the department to blacks.

The committee issued a series of recommendations, which were implemented between 1968 and 1973. At the initial selection stage, general aptitude (intelligence) tests were dropped, physical requirements were altered, and background investigation procedures and screening criteria were changed. Candidates for promotion were placed on an eligibility list ranked by scores weighting their performance ratings, departmental seniority, college credits, veterans' preference points, oral interview scores, and written examination scores. Following these policy revisions, the black proportion of the department increased to 17 percent. Even though the black proportion of the city also increased markedly (to 50 percent), the ratio of department-to-city proportions had been reduced from 1:6.44 to 1:2.94 between 1968 and 1974.

On 1 July 1974, a new city charter for Detroit became effective. Among the provisions of the charter was a requirement that a Board of Police Commissioners (BPC) be appointed to approve police promotions and to establish policies, rules, and regulations for the department. One of the first acts of the BPC was to issue a directive to the chief of police, on 31 July, that he implement an affirmative action program. The commissioners justified their order on the basis of past and present discriminatory practices in the police department. A staffing goal of 50 percent white and 50 percent black was adopted.

Problems arose because the goal could not be met in promotions to sergeant under existing procedures. The heaviest weight in promotional determination was placed on the written test. Although the test was validated, it had a differential impact on blacks. A minimum score of 70 on the test was necessary to meet eligibility requirements. On the last examination given before the implementation of the affirmative action program, in December 1973, the black failure rate was 125 percent of the white failure rate. On the first examination given after implementation, in November 1974, the black failure rate increased to 130 percent of the white failure rate. At the next administration of the sergeant's examination, in May 1976, the differential was reduced by about 5 percent but the black failure rate was still 123 percent of the white rate. Not only did blacks fail at a higher rate but those blacks who passed had lower average scores than whites who passed. Promotions based strictly on numerical rankings would not satisfy the 50-50 goal. To meet the affirmative action guidelines, the chief of police ordered the promotion list to be expanded to include all officers who attained the minimum composite passing score. The 50-50 goal was met, and no one with a written score below 70 was promoted. Based on both the November 1974 and May 1976 examinations, however, some blacks were promoted who received lower scores than some whites who were denied promotion.

Several of the white officers who were passed over for promotion sued the mayor and the city through their employees' association. They challenged the promotions on the grounds that they violated section 703j of Title VII, prohibiting racial preference, and section 703h of Title VII, which specifically allows employers to continue practices that have different consequences for protected classes if the practices are connected to "a bona fide seniority or merit system" and the differences are not the result of "an intention to discriminate." In 1976, the District Court for Eastern Michigan had enjoined the Detroit fire department from using racial quotas for promotions which disregarded the department's bona fide seniority system (*Detroit Firefighters* v. *City of Detroit*). The questions of the legitimacy of the department's affirmative action program and of the district court's final action were left unresolved, however. By the time the case reached the court of appeals, the union contract had expired and the plaintiffs had been promoted.

In the police case, the district court again accepted the reverse discrimination charge and enjoined the department from continuing its preferential treatment of black applicants for promotion. In rejecting the affirmative action program, the court held that the promotional tests were validated and that rank ordering of eligibles reflected differences in merit. In addition, the inclusion of length of service in the overall promotional decisions was based on a bona fide seniority system. On both of those grounds the regular promotional system was protected by section 703h. But the court rejected the department's claim to be attempting to redress past discrimination. It determined that blacks comprised 18.6 percent of the population of the Detroit Standard Metropolitan Statistical Area (Wayne, Oakland, and Macomb counties) yet the Detroit Police Department was 17.23 percent black. The black proportion of the department was therefore approximately 92.6 percent of the black proportion of the SMSA and clearly within the four/fifths rule.

The court thus could find no justification for the claim that the affirmative action program was intended to counter illicit practices. It went further and questioned the logic advanced by the *Doores* court that racial parallelism between the department and the city improves the quality of policing. It held that there was no prevailing public interest in discriminating against whites to improve job opportunities for blacks. No factual basis was found for the belief that more black officers and sergeants would mean better police service. On the contrary, a police officer's effectiveness as a professional law enforcement officer is dependent upon his education, skills, training attitudes, and sense of professionalism. The unalterable pigmentation of his skin has no bearing upon these factors and neither enhances nor depreciates his professional enforcement effectiveness.

The determination of the court was that the department had violated Section 703j of Title VII by disregarding bona fide seniority and merit systems; Section 706g of Title VII by establishing a system of racial preferences unilaterally because only the courts may order such preferences and even they may do so only in the face of egregious discrimination; the nondiscrimination provisions of Title VI; and Section 1981 and the Fourteenth Amendment by practicing intentional racial discrimination. The department and the city had corrupted Title VII, usurped the authority of the courts, and practiced reverse discrimination, all without reasonable cause to believe they were correcting faults of the past or laying the foundation for future benefits. Demographic representativeness was the sole aim of the affirmative action program.

On appeal to the Sixth Circuit in 1979, the district court decision was reversed. The court of appeals ruled that errors of fact and of law had been made. The major error of fact was held to be on the issue of underrepresentation of blacks in the department. The court found that, contrary to the lower court's ruling, incontrovertible evidence existed that from 1944 to 1975 there was consistent, significant racial disparity in the Detroit Police Department. The department had a residency requirement for new and continuing personnel. It provided service only in the city. Therefore, basing the department's composition on population data from the entire SMSA was inappropriate. Statistics on the city itself gave a very different picture. Blacks composed 43.7 percent of the city population and 45.8 percent of its labor market. Since the department was only 17.23 percent black, the disparity was clear.

The court ruled that Section 1981 was itself race-conscious. Use of race-conscious criteria to bring the department into conformance with constitutional mandates is, therefore, legal. It ruled that Title VI was not violated because that title forbids only discrimination that offends the Constitution. Citing *Bakke*, it said the clear legislative intent of Title VI is to proscribe only those racial classifications that violate the equal protection clause of the Fifth Amendment. On both counts the decision was that race-conscious criteria were justified because the intent was to remedy constitutional violations.

On the questions related to Title VII, the officers also lost. Section 703h was not violated because seniority was only one factor considered in promotion. On the crucial issue of reverse discrimination, Section 703j was also held not to have been violated. As in the *Weber* case, the court ruled that the primary emphasis of 703j is "require." Although employers may not be required to grant racial preferences to redress imbalances, that does not mean that voluntary preferences may not be used. In judging the legitimacy of voluntary preferential programs, the courts must consider the points articulated in *Kirkland*: Has there been a pattern of long-term egregious discrimination? Will preferential treatment for one group have a negative impact on specific members of another group?

For *Bakke*, the University of California, Davis, Medical School program failed on both counts. The Medical School had not practiced past discrimination, and there were identifiable victims of the affirmative action plan. The *Weber* and *Young* cases, however, satisfied both questions. There was clear evidence of past discrimination, and no undue burdens were placed on whites, although some identifiable whites were denied benefits. The courts have the authority to impose affirmative action under Section 706g. Since the courts may require preferential treatment in cases meeting the *Kirkland* test, they may accept the legality of voluntary programs in circumstances which meet that test.

From Equal Opportunity to Proportional Representation

American culture has always placed a high value on individual equality. Legal equality is the cornerstone of the Anglo-American legal system. Since the late nineteenth century, the primary emphasis of the civil service system has been equal, open competition for public jobs. The merit principle has been enshrined both in law and in the public consciousness. Merit testing carries with it the premise that everyone should have an equal chance to demonstrate merit. The equal employment opportunity mandate, taken at face value, amounts to a demand that the actual processes of securing public service employment meet the formal principles of equal access.

Police personnel administration has been significantly affected by enforcement of the EEO mandate. Many of the traditional considerations in hiring and promoting personnel have had to be eliminated or altered to meet the requirement that all selection and screening criteria involved in personnel administration be demonstrated to be job-relevant. Many police officers and police administrators have objected to the elimination of traditional measures of merit. "Decline of standards" has been a rallying cry to resist the changes ordered by the Equal Employment Opportunity Commission, the courts, and other agencies.

The Supreme Court explicitly stated that the intent in requiring validation of standards was not to eliminate standards. In *Griggs* it said that the aim was to ensure that only standards which accurately indicate merit be used. Other proponents of equal opportunity have taken the position that the decline-of-standards argument is a smoke screen. The assertion that elimination of the old criteria brings in unqualified personnel is said to be a convenient excuse for resisting the integration of minorities into the police force (Alex, 1976:29). Both of these positions reflect the belief that EEO has escaped the dilemma of civil service—that the processes of equal employment opportunity and the formal mandate are the same.

One of the primary arguments for EEO legislation was that the equal access emphasis of civil service did not, in fact, amount to equal opportunity. The way civil service operated was held to perpetuate exclusion of certain groups from the public service. An objective analysis of the application of the EEO mandate discloses that similar problems exist here also. The requirement that selection and screening criteria be job-relevant is less objectionable than the way in which personnel practices and policies have been evaluated. Certainly, most police administrators want to secure the best personnel for their departments and want to develop and use that personnel to its fullest extent. But they resent and resist the methods by which they are determined to have done otherwise.

In spite of the reliance by enforcers of the EEO mandate on the validation criterion, there seems to be a more important motivation for intervention into police personnel administration. That motivation is a desire to force police departments to be staffed by personnel who reflect the demographics of the local population. This motivation can be discerned by examining the basic postulate of the EEO enforcers. The nondiscrimination in employment measures aim at breaking down barriers to equal opportunity. The enforcers of those measures have taken as their point of reference the belief that over time, nondiscrimination leads to equal representation. They, therefore, work backward, uncritically assuming that underrepresentation results only from discriminatory selection.

The *Uniform Guidelines on Employee Selection* state than an employment practice that has an adverse impact on members of any race, sex, or ethnic group will be considered discriminatory (Section 3A). It also says that validated procedures are acceptable even if they have an adverse impact. In fact, the emphasis is much more on equating adverse impact with discrimination. In *Albermarle Paper Co.* v. *Moody* (1975), the Supreme Court held that "even validated tests might be a pretext for discrimination." In *McDonnell Douglas* v. *Green* (1973), the Court found that McDonnell Douglas had a legitimate reason not to rehire Green. Nevertheless, it ordered him rehired because the company had discriminated against blacks in other instances. More recently, in *Gunther* v. *Washington County* (1979), the Washington County Sheriff's Department was found not to have violated the Equal Pay Act because the pay differential between male deputies and female matrons was based on unequal work. The door was nonetheless opened for Title VII suits on the ground that equal worth of male and female employees may be a more important concern than equal work. The *Guidelines* state that enforcement agencies should examine the "bottom line" impact of employment practices. They also state that enforcement agencies may require validation of components of selection procedures even though there is no indication of discrimination in final decisions (Section 6C).

When attention is focused on affirmative action rather than only on equal opportunity, the disparity between law and administration is even more apparent. Senator Humphrey, floor manager of Title VII, explicitly stated that the title prohibits all discrimination on the basis of race. In the *McDonnell Douglas* case, the Supreme Court noted that "Title VII tolerates *no* racial discrimination." Earlier, in the landmark *Griggs* case, the Court had taken the position that the statute prohibits "discriminatory preference for *any* group *minority* or *majority*." Yet Justice Brennan could hold in the *Bakke* case that discrimination against whites is not really discrimination under Title VII. And in *Weber*, a majority of the Court upheld a selection process that was patently race-conscious.

The implications for police administration are clear. Irrespective of statutory injunctions against reverse discrimination, the EEO mandate has been transformed into a mandate to match departmental demographics to community characteristics. When *Weber* was remanded to the Fifth Circuit, Judge Thomas G. Gee said the Supreme Court was "profoundly wrong." He asked what could be more clear than that Title VII "prohibits preferential treatment for any particular group." He, too, cited Senator Humphrey's comments on Section

703j and said the section "could not be construed as the Court has now construed it" (1980). The California Supreme Court followed the United States Supreme Court's *Weber* decision with its own affirmation of a voluntary preference system in *Price* v. *Civil Service Commission of Sacramento County* (1980). Justice Stanley Mosk dissented, stating that the thrust of such decisions reflects a "combination of guilt feelings for the sins of ancestors and overzealousness by those who insist upon reconstruction of a merit society into a representative society . . . in which ability is secondary to race and sex."

Judge Gee and Justice Mosk perceive the various court decisions and EEOC guidelines to have changed antidiscrimination into antinumerical underrepresentation. *Detroit Police Officers Association* v. *Young* makes the validity of this perception for police departments clear. The Detroit Police Department used validated criteria in its selection procedures. Under an aggressive antidiscrimination program the proportion of black officers in the department was increased 283 percent between 1968 and 1974. Nevertheless, an affirmative action program which overturned that system was upheld on the grounds that the department had discriminated before 1968 with consequent gross underrepresentation of blacks. The fact that the Detroit Police Department undertook to establish nondiscriminatory procedures four years before being legally obligated to do so seemed irrelevant to the court. The affirmative action program that discriminated against whites was upheld because the goal of the EEO mandate was changed by the judiciary and the EEOC. The *Young* court held that seeking the same racial proportion among employees as in the labor force is a reasonable goal.

It matters little that there are many reasons for minority and female underrepresentation in police departments. Discrimination may be one factor, but surely it is not the only factor. Minorities and women may not be as interested in police careers as white males. Especially at a time when most employers are seeking to increase their minority and female staffs, police service may not be a high priority for those individuals most capable of meeting entry standards. Chiefs of police, nevertheless, must be prepared for challenges to their personnel systems whenever underrepresentation can be demonstrated even if discrimination cannot be shown. Continuing aggressive recruitment of minorities must be a top-priority concern. In spite of formal statements to the contrary, the implication is that standards may have to be compromised. Police administrators may come into conflict with those who establish standards if the department is underrepresentative. Such conflict emerged, for example, in *Alexander* v. *Bahou* (1980). The chief of police, fire chief, and mayor of Syracuse, New York, sued the

Civil Service Commission because New York civil service law requires selection of the three highest scorers on hiring and promotion examinations. Under that rule, the police department was 2.2 percent black and 2.2 percent female and the fire department was less than 1 percent black and 0 percent female. To forestall cutoff of LEAA and revenue sharing funds, the suit was brought to allow more minority hiring by abolishing the "rule of three," even though there was no indication of actual discrimination.

All indications are that pressures on police administrators to increase minority representation in their departments will continue. Major changes in police personnel administration procedures and criteria have already occurred. The continuing pressures to integrate police departments more fully will require fewer changes in procedures but may demand still more sweeping changes in criteria. So long as underrepresentation is sufficient to support charges of discrimination, decreasing underrepresentation by whatever means will be necessary.

Representativeness and Responsibility

The traditional approaches to securing responsible police administration emphasize form and structure. Laws and organizational checks and rules are of greater concern than are individual police officers. The contemporary alternatives that have been advanced are much more concerned with the problems of police administration that involve people.

Affirmative action is a special perspective on equating responsibility with individuals. Instead of emphasizing what individuals can do and how they fit into the police department, this perspective emphasizes who the individuals are. It equates a responsible police service with a police service that is representative of its community. This is not representation in the same sense in which representative government is considered the basis of democratic government. Representation in the context of representative government focuses on the authority of someone to act for someone else. In the most general governmental sense, elected officials are representatives of the communities that elect them. The basic ingredient making such representation legitimate is the transaction between electors and those who are elected. The electors give up some of their social power to their elected officials so that the officials may act for the electors.

The principle of a representative as an agent can also be applied to nonelected officials. The nonelected officials can be seen as agents of the elected officials who appoint them. Insofar as they are chosen by and serve under civil service systems, however, they are representatives of the government, not of the elected officials who are temporary stewards of public power. Even less, then, are they representatives (that is, agents) of particular groups or interests in the community. From this perspective, the *Report of the Board of Enquiry* on the civil service in England (1928) said that the first duty of a civil servant is to give undivided allegiance to the state at all times and on all occasions when the state has a claim upon his services (21).

In contrast to the foregoing conception of representation, affirmative action focuses on passive representation. A responsible police service is seen as a service in which the various racial and ethnic groups in society are represented in proportion to their presence in the community. It is for this reason that the courts and the EEO enforcement agencies concentrate on adverse impact rather than disparate treatment and why underrepresentation is accepted as evidence of violation of the antidiscrimination laws. Group presence, not treatment of individuals, has become the primary concern.

The actions of the EEO enforcement agencies and of the courts impose on police departments a practical necessity of monitoring their demographic composition and its relationship to community demographics. Still, there is no evidence to suggest that a demographically representative police department is a responsible police department. There is little evidence to indicate that a police officer's race or ethnicity in and of itself makes him a better or a more responsible officer. It is especially ironic that one of the arguments advanced for affirmative action is that minority officers will improve police-community relations in minority areas because the courts have held that a conscientious policy of assigning minority officers to minority areas is an illegal employment practice under EEO policy.

The efforts to match personnel with jobs, the efforts to secure equal opportunity, and the efforts to provide representative police departments do not constitute the only person-centered approaches to achieving police administrative responsibility. In the next chapter the focus of attention shifts from officers' demographic characteristics to officers' values. It examines the issue of police professionalization and the potential success of viewing responsibility as a problem of instilling a sense of moral obligation.

7 Responsibility as Moral Obligation

Professionalization of the Police

Treating responsibility as a problem of legal obedience ignores police discretion. Treating responsibility as a problem of accountability leads to checking and structuring discretion. Both of these approaches may be effective in limiting irresponsibility, but it is questionable whether controlling irresponsibility is the same as promoting responsibility. Treating responsibility as representativeness deflects attention from consideration of job performance.

Responsibility may be like liberty, which Judge Learned Hand said lies in the heart and when it dies there is irrestorable (1960:188). From this perspective, external controls—law, bureaucratic rules, equal employment opportunity, and affirmative action—are insufficient to secure responsible police. Such controls limit positive attributes of flexibility and innovation that are necessary for effective policing and effective police administration, yet they are incapable of fully limiting negative aspects of behavior that should be controlled. Because of the gap between the ideal the controls are expected to create and actual practices, it is necessary to rely on the sense of responsibility felt by individual officers and executives.

In this perspective on responsibility, the key is providing individual officers with an internalized commitment to serve social interests. Leadership does not mean simply setting up rules and systems of punishment. It means providing positive role models and articulating the goals of the police institution and of the controlling social values that relate to the police mission. Responsibility should result from the officers' pursuit of the goals in conformance with the values. The officers should be impelled by a desire to reduce the gap between idealized police behavior and the realities of police work.

Proponents of such a position assume that everyone who has authority over others has an idea of what he hopes to achieve by using his power—using it to further only his own good, or to promote public interest (De Jouvenel, 1957:xii). They further assume that pursuit of the common interest can be assured only by directly influencing the internalized role prescriptions of individual police officers. Their basic point is that no matter how severe the penalties or how rigorous the disciplinary procedures, people cannot be forced to be responsible.

They also assume that a professionalized police service leads to administrative responsibility by establishing value consensus among technically competent officers. The individual officer, as a member of a professionalized occupational group, interprets his duty according to group-defined standards, which are derived from more general societal standards and interests. With his dual commitment to competence and social obligation, the professional can make sure that police action is not only technically correct but is accepted as correct by the public.

This chapter will first discuss the significance of police discretion, analyzing the conflict between the ministerial myth of policing (the false hope of attaining responsibility through legal obedience) and the need for and use of discretion. Then it will consider the prospects for successful professionalization of the police and for achieving police responsibility through development of a sense of moral obligation.

The emphasis placed on responsibility as obedience or as accountability may derive from a desire to eliminate police discretion in the belief that discretion is undesirable because it introduces uncertainty into the standards by which officers may be judged. The underlying premise is that the clearer the restraints on the exercise of power are, the easier it is to recognize when power is abused. This view, however, is out of touch with the reality of public administration in general and grossly out of touch with the reality of policing and police administration. Discretion arises whenever there is indefiniteness in how to pursue a course of action. Any official who has a duty to perform or a goal to achieve and who cannot rely on specific predetermined guidelines has discretion.

A political system that is organized to follow the demands of its citizenry must sacrifice uniformity in the operation of its enforcement system. The system is basically set into operation only in response to those citizens who call on it. It largely ignores those instances and forms of illegality that the citizens choose to ignore. Were the system to strive for universality in the application of law, it would have to refuse to follow the diverse desires of the populace. A government committed to controlling itself and being controlled as well as to controlling the governed cannot be operated by individuals narrowly focused on negative strictures as embodied in law. Administrators, including police, in a democratic society have a commitment to pursuing positive purposes of the society; these are not necessarily to be achieved through arresting lawbreakers in every instance when a law is broken.

Since 1930, discretionary law enforcement has been acknowledged in the United States. Schuyler Wallace, in a survey of U.S. district attorneys in the late 1920s, found that over 90 percent of those responding admitted that nonenforcement and nonprosecution were official policy. Prosecutors gave four reasons for their practice of nonenforcement, two focusing on justness and two stemming from public desire. Substitution of reasonable discretion was thought to have better social effects than strict enforcement. The prosecutors also were convinced that enforcement of some laws would be directly contrary to the interest of justice. The most frequently cited reason for selective or nonenforcement was, however, a straightforward desire to make actions conform to local public opinion. A closely related reason was a belief that it would be a waste of time, effort, and money to prosecute cases, no matter how strong, that were likely to result in acquittal by a jury (1930:358).

Data on police discretion do not go back as far as the prosecutor study, but a wealth of similar data has been generated since the 1960s. A nationwide sample of American police officers of all ranks and from a variety of divisions found that, in spite of statutory proscriptions, they believed discretion to be a necessary part of their work. As can be seen in Table 7-1, a majority of police agreed that as long as a law is on the books, they *must* enforce it. A substantial majority agreed, however, that to keep the peace the police need the authority to control certain public behavior even when a law is not being violated.

In the exercise of their duties police officers face many emergency, crisis, or potentially crisis situations; the unusual, the hazardous, the unpredictable, and the disruptive are the everyday experience of the patrolman. There is never enough money available for full enforcement of the law. Even the large metropolitan cities do not have enough police to enforce all the laws and provide all requested services. More significantly, police work is complicated because they serve and are in direct contact with a disparate population rather than a uniform or coherent community. The police must contend with a

Table 7-1. Police Officers' Views of Police Discretion (percent)

As long as a law is on the books police must enforce it	63
The best officer knows when to depart from standard procedures to get the job done	68
Preservation of the peace requires police to have the authority to make people move along or break it up even if no law is being violated	71

Source: Watson and Sterling, 1969:57, 132, 69.

great variety of expectations about their role. The law, the department, the local government, public opinion, and individual clients all have different requirements and different views of the police. Both the police officers as individuals and the police department as an organization must make accommodations with these differential expectations. The mechanism of accommodation is discretionary enforcement and resource allocation.

As a consequence, police officers' discretion extends throughout the full range of their duties, as has been demonstrated in empirical studies. Discretionary decision making is evident through all the steps from the initial response to a call for service to determination of whether to file a felony charge against a suspected offender. The decision to dispatch a unit to a call has been found to be affected by the rate of calls (Cumming et al., 1965:188) and the service or offense involved in a call (Cumming et al., 1965; Bercal, 1970:682; Shearing, 1974:83; J. Q. Wilson, 1975:19). Broad discretion is exercised in handling juvenile offenders (Piliavin and Briar, 1964; McKeachern and Bauzer, 1967; Terry, 1967; Black and Reiss, 1970; Steer, 1970; Lundman et al., 1978), in handling the mentally ill (Bittner, 1967a; Matthews, 1970; Mehlman, 1972; Snibbe, 1973; Jacobsen et al., 1973; Handberg and Pilchick, 1980), in enforcing traffic laws (Preiss and Ehrlich, 1966; Gardiner, 1968; Campbell and Ross, 1968; Petersen, 1971; Lundman, 1979), in enforcing misdemeanor victimless crime laws such as public drunkenness (Bittner, 1967b; Sullivan and Siegel, 1972; Lundman, 1974; Pastor, 1980), and even in enforcing felony law (LaFave, 1965; "Police Discretion . . . Rape in Philadelphia," 1968; Black, 1980; Skolnick, 1975).

Clearly, the wrong question is frequently asked. Instead of debating whether the law should be selectively enforced, attention should be focused on how selectivity is to be governed. The great problem of discretion is not that it exists but the frame of reference within which it is exercised. Unguided discretion provides an opening for illicit discrimination that can lead to serious social injustice. Discretion must be exercised in accordance with the desires of the citizenry and with applicable technical requirements and accepted decision-making processes. Responsible exercise of discretion is not arbitrary, capricious, selfish, wanton, or careless.

To provide the proper frame of reference for the exercise of discretion, proponents of professionalization of the police stress the need for adherence to appropriate social values. If police officers merely carried out the laws and the policies and procedures established by their superiors, there would be no conflict of values. The legislators, judges, and top-level administrators would have values; the police would have only programmed responses. But effective law enforcement and efficient peace keeping depend on discretion. Police officers must therefore be controlled by values that support the ends of a democratic society.

There is, nevertheless, a problem with seeing professionalization of the police as the key to responsible police. Professionalization of the police has long been a major goal of progressive police administrators, but it has not been developed into an operational program. The various efforts undertaken in the name of professionalization have lacked a unified focus. The calls for professionalization have in many cases been based on misinterpretation, misapplication, misrepresentation, and miscalculation.

The meaning of the terms "profession" and "professional" has been misinterpreted. Police professionalization lacks coherence as a movement because its proponents have often failed to recognize that professional status is not the same for all occupational groups. The term "professionalization" has been misapplied to developments in police administration because the general usages of "professional" are not directly applicable to the police. Police-specific usages are not always reasonable adaptations of the general perspectives. The fact that the social and political environments of police departments limit the possibilities for intradepartmental processes has been misunderstood. Professionalization in any sense may not be a realistic prospect in certain departments. In other departments the form professionalization takes will be largely controlled by extradepartmental factors. The rewards that may accrue from professionalization have been miscalculated. Professional status for an occupational group has different implications for society as a whole than for the group involved. Police professionalization has tended to emphasize pursuit of professional status in order to obtain its perceived rewards for the occupational group, neglecting to provide society with its rewards of professionalism. Ultimately, the course of police professionalization must be evaluated in terms of the potential of society to reward such professionalism as is developed by the police.

Professionalism and the Police

Efforts at professionalizing the police aim at an elusive goal because there are no set criteria. Before evaluating the potential success of police professionalization, it is necessary to outline the dimensions of professionalism and identify the criteria by which professional status is judged. There is no clearly recognized definition of a profession in American society. Attempts to delineate the nature of professions have produced two different sets of criteria, each with a different focus and emphasizing a different basis for claiming professional status. The first, referred to here as type one, the ideational focus, emphasizes an occupational group's subscription to social ideals. The second, type two, the expertise focus, emphasizes the nature of the tasks performed by an occupational group and the way the tasks are carried out.

From the perspective of the ideational focus, professionalism is an effort to improve society. This focus is exemplified by Harold L. Wilensky's statement, "The service ideal is the pivot around which the moral claim to professional status revolves" (1964:140). The work of the professional in this view is infused with moral value beyond the results clients receive. This model is largely based on the three classical professions, law, medicine, and theology, in which professionals deal with matters of great importance with great discretion and without direct supervision. They handle emergencies and have access to intimate information about guilt and transgression, and they make decisions involving life and death and honor and dishonor.

Because matters of life and death and honor and dishonor arise in infinite variety, professionals are trained to individualize the services they provide. Each person who consults a physician, lawyer, or minister expects to be treated as a unique individual with special problems. This does not deny that there are many common illnesses, lawsuits, and sins that may be dealt with through predetermined treatments, but the professional is expected to be prepared for and capable of dealing with the uncommon and perhaps the unique. He must be capable of creative, innovative action to define and solve the problems he confronts.

The need for innovative treatment has two major consequences for the social definition of professional status. One consequence is in the area of relationships between professionals and clients. The other has to do with the organization of the profession as a social institution and the patterns of relationships within the professions. The necessity of long preservice education and training as preparation for professional practice and the reality of uncommon cases requiring specialized insight and innovative treatment means that the layman client is often unable to judge the appropriateness of the professional's course of action. The client is compelled to accept the measures decided upon by the professional because of the authority of the professional. But the professional's authority is not backed by negative sanctions (Parsons, 1951:463); it rests largely on the trust and faith of the client.

The client suspends much of his autonomy in the area in which he consults the professional. He may choose to get a second opinion. But once the client decides to accept the counsel of his physician, lawyer, or minister he is expected to follow instructions with implicit faith in their rightness. In medicine, according to Talcott Parsons, this means the patient must put his confidence in his doctor, and if he loses confidence, he must find a different physician (1951:464). The ultimate significance is that the patient must recognize an obligation to define himself as Dr. X's patient. The willingness of most people to do so is only partially explained by the medical profession's assumed scientific foundation. In fact, medicine, law, and theology have common roots in prescientific mysticism and magic.

The relationship between the professional and his client in these classical professions is personal. Laymen recognize that patients die, that litigation fails, that souls are lost, in spite of the best efforts of the professional, and that the blame may not belong to the professional. Death, damnation, and/or legal penalty may be accepted as a consequence of the nature of the case rather than of failure on the part of the physician, minister, or lawyer. Very early in their careers the practitioners of these classical professions recognize the implications of this fact.

Since the layman lacks competence to judge professional ability and since results may not be indicative of ability, the personality of the professional becomes a dominant concern. Wagner Theilens, Jr., found a large degree of correspondence between medical and law students' appraisals of the attributes of good practitioners. Seventy-three percent of both medical and legal students identified high intelligence as the most important factor for making a good doctor or lawyer. Pleasing personality was ranked second by 40 percent of the medical students and by 43 percent of the law students (1958:148).

Even before completing their training for professional practice, the would-be physicians and attorneys are aware that the trust and faith of their clientele are often unrelated to rational considerations of technical competence. The persistence of the sense of awe that provides the impetus for deference to and faith in the professional thus is one of the primary factors marking professional status.

The need for creative, innovative action in an area requiring special knowledge and skills contributes to development of professional criteria in a second way. Since the practice of the profession is so dependent on insight into the uniqueness of individual cases and the consequent need for individualized treatment, it is assumed that the best judges of professionals are their peers. Just as the individual surrenders some of his autonomy to his counselor, the normal organs of social control surrender some of their oversight authority to organized professional groups.

Organized professional groups are formally committed to the service ideal. They use the delegated authority of the state to maintain high standards of the professions at large by enforcing individual high standards. Through their professional organizations the members of professions are involved in self-government. They screen out the unfit by establishing the criteria by which an individual may enter the profession. They attempt to reinforce the traditional sense of clientele deference by certifying that members of the profession meet the standards which originally gave rise to that deference. The professional is certified to have obtained the knowledge and skills that are necessary for technical excellence. He is also certified to have accepted the responsibility to uphold the profession's code of ethics and to have agreed to subject himself to peer evaluation of his loyalty to the code. He is thus certified to be an expert in his area of specialization and to be a person of good character.

Members of a self-governing profession are also assumed to find their primary rewards to be satisfaction from providing service and from peer acceptance. Members of the profession are expected to be held to the highest standards by fear of professional sanctions (especially loss of respect from the other members of the profession and, most seriously, expulsion from the profession). The maintenance of internal disciplinary mechanisms is expected to have two functions. On the one hand, it provides a form of support for those who are unjustly accused of malpractice by clients. In a professional forum, the legitimacy of actions taken that have had negative results may be established through review by people competent to recognize the circumstances involved. On the other hand, it provides a mechanism to demonstrate to the public that malpractice will be dealt with by the profession without need for outside oversight.

The foregoing description, of course, does not give a true picture of the real world of the classical professions. The service ideal clearly does not provide the sole motivation for individuals or for the profession at large. Physicians and lawyers, for the most part, seek to maximize their incomes. Some are amoral and concerned only with personal gain irrespective of a pledge to adhere to a code of ethics. Professional associations protect their members from justified as well as from unjustified censure. When professionals are organized into large organizations (such as hospitals and large law offices and legal agencies) they are every bit as sensitive to inevitable gradations of distinction and achievement as are nonprofessional workers (Goss, 1963). Still, the service ideal and the image of moral authority are the basic elements that characterize type one professionalism.

The second focus that has emerged from efforts to delineate the essential nature of professions may be termed the technical-managerial or expertise focus (type two). The emphasis in describing professions in this category is on an occupational group's tasks and the way the tasks are carried out. From the perspective of this focus, professionalism is a matter of applying specialized skills in the most effective manner. Like the ideational focus, this perspective emphasizes a claim to special competence acquired through extensive training to handle a specified task. Also, like the first focus, this perspective recognizes that practitioners are to treat clients impartially and without personal prejudice and to view problems objectively.

The major point of divergence between the two types of professionalism is in the relationship between the professional practitioner and the client. The personal moral authority of the practitioner in the expertise view of professionalism is valued more for what he can do than for what he is. The professional here is expected to be judged by the results he accomplishes. A physician may not be held blameworthy when a seriously ill patient dies, but an engineer whose bridge collapses during an earthquake is held responsible.

From this perspective, the professional is basically a technician. He has a body of skills and knowledge at his disposal which has been developed more or less systematically. He is trained to follow established rules to solve problems in his area of expertise. He is expected to treat clients fairly and to adhere to the group's code of ethics. He is expected to be motivated by a desire to perform well and to find primary job satisfaction in problem solving and work well done. Professionals are expected to have higher status, higher income, and superior interorganizational mobility than nonprofessionals.

Based on these considerations, a type two profession is a reasonably clear-cut occupational field, which requires extensive training and offers a lifelong career of growth and development to its practitioners.

This definition does not require the surrender of autonomy by the client that the first perspective emphasizes. Rather, it places much more emphasis on the professional as a provider of services to the client. The value of the professional may even be said to lie in the reliability of his actions. Charles Perrow states: "The eunuch in the harem is the prototype of the modern professional: he is competent to do all but that which he should not do" (1972:17).

This second focus corresponds to the census bureau's definition of a professional worker: one who performs work based upon the established principles of a profession or science, which requires training through academic study or extensive practice or both. The keystone of this focus is technical competence in a complex field guided by a set of procedural rules for problem identification and solution.

A composite description of a profession based on the two perspectives would emphasize technical competence mobilized for valued social ends. The elements of a profession would be intellectual training, specialized knowledge, operational utility, a service ideal, and a code of ethics. Actual professional status would, however, be a function of public perceptions of the value of the services provided by the occupational group in question. Professional status would come about only if the public were to accept that the professional knows more about what is good for his clients than do the clients themselves. Technical competence through academic and occupational training confers professional status only when there is public recognition of the high social value of the services provided and of the integrity of the service providers.

The mere existence of a formal professional ethic cannot forge the vital linkage between technical competence and public acceptance which is a prerequisite to professional status. The subordinate norms of the service ideal—that the professional be impersonal, impartial, and objective—are attributes of the professional worker (the second model of professionalism) and, therefore, do not distinguish the professional (in the classical sense) from the nonprofessional. Nor can a code of professional conduct, by itself or combined with the foregoing behavioral norms, raise an occupational group to type one professional status.

The necessity of instilling an identification with the tenets of democracy has long been recognized by at least some law enforcement officials. The law enforcement code of ethics adopted by the California Peace Officers Association in 1956 and by the International Association of Chiefs of Police in 1957 states: "As a Law Enforcement Officer, my first duty is to serve mankind; to safeguard lives and property; to protect the innocent, the weak and the peaceful; and to respect the Constitutional rights of all men to liberty, equality and justice." But the link between the formally stated service ideal and police operations has not yet been forged in the public mind.

In large part, this can be seen as a consequence of the perceived superficiality of the formal code. Beyond the general agreement that professionalization of the police means developing a commitment to democratic values, there seems to be little consensus as to what constitutes professionalization, professionalism, or even the profession of police officer. For some police officers, mainly those with long tenure but still in lower ranks, professionalism is a superficial, procedural, mainly public relations ploy. As an instructor at a police academy said, "We can't take them out and kick them in the balls. Today we have to use professionalization" (Harris, 1973:48). Such attitudes point up the fact that commitment to democratic values as a professional obligation has not created a meaningful service ethic at the lowest levels of police departments.

There is, in short, a lack of correspondence between the model of professionalism based upon the three venerable professions and the common police image of professionalism based upon a relatively narrow concern with managerial/administrative efficiency and organizational autonomy. To understand the potential for professionalism to provide socially responsible policing, it is necessary to undertake a phenomenological study of police professionalism. That is, it is necessary to examine how the occupational membership itself defines a profession, a professional, professionalism, or professionalization.

The Police View of Professionalism

The initial efforts to establish policing as a profession were aimed at the department and its subunits rather than the individual line officers (Caiden, 1977:chapter 1). Professionalization for the early reformers meant bureaucratization. The goal was to make the organization responsive and dutiful.

The advocates of this position believe that nonprofessional police do not follow the rules. The logical solution, therefore, would be to increase the specificity of the rules and their enforcement. Administrators subscribing to this view see their duty to be minimization of individual behavior which is contrary to the interests of the department. In practice, this means reducing the amount of discretion exercised by officers in the field away from the eye of superiors. Overall department policies would have to be developed that would provide a framework for the proper and consistent exercise of discretion.

Historically, however, police departments have responded to policy dictates from outsiders such as courts and political officials. Policy formulation within the departments has been largely confined to relatively minor areas of concern such as the care of equipment, standards of off-duty behavior, scheduling of court appearances, and handling of prisoners' property. The early proponents of professionalism, therefore, had as one of their primary goals the centralization of authority within the department with regard to internal operation and departmental autonomy vis-a-vis outside agencies.

The watchword of professionalizing reformers has been efficiency in control and in operation. With control of the organization firmly in the hands of the upper-level administrators, emphasis could be put on establishing formal rules based upon expert knowledge. Technical competence, specialization, and impartial execution of duty would be substituted for nonprofessional concerns associated with political control.

The police administrators perceived a basic conflict between professionalism and politics. Professionalism, with its broad orientation, was seen to rest upon knowledge, science, and rationality and, therefore, to be concerned with the correct ways of solving problems and performing duties. Politics was seen, in contrast, to be based upon negotiation and compromise by subject-area amateurs. A professional police department was seen as one that emphasized efficiency and rationality to the exclusion of political criteria as the bases of decision making.

Within the department the counterpart of the drive for objective, standardized performance criteria, which highlighted the professional-political conflict, was a drive for impartial officers. From this perspective, police professionalism was designed to encourage the development of competent officers who would apply the law according to impersonal standards. The professional officer is expected to use special expertise within an area of discretion bounded by department policies based upon expert knowledge. General, impartial, impersonal rules would regulate the patrolman, and he would apply general, impartial, impersonal standards in dealing with the public. This view is related to type two professionalism. It rests, however, on a conception of the professional police officer which is analogous to Weber's ideal bureaucrat who through specialized training and constant practice becomes more and more proficient and discharges his duties impersonally according to prescribed rules (1973:15).

Latter-day reformers still cling to the emphasis on bureaucratic operation. The American Bar Association, in its *Standards Relating to the Urban Police Function*, for example, maintains that since individual police officers make important decisions without direct supervision and without departmental uniformity, discretion should be structured and controlled and police administrators should give the highest priority to the formulation of administrative rules governing the exercise of discretion (1973:4.2, 4.3). The essence of the perspective has been altered, however. The bureaucratic vision of professionalism has been tempered, even within police circles, by elements of the type one construction. Strict bureaucratization has given way to a more sophisticated movement toward a type two professionalism as a result of this effort to blend bureaucracy and the classical view of professions.

This expansion of the traditional reform emphasis on bureaucratic control is significant. The premise upon which it rests is that police officer discretion is inevitable and is not necessarily contrary to responsible policing. The President's Commission on Law Enforcement and Administration of Justice, for instance, maintained that the exercise of discretion within appropriate legal guidelines, subject to review, better protects basic individual rights than does the routine, uncritical application of rules, which are often procedurally explicit but substantively imprecise (1967:18).

There are two police-generated views of professionalism just as there are two general views. The first is the command orientation, focusing on departmental structure and processes. This orientation assumes that officers' conduct can be closely and specifically controlled by norms and policies established by the formal central command. The second is the discretion orientation, which recognizes the need for and legitimacy of the exercise of broad discretion by officers at the lowest levels of the agency.

From the perspective of the command orientation, the process of professionalization is a matter of organization. This orientation leads to restructuring the rank system to provide for police-assistant grades and assigning routine and clerical duties to civilians. The essence of police work is seen to be crime prevention and detection. Those who subscribe to this orientation hope that through elimination of traffic and parking duties, warrant serving, responsibility for alcohol and drug treatment programs, and the like, police officers will be able to concentrate on "real" police work.

An officer in a department with a command orientation is expected to be process-oriented. The officer is to do a good job procedurally within his area of competence and not to be concerned about the final disposition of the events in which he takes part. He is taught to be impartial and to go by the book, which means that he is expected to use the techniques and skills of his profession to enforce laws uniformly, without regard for persons. The department admits that discretionary activity takes place but attempts through technical-managerial efficiency to provide firm guidelines for the exercise of that discretion. This means that although some discretion may be recognized to be inevitable and even necessary, the breadth of discretionary operation is subject to constant constriction. The Law Enforcement Code of Ethics reflects this orientation by rejecting officiousness and decision making based on personal feelings, prejudices, animosities, or friendships and by asserting a commitment to relentless prosecution of criminals and enforcement of the law "without fear or favor, malice or ill will, never employing unnecessary force or violence and never accepting gratuities" (California Commission on Peace Officer Standards and Training, 1974:31). The paradox in this orientation is that law enforcement is only part of the policeman's duty and in the aspect of his job that involves maintenance of order there are few general rules that can be uniformly applied.

In marked contrast, in a department dedicated to encouraging the development of discretionary professionalism it is recognized that the individual officer bears the burden of deciding the proper measures to apply to given situations. It is assumed that broad discretion must be allowed because the command structure cannot supervise or foresee the circumstances of all encounters between policemen and citizens. Such a department expects its officers to be outcome-oriented. The officer is to see his actions as part of an overall system. He is encouraged to use his judgment and to improvise (within legal limits) to keep the peace. He is encouraged to recognize that good police work is not simply a matter of making good busts. Law enforcement is not ignored, but peace keeping is viewed as no less valuable than crime fighting. The department recognizes that peace keeping cannot be organizationally defined and controlled. Procedural efficiency is seen as secondary to effective order maintenance.

This orientation seeks to nurture a certain attitude or philosophy that would support the position that the police task is the maintenance of legality and public security. This focus would cover peace keeping, law enforcement, and service work. Only with such an expanded view of their role, according to this orientation, can the police win public respect and ultimately professional status. (This view is clearly reflected in the growing concern in academic criminal justice with ethical education [Potts, 1981; Heffernan, 1981].)

The two occupationally specific orientations to police professionalism differ from but are related to the two general perspectives on professionalism. The command orientation is a modification of type two professionalism (technical-managerial focus). The discretionary orientation is a partial approach to type one professionalism (ideational focus). There are thus both multiple general definitions and multiple police-generated definitions of professionalism. Since the two sets of definitions are not fully compatible, it is to be expected that a quest for police professionalism will be more a source of friction than of productive cooperation unless the discrepancies are acknowledged.

The Social and Organizational Context of Police Professionalization

Examination of the police role indicates that in several respects police work meets the criteria of the professions set out earlier. Those who claim that police should be accorded professional status based on the role they perform assert that police officers are skilled specialists with unique competence who ply their skills in the public interest. They hold that the essence of professional work is individual discretion and that discretion is the essence of police work. This view recognizes that the police are required to encounter a vast range of emergency situations involving an equally vast range of circumstantial factors. The individual police officer is required to assess volatile, unstable situations and to determine his response quickly and without consultation or assistance.

The emphasis on judgment, the lack of clear guidelines to cover most circumstances, the necessity for reactive or self-activated behavior, the stress on personal assessment of emergency situations all seem to support police work as a candidate for professional status. Police work is, nevertheless, inherently different from the work of the traditional professions.

The police confront a major dilemma in their quest for professional status which also confronts another occupational group with a similar apparent claim to that status. Like police officers, social workers share with the recognized professions a role in handling vital matters that require access to intimate information. Still, the authors of "The Emergence of a Social Work Profession" note that social workers lack a "clear area" of technical competence (Wilensky and Lebeaux, 1965:278). Technical competence alone is not the issue. It is the claim to "*exclusive* possession of competence in a specified area" that supports a claim to professional status (ibid.:284; emphasis in original). The police, no less than social workers, are inhibited in their movement toward professional status by that lack of a clear, exclusive area of competence. Police can no more claim an exclusive role in public safety than can social workers claim an exclusive role in human welfare.

At perhaps an even more basic level, the social role of the police differs from the social role of the recognized professions. This difference is rooted in the bases of legitimacy for the exercise of authority by the various occupations. Physicians and lawyers base their claim to authority on personal expertise, whereas police base their claim to authority on societal delegation. Other professionals can and do dump their problems on the police. The police have to deal with almost anyone who chooses to call upon them and with clients who not only do not call upon them but who resist. While other professions rely on authority and must call the police to exercise power when authority fails, the police have direct access to power when their authority fails. Furthermore, while other professionals are trained and socialized before beginning practice, even though they may practice their profession within a bureaucracy, the police are trained and socialized within the bureaucracy.

This fact of police employment in a bureaucratic agency must be borne in mind when assessing the potential for police professionalization. Police officers will not become independent operators affiliated with large organizations (as doctors are with hospitals) or free professionals (as lawyers are in private practice) or collegially governed professionals (as university faculties are). A realistic approach to police professionalization must cultivate the positive attributes of professionalism (technical competence guided by a service ethic) within the context of bureaucratic employment.

Proponents of professionalism have to recognize that there is a dynamic tension between the societal goals of professionalism and the police occupational goals of professionalization. The basic societal goal of professionalism is validly applicable to police. Society in general benefits from professionalism when "professional" means a high level of technical competence in dealing with vital interests, delivered by individuals committed to a service ethic, who are organized into a self-governing institution, which is committed to preservation and improvement of competence and ethical integrity. Police officers should be guided by a sense of moral obligation to perform their duties effectively, impartially, and in conformance with the values, beliefs, and wishes of the public.

The occupational goals of the police in advocating professionalization run in a different direction. Rather than seeing professionalism as a point to be reached, many proponents of police professionalization see professional status as a reward to be conferred. They insist that the practice of policing is professional work and that police officers deserve the rewards provided to other professionals. Therefore, in comparison with the current situation police officers deserve higher pay, greater social status, greater public respect and deference, and, above all, operational autonomy because the right to make decisions is the most zealously guarded of professional prerogatives (Hughes, 1958:94). They do not deny that efforts must continue to upgrade the quality of policing, but they emphasize that the basic elements of professionalism have been achieved.

Higher pay and better social standing for police officers may be fully justified without regard to the issue of professionalism. The po-lice-generated definitions of professionalism are valid adaptive approaches for recognition of the complexity and importance of po-lice work which merit greater reward for police service. They are adaptive in that they are rooted in the general perspectives on profes-sionalism but recognize the organizational context of police employment.

The two general perspectives on professions developed in response to social and cultural factors. The type two perspective developed to take account of the rise of new professions that did not meet the criteria applied to law, medicine, and theology. In the case of orienta-tions to police professionalization, only one occupational group is in-volved, but the fragmentation of the police service in America into thousands of municipal, county, state, and federal agencies has, to a large extent, blocked formation of a unified concept of professional-ism. The potential success of police professionalization efforts must be judged in light of this fragmentation.

The local political culture in which each police department exists has an impact on the nature of the police occupation. The attitudes, values, and beliefs of the public in each jurisdiction affect the way local governments operate. As an agency of the local government, the police departments are affected by public sentiment. Both the poten-tial for professionalization and the kind of professionalism that is sought are subject to local variations. This does not mean that there can be no general effort toward professionalization; it only means that evaluation of professionalization efforts must consider the influence of factors beyond the control of the department.

The police-generated definitions of professionalism recognize that variations in professionalism are to be expected. Not every depart-ment is unique, however. There are several general patterns of inter-play between local environments and police services. James Q. Wilson's (1975) scheme of police responses to local conditions can be adapted to examine professionalization. A typology of the relation-ships that may exist between the impact of the local political culture

Figure 7-1. Variations in Police Professionalism

Source of Role Definition	Role Emphasis	
	Order Maintenance	Law Enforcement
Local	I Nonprofessional	II Quasi-professional
Occupation-wide	III Command professional	IV Discretionary professional

Increasing Direct Departmental
Control over Individual Behavior

on police operations and the form professionalization takes can be developed.

Wilson identified three types of police departments: the watchman style, the legalistic style, and the service style. Each of the three styles is a function of the social conditions in the city, the variety of demands for service made on the departments, and the local political culture. Against these factors can be compared the orientations of the police administrative and executive personnel with regard to the nature of the police role. A fourfold typology of police professionalism can be constructed from these factors (Figure 7-1).

The four forms of police professionalism are, of course, not all-inclusive. The typology is limited in scope, as is true of any theoretical framework that attempts to categorize complex interrelationships. The typology is intended to illustrate salient factors that contribute to variations in police professionalism. General patterns of local political culture and police responses are the focus of concern. There is no way to account for every possible impact of local politics on the form or degree of professionalization. Furthermore, the typology does not attempt to account for characteristics of individual officers. It addresses only generalized organizational responses to certain circumstances. And the typology does not imply that every officer or every division within a given department will fall into the pattern that is characteristic of the department as a whole.

In the first cell of the figure is the nonprofessional officer. The typical officer in this category meets the criteria of none of the perspectives or orientations; he is not motivated by either service to society or high technical competence. His policing style is most likely to fit Wilson's watchman category. He is concerned primarily with the order-maintenance (Wilson) or peace-keeping (Banton, 1964) function of the police. He wants to keep his beat quiet. He seeks to avoid using the formal sanctions of the law because going to court and making a case takes time. When he is in contact with lawyers and judges, he is the subordinate. On the streets he is the boss of his beat, and that is what he sees as his proper position. He will make felony arrests because that is the source of departmental rewards and because that enhances his self-image as protector of his turf.

This officer's source of role definition is local. He may not like the local power holders, and he may resent their power over him, but he recognizes that they make it possible for him to be a police officer. The formal authority figures of the department also recognize that the local power holders control police policy. Neither the departmental hierarchy nor the individual officers want to rock the boat. The superior officers want to protect their positions, and the street officers want to protect their territorial rights. The result is that political pressure on the department is combined with peer group pressure within the department to override departmental supervision of individual officers. The meaning of the term "professional officer" is simple and is not related to the criteria that qualify occupational groups for professional status. A professional police officer is simply a person whose occupational status is that of policeman; that is, professional means only not amateur. Professional ethics, science-based technical expertise, and most aspects of departmental discipline are extraneous to field operations in low-visibility circumstances.

In cell II is the quasiprofessional officer. The typical officer in this category meets the criteria of the model bureaucrat. He is motivated by the rewards conferred by the department, which are provided for faithful service. His policing style is most likely to fit Wilson's legalistic category. He is concerned with the law enforcement function of the police. He wants to be productive. Even in low-visibility circumstances he is willing to invoke the formal sanctions of the law. Tickets, arrests, field contact reports, and the like are seen as tangible proof of his productivity. He is unlikely to form personal relationships with the citizens on his beat. His beat is no more than a place where he executes his duties.

This officer is a product of the traditional reform movement, which sought to free police departments from political control by centralizing authority for police policy and operations to promote efficiency and rationality and to combat corruption. The movement was little concerned with professionalizing individual officers. In fact, the goal of the movement has been described as replacement of the "flatfoot cop on the take" with "cadres of . . . snappy operatives working under the command of bureaucrats-in-uniform" (Bittner, 1978:43).

The role definition for this officer is established by his departmental superiors and is, therefore, locally determined. A very significant difference between the role definition process for the nonprofessional and the quasi-professional is that in the latter, the partisan political powers have relinquished their control over most aspects of police policy. The departmental hierarchy is relatively freed from political pressures to maintain the dominant factions in power. (This situation can be contrasted to the political factors perpetuating a nonprofessional department in Wincanton as described by Gardiner, 1967.) With this freedom the hierarchy seeks to maintain tight discipline over the line personnel. Strict standards of behavior and performance are established, and punishment is exacted for breaking the rules. The officer can be expected to strive for effectiveness and impartiality. He is a quasi-professional because his concern for effectiveness and impartiality is a reaction to stringent discipline. This officer is a bureaucrat, not a professional. He seeks to keep out of trouble by doing what the department considers to be a good job. He may act as would a professional, according to the general sets of criteria for professionalism, but he lacks the personal commitment to the service ethic which is presumed to provide internalized guides to thought and action.

In cell III is the command professional. The typical officer in this category meets the criteria of the police-defined equivalent of the professional worker. He is the police version of a type two professional—the technical-managerial professional. He is motivated by a desire to perform well in his job as defined by the department but also by a desire to live up to his generalized image of a good police officer. That is, he is motivated both by what he believes he should do and by what he believes he should be. His policing style is also most likely to fit a legalistic category. Like the quasi-professional, he is concerned primarily with the law enforcement function of the police. He has a firm belief in the need to work through the formal system. Similarly, he accepts the need for and legitimacy of formal departmental performance standards.

This officer is distinguished from the nonprofessional and the quasi-professional by his identification with "the police profession." He believes that there are standards of good police work that extend beyond his own department. In line with the technical-managerial perspective, he has faith in science. He adheres to the norms of impartiality, impersonality, and objectiveness. He also recognizes the need for police officers to uphold high personal standards of integrity and public service. He accepts the fact of stringent departmental discipline but views it as appropriate only insofar as it operates to uphold professional standards. While the quasi-professional sees the disciplinary system as a threat, the command professional sees it as a support ensuring that the department as a whole is held to high standards.

Command professionalism is most likely to arise in circumstances similar to those that produce quasi-professionals. The partisan political influence that perpetuates the nonprofessional department will be missing. There will likely be more support from the political system than in the bureaucratic department and as a result, better access to trained and educated officers. Instead of the department being isolated from the rest of local government, it has autonomy in its area of responsibility and is expected to be technically competent. The local political culture in instances where quasi-professional officers are developed is essentially opposed to politics. The department may be left to devise its own standards and policies because of fear that politicians would exploit the department. The political officeholders are expected to ensure that technical competence and integrity are maintained. Their attitude toward the department is basically favorable.

At the individual level, the command professional differs from the quasi-professional in his sense of commitment. He believes in actively seeking to upgrade the public image of the police by proving how effective they can be and by showing how much they contribute to society. He is concerned with developing job-specific skills but also believes that technically competent performance leads to socially valued outcomes.

Finally, in cell IV is the discretionary professional. The typical officer in this category is most likely to be found in Wilson's service department. This officer is a police equivalent of the traditional professional. He is motivated by the ethic of social improvement, which is the key element distinguishing the ideational focus from the technical-managerial focus. He sees the police role in its broadest sense. He is committed to the use of police power to deal with social problems. He emphasizes preservation of social order. He is likely to see prepa-

ration for police work as both training and education and to have
more faith in the latter than does the command professional. He has
an occupationwide frame of reference for development of profes-
sional standards. He is most likely to find the legitimacy of the depart-
mental hierarchy to lie in its role as securer of resources for good
police work and as articulator of professional standards. Accordingly,
he is unlikely to view standards based on quantifiable measures such
as numbers of citations and arrests as appropriate indicators of police
performance.

Like the command professional, he values both skill development
and achievement of socially valued outcomes. He differs in that his
primary concern is with the societal outcomes. He is much more con-
cerned with using nonpolice community resources to deal with police-
related problems and is much more flexible in his definition of police
skills. The department does not relinquish direct control over the
discretionary professional but does grant him greater latitude in
choosing his course of action, placing less emphasis on bureaucratic
rules. Overall, the impression is that harmony is the key. The local
political culture must support a relationship of trust between the com-
munity and the political officeholders, between the community and
the police, and between the officeholders and the police. Only then
can the fear of exploitation, which gives rise to rigid bureaucracy and
strict control, be overcome.

The importance of this typology is to make clear that professional-
ization of the police cannot be viewed simply as a progression from
nonprofessional to bureaucrat to technical-managerial professional to
professional. The localized, bureaucratized control of police officers
limits the professional development that can occur. The discretionary
professional, as a version of the traditional professional, is likely to
evolve only where the service type of police department can develop.
Professionalizers cannot ignore the social and political realities of
policing.

The Limits of Police Professionalism

Proponents of responsibility through moral obligation hold that ex-
ternal controls cannot fully comprehend the entire range of
undesirable behavior. Because of the gap between controls and prac-
tices, it is necessary to rely on the individual's good judgment. Since
such reliance is inevitable it should be developed. Development of
technical skills along with recognition of higher social values and the
need for joining the two is seen as the essence of professionalism.

Development of a sense of moral obligation to uphold societal values is a necessary ingredient in responsible policing. Not only does the retreat to technology set up barriers between political leaders and administrative leaders but it can also misdirect personal conceptions of duty by individual agents. Under a democratic system of government it is not enough that the state perform its directive and control activities well. The development of proper governmental and administrative policy in a democracy implicitly requires adherence to values more basic than those involved in the pursuit of efficiency. There must also be adherence to values that relate to the use of force and coercion in a free society.

A democratic policing system requires a blending and coexistence of apparent contradictions. On the one hand, the police must compel behavior by citizens. On the other hand, the police must be responsive; they must behave in accordance with the will of the citizenry. The police must ensure order, but it must be order under law. Order under law is concerned not merely with the achievement of regularized social activity but the means used to attain peaceable behavior.

The easiest way to ensure predictability and reliability in the social environment is to chain everyone to routine. That, however, is diametrically opposed to the principles of liberal democracy. The government not only has to resolve conflict and repress disturbances but must foster conditions that encourage initiative. Law and order are frequently in opposition. Law imposes rational constraints on the methods used to attain order. If order becomes the paramount concern, prohibitions are established against actions, examples, and suggestions that may stimulate variations (and, therefore, unpredictability) in individual behavior. Such a development is a real possibility if the retreat to technology is too complete; the control aspect of the police could become the sole point of validation.

A constant process of social and governmental adjustment and readjustment must be maintained. Government cannot be expected always to be reactive. The individuals who staff the coercive institutions always retain some degree of independence from the institution. Their beliefs and their own idiosyncratic views about their authority and its exercise may not completely mesh with the principles officially embodied in the Constitution and the laws. These individuals cannot be expected to find their social position weakened while refraining from using their official power for self-protection.

No social system is completely integrated, and the fact of malintegration may impose role conflict on the individual. Police officers are especially vulnerable to institutional role conflict. Every institutionalized role involves a sense of obligation to the system as a unit and to its members. Each member defines certain actions as beneficial to the integrity of the system and certain other actions as detrimental to that integrity. Because of malintegration, divergent patterns of behavior may all seem beneficial if viewed from different role perspectives. As a result, an individual may be unable to act in any way because of the cross-pressures.

The view that responsibility is solely a matter of conscience does not suffice: "Liability is the beginning of responsibility. . . . The individual is held accountable for what he has done in order that he may be responsive in what he is going to do" (Dewey, 1922:474). Even from the perspective of professionalism, then, the issue returns to accountability. Administrators, to be responsible, must be answerable. They must be compelled to render an accounting of what they do and how they do it. Their conduct must be susceptible to rational explanation and to identification of causal responsibility. This requires both someone to determine standards of proper and improper conduct and some mechanism to enforce the standards.

Proponents of this position do not deny that internalized values are important. They accept that there is an inevitable gap between controls and behavior patterns and that in the gaps it is necessary to rely on individuals' senses of obligation and professional orientation. The primary concern, however, is to ensure that, although proper latitude is allowed for administrative flexibility and innovation, when behavior exceeds acceptable bounds, a corrective mechanism can be applied. Internal controls must be augmented and influenced by external controls. A sense of moral obligation, professional standards, and pursuit of technical efficiency may be important elements in sound administration, but they are not continuously operative. Moral obligation, especially, "is likely to operate in direct proportion to the strictness and efficiency of political responsibility" (Finer, 1941:350). No matter what the form of government or the outlook of its personnel, internalized standards are only partially the answer to responsibility.

The traditional American police system developed without a clear definition of what constitutes good police work or how police work fits into democratic society. As a result, an informal occupational code has developed which sanctions illicit behavior. Even police officials committed to eradication of that code do not agree on a definition of police professionalism or how to achieve it. Most important, there is no general agreement as to whether police professionalism in some ideal form would be beneficial to the larger society.

Professionalism, in a limited sense of commitment to higher values, is important to the development of administrative responsibility among police. But this form of professionalism is only one ingredient in responsible administration. Inculcation of higher values and loyalty to social and political goals are esteemed, and development of professionalism is considered a prime concern of administrative superiors. Constant invocation of punitive control mechanisms is recognized to be self-defeating and ultimately self-destructive, but administrative superiors must be able to exercise control. The key to responsible police administration seems to lie in the existing arrangements, but those arrangements need to be altered.

8 The Police and Administrative Responsibility

Three broad conceptions of administrative responsibility have been applied to or recommended for American urban police. First, the view that administration should be a ministerial function considers responsibility as a problem of obedience. Policy makers decide what is to be done and how it is to be done. The administrators merely execute the policy. Their performance is monitored to assure that it conforms to the policy makers' mandate. In line with this position, common law and American statutory law prescribe that police must enforce all laws all the time and that they are subject to legal sanction if they fail to act accordingly.

Second, the view that discretion is inevitable in administration but that it should be severely limited and controlled holds that responsibility will result if discretion is allowed only according to prescribed calculable rules. This view sees responsibility as a problem of answerability and accountability. Policy makers decide what goals they want to achieve and establish formal organizations to develop and implement technically correct procedures for attaining those goals. The administrators carry out set policies according to guidelines specified by the agency. The agency then has a duty to check on individuals' behavior to ascertain whether the officially prescribed procedures are being followed. In line with this approach, police departments have been organized according to the precepts of bureaucracy.

Third is the view that responsibility depends on individuals. There are three person-centered approaches in police administration. The first emphasizes the need to match individuals to organizational mission, rationalizing the personnel administration cycle to require that the work to be done by police officers be clearly identified, that the personnel policies used be job-relevant, and that police officers be managed so as to provide a maximum contribution to departmental goals throughout their term of employment. The second variation builds upon the notion that administrative officials should be representative of their community, just as elected officials are representative of their constituents. The concept of affirmative action has led to confusing the idea of being representative with the idea of being a representative. The latter implies delegation to individuals based on active representation, whereas the former is based on demographic composition, or passive representation. The third person-centered approach emphasizes the need for mutually reinforcing police officers' commitment to social values and to technical skills. Its basic premise is the belief that responsibility is primarily a problem of inner discipline or sense of moral obligation. It is the alternative of police professionalization.

The facts of police work are completely at odds with the first position (police as discretionless law enforcers). The extreme person-centered alternative (professionalization) seems equally incapable of providing an adequate solution to the problem of securing responsible police administration. External sanctions may not be totally effective without internalization of moral standards, but they are necessary nonetheless. Reliance solely on internalized values is equally inadequate. Professional standards can easily be reduced to exhortation and unanalyzed abstractions and substituted for reasoned consensus on goals; unanalyzed abstractions cannot provide guidance in complex environments. The result is the opposite of guidance—it is expediency (Selznick, 1949:59). Exhortation is not enough. The guiding principles have to be backed up by recognized sanctions.

Responsibility can be achieved only through a predictable and regularized process of accountability for administrative behavior. The failure of bureaucracy is not reliance on organizational accountability but excessive reliance on bureaucratic structures without recognition of the need for flexibility in their application. Over-reliance on hierarchy has encouraged the use of command instead of leadership and guidance. The command emphasis has led to belief in self-enforcing orders from top-level officials and in the efficacy of detailed regulations promulgated by fiat. This emphasis has failed to promote administrative responsibility.

Abolition of bureaucracy is not the primary requisite for police administrative responsibility. The problems of departmental operation can be dealt with without significant structural innovation. Fundamental structural innovation is not likely to be accomplished; indeed, and more important, it is unnecessary. Responsible policing may be achieved in other ways by means of relatively easy adjustments.

Institutional Direction for Police Responsibility

One of the chief tenets of American democracy, as stated in the Declaration of Independence, is that "governments are instituted among men, deriving their just powers from the consent of the governed." Government power in a democracy, therefore, must always be limited. The urban police department, more than almost any other government entity, is founded upon the use of force. It is a manifestation of the state's legitimate monopoly of coercive power to enforce its rules. Yet it must be responsible to those whom it is empowered to coerce.

As part of the government system, the police are involved in society's collective goal achievement. They are an institution of the community entrusted with great power to provide a safe, orderly, and just social environment. But they cannot be allowed to decide unilaterally how they will fulfill that task. Even though the police perspective may be understandable and a valuable aid to the formation of public policy with regard to crime and disorder, the police cannot, in a democratic society, be allowed to dictate public policy in those areas.

The police have an important social and governmental role, but many aspects of that role are contradictory or ambiguous. The police suffer from the general debilities of all government agencies in a democracy because they must control yet be controlled by the citizenry. The dilemma of democratic government is, however, more acute for the police than for most other institutions because they possess the ultimate manifestation of the state's preemption of legitimate force; they possess the power of life and death, which they are expected to exercise in unstable, often hostile, circumstances.

Several mechanisms have been, and are being, used in an attempt to control the police. As a part of the government, they are subordinate to the elected representatives of the people. They are responsible to and supervised by the mayor or manager, who is in turn responsible to the council and the people. The rule of law is regarded as superior to the police and, therefore, police conduct is subject to judicial oversight through criminal prosecution, tort liability, and the exclusionary rule for evidence. In addition to political and judicial oversight, such supplementary devices as internal affairs investigation and civilian review board investigation of citizen complaints against officers have been proposed and used. All of these mechanisms contain defects. Political leaders have often either used the police for partisan purposes and have opened the departments to a wide range of corrupt practices, or they have so feared potential allegations of misuse of police power that they have abdicated responsibility and left departments to their own devices. The courts and both internal and external review procedures have been reactive rather than proactive, limiting their ability to control police conduct.

The key to ensuring administrative responsibility in the police is recognition that administrative responsibility is essentially a political problem. Because of the nature of the police role, the ability to maintain administrative responsibility is a test of the political capacity of democratic society. Administrative responsibility cannot be viewed solely as a problem of personal behavior and moral obligation of individuals. As in all government institutions, the police department's relationship with the larger political system and with the public has to be the focus of responsibility in executing discretionary coercive power.

Police administrative responsibility is a problem of guidance or direction. Requiring new reactive control mechanisms such as civilian review boards may only make perceptions of nonresponsibility more acute because the mechanisms cannot live up to expectations. Establishing new authority structures is clearly an illusory solution. Mayors, city managers, directors of public safety, police commissioners, city councilmen, grand juries, district attorneys, attorneys general, governors, judges, magistrates, ombudsmen, sheriffs, chiefs of police, and others all have some degree of formal authority over police agencies, and yet police irresponsibility remains a chronic problem.

In spite of acknowledged defects, the system has within itself the seeds of its own reform. Its positive features need to be accentuated and more fully mobilized. The foremost need is for the officials formally charged with direction of the police department to fulfill their function. The mayor, city manager, and city councilmen must recognize that as representatives of the people they are responsible for the direction of all aspects of local government including police service. This means that the municipal chief executive, the police commissioner or the director of public safety, and the chief of police must work together to develop the broad outlines of police policy with regard for the legal setting, public sentiment, council approval, departmental capabilities, and professional competences.

The emphasis must be on institutional relationships. The officials charged with directing the police agency must remain attentive to their gatekeeper function. They must recognize that they need to work in concert but that they must represent diverse interests. Through the representation of these differing societal needs they assure that policy making will be democratic.

Democratic policy making alone, however, does not provide the whole answer. Institutional direction of the police also requires effective leadership. The municipal chief executive needs to be able to recruit the chief of police from outside the local department and perhaps from outside the police profession. He must be able to depend on the loyalty and cooperation of all his staff including the chief of police. The chief must have effective control of the operation of the department. He must be able to ensure that the policies made will guide the department's action. That assurance can come only if he is able to build a staff loyal to him rather than to the force. He must have the freedom personally to select his principal subordinates and staff advisers. He must also be able to build up and maintain a competent research capacity for internal intelligence to enhance his role in the policy-making and implementation process.

Recognition of the relationship between police administration and the nature of the political system also carries with it a view of the internal role of the chief that differs from the traditional view. From this perspective effective executive leadership is not the same as command and rigorous discipline. Excessive reliance on external discipline may kill initiative and diminish morale. Command diminishes subordinate responsibility (Barnard, 1950:1002–03). Only through delegation and participation in decision making can responsibility be encouraged.

As the chief and the political overseers of the department develop the broad outlines of police policy, administrative rule-making procedures can be used to fill in the details. Administrative rule making based on rank-and-file participation is vastly different from the traditional police rule-making practice. The aim is to develop positive inducements as well as to establish negative restraints. Through rank-and-file participation the rule-making process will be made relevant to the exigencies of field work. Since the rule-making process will grow out of a more realistic understanding of immediate needs because it is based on widespread participation, it can be expected to bring with it increased acceptance of the rules. In contrast to the traditional command rule making, this approach has an educative and support-building effect.

The processes of institutional guidance, executive leadership, and participative administrative rule making can all be further supported by a new orientation to the internal review system. At present most such systems focus narrowly on investigation and censure of misbehavior. Internal affairs divisions can play a valuable role in the policy- and rule-making processes. By expanding their concern from reaction to misbehavior to active examination of all aspects of internal operation the IAD can identify areas in which rule and policy making should be undertaken and can serve as a feedback loop after policies and rules have been made. Furthermore, by taking an active interest in civilian complaints through impartial acceptance of all complaints and prompt, thorough investigations followed by reports back to complainants, the IAD can play an important role in building public confidence. An IAD with such a positive orientation is a much more viable alternative than external review agencies. The reformed IAD will play a significant role in institutional guidance and executive leadership, a role in which external review would be much less effective. Like administrative rule making, a positive IAD can build rank-and-file support for the general policies made by the political overseers.

There is, of course, always a possibility that the IAD could be co-opted by the other elements of the police department, which would weaken rather than reinforce the process of institutional direction. To guard against such an eventuality and to promote administrative responsibility by protecting the credibility of the institutional level of decision making, an external auditing system to investigate and adjudicate IAD actions could be established. The auditing process would not be a *de novo* review of specific cases but an examination of procedures and consistency of outcomes. To remove the auditing units further from the specter of civilian review boards, they could be given a general function of reviewing police departments' operational practices as do the Inspectors of Constabulary in Great Britain and the Ontario Police Commission in Canada.

Rather than focusing on individual misconduct, the reports of inspectors could highlight the accomplishments of departments. At the same time, because they represent an outside check on the internal review system, the audits could help legitimize the internal review system by preempting charges of bias. Such an inspectorate could be organized statewide under the direction of the attorney general or at the county level under the sheriff or district attorney. In either case, if the auditors are assigned to various departments on rotating bases, the charges most often leveled against outsiders could be avoided.

The proposals advanced may not seem to constitute a solution to the problem of ensuring responsible policing. The fact that these proposals are not dramatic or radical does not mean they are not conducive to reinvigorization of the police service. The radical alternatives that have often been advanced to deal with perennial problems frequently provoke such animosity that no change results.

The key to effecting administrative responsibility among the American police is the willingness of the political overseers of the police to take the necessary steps toward reform. In several notable instances, chiefs of police have been highly successsful in reorienting their departments. But thoroughgoing reform is far beyond the power of the chiefs. A strong executive is a necessary but not a sufficient element in administrative responsibility.

Management of the police institutions must be viewed as a problem of political guidance. The police must perform a variety of important social tasks. As government agents they must operate in accordance with the values, ideals, and desires of the polity. Consequently, "responsibility can never be confined to the efficient performance of a specialized function"; it rests upon coordination of multiple factors and contingencies "in the interest of collective goals" (Parsons, 1951:100).

When the political overseers, the department leaders, the individual officers, and the public recognize the need for an open and cooperative role in establishing police policy, the department can be expected to play a leading role in structuring discretion and developing substantive understanding among all the principals about the guiding principles and operating goals of the department and how they relate to general social objectives—which is the essence of administrative responsibility.

Appendix

Cases Cited

Adams v. Williams, 407 U.S. 143 (1972)

Albermarle Paper Co. v. Moody, 422 U.S. 405 (1975)

Alexander v. Bahou, 86 F.R.D. 194 (1980)

Alvarez v. Wilson, 431 F. Supp 1261 (1977)

Arnold v. Ballard, 390 F. Supp 723 (1976)

Askay v. Maloney, 179 P. 899 (Ore. 1919)

Association Against Discrimination v. City of Bridgeport, 454 F. Supp 751 (1978)

Berberian v. Mitchell, 321 A.2d 431 (R.I. 1974)

Bilick v. Dudley, 356 F. Supp 945 (1973)

Blake v. City of Los Angeles, 595 F.2d 1367 (1979)

Boston Chapter NAACP v. Beecher, 504 F.2d 1017 (1974)

Boyd v. United States, 116 U.S. 616 (1886)

Brewer v. Williams, 430 U.S. 387 (1977)

Bridgeport Guardians v. Bridgeport Police Department, 431 F. Supp 931 (1977)

Briethaupt v. Abram, 352 U.S. 432 (1957)

Brown v. General Services Administration, 425 U.S. 820 (1976)

Brown v. Illinois, 422 U.S. 590 (1975)

Brown v. United States, 256 U.S. 335 (1921)

Carey v. Piphus, 435 U.S. 247 (1978)

Celmer v. Quarberg, 203 N.W.2d 45 (Wisc. 1973)

Cole v. Johnson, 17 Cal. Rpt. 664 (Cal. 1961)

Commonwealth v. Ruckinger, 239 Pa. Super. 520 (Pa. 1976)

Commonwealth of Pennsylvania v. Flaherty, 477 F. Supp 1263 (1980)

Coolidge v. New Hampshire, 403 U.S. 443 (1971)

De Castro v. State, 359 So. 2d 551 (Fla. 1978)

Delong v. City of Denver, 530 P.2d 1308 (Colo. 1974)

Detroit Firefighters v. City of Detroit, 17 F.E.P. 186 (1976)

Detroit Police Officers Association v. Young, 446 F. Supp 979 (1978)
Diamond v. Marland, 395 F. Supp 432 (1975)
Dillenbeck v. City of Los Angeles, 72 Cal. Rpt. 321 (Cal. 1968)
Dixon v. United States, 296 F.2d 427 (1961)
Doores v. McNamara, 476 F. Supp 987 (1979)
Doyle v. Ohio, 426 U.S. 610 (1976)
EEOC v. American Telephone and Telegraph, 556 F.2d 167 (1977)
EEOC v. Detroit Edison Co., 515 F.2d 301 (1975)
EEOC v. Murphy Motor Freight Lines, 448 F. Supp 381 (1980)
EEOC v. Radiator Specialty Co., 610 F.2d 178 (1980)
EEOC v. United Virginia Bank/Seaboard National, 615 F.2d 147 (1980)
Escobedo v. Illinois, 378 U.S. 478 (1964)
Ex parte Dillon, 186 P. 170 (Cal. 1919)
Ex parte Virginia, 100 U.S. 339 (1879)
Gill v. Monroe County Department of Services, 79 F.R.D. 316 (1978)
Glover v. City of New York, 401 F. Supp 632 (1975)
Griggs v. Duke Power Co., 401 U.S. 424 (1971)
Grundt v. City of Los Angeles, 468 P. 2d 825 (Cal. 1970)
Guardians Association of the New York City Police Department v. Civil Service
    Commission, 431 F. Supp 526 (1977)
———, 484 F. Supp 785 (1980)
Gunther v. Washington County, 602 F.2d 882 (1979)
Hampton v. Chicago, 339 F. Supp 695 (1972)
Hardwick v. Hurley, 289 F.2d 529 (1961)
Harmon v. San Diego County, 477 F. Supp 1084 (1980)
Harris v. New York, 401 U.S. 222 (1971)
Hausman v. Tredinnick, 432 F. Supp 1160 (1977)
Hill v. Western Electric Co., 596 F.2d 99 (1980)
International Brotherhood of Teamsters v. United States, 431 U.S. 324 (1977)
Jencks v. United States, 353 U.S. 657 (1957)
Johnson v. Hacket, 284 F. Supp 933 (1968)
Kawananakoa v. Polybank, 205 U.S. 349 (1907)
Kerr v. Illinois, 119 U.S. 436 (1886)
Kirkland v. New York State Department of Correctional Services, 520 F.2d
    420 (1975)
Kuruma v. The Queen, AC 197 (1955)
Lawrie v. Muir, JC 19 (1950)
Lindsay v. City of Seattle, 548 P.2d 320 (Wash. 1976)
Linkletter v. Walker, 381 U.S. 618 (1965)
Lord v. Kelley, 223 F. Supp 684 (1963)
Louisiana v. United States, 380 U.S. 145 (1965)
Maehren v. City of Seattle, 599 P.2d 1255 (Wash. 1979)
McDonnell Douglas v. Green, 411 U.S. 792 (1973)
McGilvery v. State, 533 S.W.2d 24 (Texas 1976)
McShane v. Moldvan, 172 F.2d 1016 (1949)
Mapp v. Ohio, 367 U.S. 643 (1961)
Marshall v. Sawyer, 301 F.2d 639 (1962)

Massiah v. United States, 377 U.S. 201 (1964)
Mathis v. United States, 391 U.S. 1 (1968)
Miller v. United States, 404 F.2d 611 (1962)
Miranda v. Arizona, 384 U.S. 436 (1966)
Monell v. Department of Social Services of the City of New York, 436 U.S. 658
   (1978)
Monroe v. Pape, 365 U.S. 167 (1961)
Montgomery v. State, 145 Tex. Cr. 606 (Texas 1943)
Moor v. Alameda County, 411 U.S. 693 (1973)
Morgan v. Labiak, 368 F.2d 338 (1966)
Morita v. Southern California Permanente Medical Group, 541 F.2d 217
   (1976)
Muetze v. State, 243 N.W. 2d 393 (Wisc. 1980)
Mullens v. Davidson, 57 S.E. 2d 1 (W. Va. 1949)
Mullins v. River Rouge, 338 F. Supp 26 (1972)
Muskopf v. Corning Hospital District, 11 Cal. Rpt. 89 (Cal. 1961)
NAACP v. Allen, 493 F.2d 619 (1974)
Nesmith v. Alford, 318 F.2d 110 (1963)
Nugent v. Sheppard, 318 F. Supp 314 (1970)
Officers for Justice v. Civil Service Commission, 395 F. Supp 378 (1978)
Olmstead v. United States, 227 U.S. 438 (1928)
Orozco v. Texas, 394 U.S. 324 (1969)
Oyler v. Boles, 368 U.S. 448 (1962)
Paul v. Davis, 424 U.S. 693 (1976)
Peak v. State, 342 So. 2d 98 (Fla. 1977)
People v. Cahan, 283 P.2d 905 (Cal. 1955)
People v. Davies, 188 N.E. 337 (Ill. 1934)
People v. Defore, 242 N.Y. 13 (N.Y. 1926)
People v. Seymour, 398 N.E. 2d 1191 (Ill. 1979)
People v. Smith, 163 Cal. Rpt. 322 (Cal. 1980)
People v. Summers, 82 N.Y.S. 297 (N.Y. 1903)
Pierson v. Ray, 386 U.S. 547 (1967)
Plessy v. Ferguson, 163 U.S. 537 (1896)
Price v. Civil Service Commission of Sacramento County, 161 Cal. Rpt. 475
   (Cal. 1980)
Quern v. Jordan, 440 U.S. 332 (1979)
R. v. Commissioner of Police of the Metropolis, ex parte Blackburn, 2 QB 118
   (1968)
R. v. Howe, 100 Common. LR 448 (Aust. 1958)
R. v. Turner, Vict. R. 30 (Aust. 1962)
R. v. Wray, SCR 272 (Can. 1971)
Refoule v. Ellis, 74 F. Supp 336 (1947)
Regents of the University of California v. Bakke, 438 U.S. 265 (1978)
Reneau v. State, 70 Tn. 720 (Tenn. 1879)
Rhode Island v. Innis, 446 U.S. 291 (1980)
Richardson v. Newark, 449 F. Supp 20 (1978)
Richardson v. Snow, 340 F. Supp 1261 (1972)

Rios v. Enterprize/Associated Steamfitters Local 638, 501 F.2d 622 (1974)
Rochin v. California, 342 U.S. 165 (1952)
Santa Clara County v. Southern Pacific Railroad, 118 U.S. 394 (1886)
Schmerber v. California, 384 U.S. 757 (1966)
Schneider v. State, 353 So. 2d 870 (Fla. 1977)
Screws v. United States, 325 U.S. 91 (1945)
Semayne's Case, 77 ER 194 (1603)
Smith v. Ambrogio, 456 F. Supp 1130 (1978)
Somers v. Strader, 435 F. Supp 1184 (1977)
Stacey v. Emery, 97 U.S. 642 (1878)
State v. Armfield, 9 N.C. 246 (N.C. 1822)
State v. Byrne, 595 S.W. 2d 301 (Mo. 1979)
State v. Clark, 2 Del. Cas. 210 (Del. 1793)
State v. Fontenot, 383 So. 2d 365 (La. 1980)
State v. Fortier, 553 P. 2d 1206 (Ariz. 1979)
State v. Leathers, 31 Ark. 44 (Ark. 1876)
State v. Pruitt, 212 S.E. 2d 92 (N.C. 1975)
State v. Riddick, 230 S.E. 2d 506 (N.C. 1976)
State v. Rollwage, 533 P. 2d 831 (Ore. 1975)
State v. Strickland, 225 S.E. 2d 531 (N.C. 1976)
State v. Wagstaff, 105 S.E. 283 (S.C. 1920)
Stengel v. Belcher, 522 F.2d 438 (1975)
Stringer v. Dilger, 313 F.2d 536 (1963)
Stryker v. Register Publishing Co., 423 F. Supp 476 (1976)
Swann v. Charlotte-Mecklenberg Board of Education, 402 U.S. 1 (1971)
Thompson v. State, 342 So. 2d 306 (Miss. 1977)
Thornton v. Buchmann, 392 F.2d 870 (1968)
Toomey v. City of Fort Lauderdale, 311 So. 2d 678 (Fla. 1975)
United States v. City of Buffalo, 472 F. Supp 478 (1979)
United States v. City of Chicago, 549 F.2d 415 (1977)
United States v. City of Philadelphia, 573 F.2d 802 (1979)
United States v. Classic, 313 U.S. 299 (1941)
United States v. Commonwealth of Virginia, 620 F.2d 1018 (1980)
United States v. Cooper, 428 F. Supp 652 (1979)
United States v. Di Re, 332 U.S. 581 (1948)
United States v. Edwards, 415 U.S. 800 (1973)
United States v. Lynch, 189 F.2d 476 (1951)
United States v. Mesa, 487 F. Supp 562 (1980)
United States v. Peltier, 422 U.S. 531 (1975)
United States v. Price, 380 U.S. 787 (1966)
United States v. San Diego County, 21 F.E.P. 402 (1979)
United States v. Schipani, 315 F. Supp 253 (1970)
United States v. State of New York, 474 F. Supp 1103 (1979)
United States v. Watson, 423 U.S. 411 (1976)
United States v. Wood, Wire and Metal Lathers International, Local 46, 417
     F.2d 408 (1973)

United States ex rel Accardi v. Shaughnessy, 347 U.S. 206 (1954)

United Steelworkers of America v. Weber, 443 U.S. 193 (1979)

Vulcan Society of New York v. Civil Service Commission of New York City, 490 F.2d 1042 (1973)

Walder v. United States, 347 U.S. 62 (1954)

Washington v. Davis, 426 U.S. 229 (1976)

Waterhouse v. Saltmarsh, 80 ER 409 (1724)

Weber v. Kaiser Steel, 611 F.2d 132 (1980)

Weeks v. United States, 232 U.S. 383 (1914)

Whirl v. Kern, 407 F.2d 781 (1968)

Wiley v. Memphis Police Department, 548 F.2d 1247 (1977)

Wolf v. Colorado, 338 U.S. 25 (1949)

Won Sun v. United States, 371 U.S. 471 (1963)

Yanez v. Romero, 619 F.2d 851 (1980)

References

Alex, N. 1976. *New York Cops Talk Back: A Study of a Beleaguered Minority*. Wiley, New York.

Allen, D. N. 1982. "Police Supervision on the Street: An Analysis of Supervisor/Officer Interaction during the Shift." *Journal of Criminal Justice* 10:91–110.

American Bar Association Project on Standards for Criminal Justice. 1973. *Standards Relating to the Urban Police Function*. American Bar Association, New York.

American Civil Liberties Union of Southern California. 1969. *Law Enforcement: The Matter of Redress*. Institute of Modern Legal Thought, Los Angeles.

Appleby, P. H. 1952. *Morality and Administration in Democratic Government*. Louisiana State University Press, Baton Rouge.

Baldus, D. C. and J. W. L. Cole. 1980. *Statistical Proof of Discrimination*. Shepard's/McGraw-Hill, New York.

Banton, M. 1964. *The Policeman in the Community*. Basic Books, New York.

Barnard, C. I. 1950. "Bureaucracy in a Democracy." *American Political Science Review* 43:990–1004.

Bercal, T. E. 1970. "Calls for Police Assistance: Consumer Demands for Governmental Service." *American Behavioral Scientist* 13:681–91.

Bittner, E. 1978. "The Functions of the Police in Modern Society." In *Policing: A View from the Street*, ed. P. K. Manning and J. Van Maanen. Goodyear, Santa Monica.

————. 1970. *The Functions of the Police in Modern Society*. Public Health Service Publication 2059. National Institute of Mental Health, Chevy Chase, Md.

————. 1967a. "Police Discretion in Emergency Apprehension of Mentally Ill Persons." *Social Problems* 14:278–92.

————. 1967b. "The Police on Skid-Row: A Study of Peace Keeping." *American Sociological Review* 32:699–715.

Black, D. J. 1980. "Production of Crime Rates." In *Police Behavior*, ed. R. J. Lundman. Oxford University Press, New York.

—— and A. J. Reiss, Jr. 1970. "Police Control of Juveniles." *American Sociological Review* 35:63–77.

Blackstone, W. 1765. *Commentaries on the Laws of England*. Edited by G. Chase. Banks and Brothers, New York.

Blumberg, A. S. 1967. "The Practice of Law as a Confidence Game: Organizational Cooptation of a Profession." *Law and Society Review* 1:15–39.

Bureau of Justice Statistics. 1982. *Sourcebook of Criminal Justice Statistics*. U.S. Department of Justice, Washington, D.C.

Burger, W. 1964. "Who Will Watch the Watchman?" *American University Law Review* 14:1–23.

Caiden, G. E. 1977. *Police Revitalization*. D. C. Heath, Lexington, Mass.

Cain, M. 1971. "On the Beat: Interactions and Relations in Rural and Urban Police Forces." In *Images of Deviance*, ed. S. Cohen. Penguin, Harmondsworth.

——. 1973. *Society and the Policeman's Role*. Routledge and Kegan Paul, London.

California Commission on Peace Officer Standards and Training. 1971. *The San Jose Police Department Management Survey*. State of California, Sacramento.

——. 1974. *POST Administration Manual*. State of California, Sacramento.

Campbell, D. and H. L. Ross. 1968. "The Connecticut Crackdown on Speeding." *Law and Society Review* 3:33–53.

Carter, J. E. 1978. *Message from the President of the United States: Civil Service Reform*. U.S. Government Printing Office, Washington, D.C.

Churchman, C. W. 1968. *The Systems Approach*. Dell, New York.

Citizens' Committee to Study Police Community Relations in the City of Chicago. 1967. *Police and Public*. City of Chicago, Chicago.

Cohen, B. 1970. *The Police Internal Administration of Justice in New York City*. Rand Corporation, New York.

Cohen, B. and J. M. Chaiken. 1972. *Police Background Characteristics and Performance*. Rand Corporation, New York.

Congressional Research Service. 1976. *History of the Civil Service Merit Systems of the United States and Selected Foreign Countries*. U.S. Government Printing Office, Washington, D.C.

Coxe, S. 1961. "Police Advisory Boards." *Connecticut Bar Journal* 35:138–55.

Cumming, E., I. Cumming, and L. Edell. 1965. "The Policeman as Philosopher, Guide and Friend." *Social Problems* 12:184–92.

Davis, K. C. 1975. *Administrative Law and Government*. West, St. Paul, Minn.

——. 1974. "An Approach to Legal Control of the Police." *Texas Law Review* 52:703–25.

Decker, S. H. and R. L. Smith. 1980. "Police Minority Recruitment: A Note on Its Effectiveness in Improving Black Evaluations of the Police." *Journal of Criminal Justice* 8:387–94.

de Jouvenel, B. 1957. *Sovereignty: An Enquiry into the Political Good*. University of Chicago Press, Chicago.

Dewey, J. 1922. "Morals and Conduct." In *The Social Philosophers* (1947), ed. S. Cummins and R. N. Linscott. Random House, New York.

Dimock, M. E. 1936. "The Role of Discretion in Modern Administration." In *Essays on the Law and Practice of Governmental Administration*, ed. C. G. Haines and M. E. Dimock. Greenwood Press, New York. Reprint, 1968.

Eisenberg, T., D. A. Kent, and C. R. Wall. 1973. *Police Personnel Practices in State and Local Governments*. International Association of Chiefs of Police, Police Foundation, Washington, D.C.

Emery, F. E. and E. L. Trist. 1972a. "The Causal Texture of Organizational Environments." In *Systems Thinking*, ed. E. L. Trist. Penguin, Harmondsworth.

———. 1972b. "Socio-technical Systems." In *Systems Thinking*, ed. E. L. Trist. Penguin, Harmondsworth.

Equal Employment Opportunity Commission. Annual. *Job Patterns for Minorities and Women in Private Industry*. U.S. Government Printing Office, Washington, D.C.

———. 1979. *Affirmative Action Appropriate under Title VII of the Civil Rights Act of 1964, as Amended*. U.S. Government Printing Office, Washington, D.C.

———. 1974. *Minorities and Women in State and Local Government*. U.S. Government Printing Office, Washington, D.C.

FBI Uniform Crime Reports. 1981. *Crime in the United States, 1980*. U.S. Department of Justice, Washington, D.C.

Federalist Papers. 1787. Edited by A. Hacker. Pocket Books, New York. 1971.

Finer, H. 1941. "Administrative Responsibility in Democratic Government." *Public Administration Review* 1:335–50.

Foote, C. 1955. "Tort Remedies for Police Violations of Individual Rights." *Minnesota Law Review* 39:493–516.

Frankel, L. and M. A. Allard. 1972. "Personnel Policies in Municipal Police Departments." *Urban Data Service* 4, no. 8.

Freedman, M. 1970. "Professional Responsibility of the Criminal Defense Lawyer: The Three Hardest Questions." *Michigan Law Review* 64:1469–84.

Friedrich, C. J. 1950. 3d ed. *Constitutional Government and Democracy*. Ginn, Boston.

Gain, C. R. and R. T. Galvin. 1973. "Police Management: Critical Elements for City Managers." *Public Management* 55:14–17.

Gardiner, J. A. 1968. "Police Enforcement of Traffic Laws." In *City Politics and Public Policy*, ed. J. Q. Wilson. Wiley, New York.

———. 1967. *Wincanton: The Politics of Corruption*. U.S. Government Printing Office, Washington, D.C.

Goldner, N. S. and R. Koenig. 1972. "White Middle-Class Attitudes toward an Urban Policemen's Union." *Crime and Delinquency* 38:168–75.

Goodnow, F. J. 1900. *Politics and Administration: A Study in Government*. Macmillan, New York.

Gouldner, A. W. 1955. "Metaphysical Pathos and the Theory of Bureaucracy." *American Political Science Review* 49:496–507.

———. 1954. *Patterns of Industrial Bureaucracy*. Free Press, New York.

Goss, M. E. W. 1963. "Patterns of Bureaucracy among Hospital Staff Physicians." In *The Hospital in Modern Society*, ed. E. Freidson. Free Press, New York.

Grosman, B. A. 1975. *Police Command: Decisions and Discretion*. Macmillan of Canada, Toronto.

Gwartney, J. 1979. "Statistics, the Law and Title VII." *Notre Dame Lawyer* 54:633–58.

Halpern, S. C. 1974. "Police Employee Organizations and Accountability Procedures in Three Cities." *Law and Society Review* 8:561–82.

Hand, L. 1960. *The Spirit of Liberty*. Knopf, New York.

Handberg, R. and S. Pilchick. 1980. "Police Handling of Mental Patients: Crisis Intervention Requirements and Police Behavior." *Criminal Justice Review* 5:66–73.

Handbook of Labor Statistics. Annual. U.S. Department of Labor, Washington, D.C.

Harding, R. W. 1975. "Changing Patterns of the Use of Lethal Force by Police in Australia." *Australian and New Zealand Journal of Criminology* 8:125–36.

———. 1972. "Police Disciplinary Procedures in England and Western Australia." *University of Western Australia Law Review* 10:195–222.

Harris, R. 1973. *The Police Academy: An Inside View*. Wiley, New York.

Haworth, J. G. and C. T. Haworth. 1980. "Statistical Analysis and Equal Employment Opportunity." In *Ninth Annual Institute of Equal Employment Opportunity Compliance*. Practicing Law Institute, New York.

Heaphy, J. F., ed. 1979. *Police Practices*. Police Foundation, Washington, D.C.

Heffernan, W. C. 1981. "Criminal Justice Ethics: An Emerging Discipline." *Police Studies* 4:24–28.

Hirschel, J. D. 1979. *Fourth Amendment Rights*. Lexington Books, Lexington, Mass.

Hudson, J. R. 1972. "Organizational Aspects of Internal and External Review of the Police." *Journal of Criminal Law, Criminology and Police Science* 63:427–33.

Hudson, J. R. 1970. "Police-Citizen Encounters that Lead to Citizen Complaints." *Social Problems* 18:179–93.

Hughes, E. C. 1958. *Men and Their Work*. Free Press, New York.

International City Management Association. 1981. *Municipal Yearbook*. ICMA, Washington, D.C.

———. 1980. *Municipal Yearbook*. ICMA, Washington, D.C.

———. 1979. *Municipal Yearbook*. ICMA, Washington, D.C.

———. 1970. *Municipal Yearbook*. ICMA, Washington, D.C.

Jacobson, D., W. Craven, and S. Kushner, 1973. "A Study of Police Referral of Allegedly Mentally-Ill Persons to a Psychiatric Unit." In *The Urban Policeman in Transition*, ed. J. R. Snibbe and H. M. Snibbe. Charles C. Thomas, Springfield, Ill.

Kansas City (Missouri) Police Department. 1971. *A Survey of Citizen Complaint Procedures*. City of Kansas City, Kansas City.

Kelly, M. J. 1975. *Police Chief Selection: A Handbook for Local Government*. Police Foundation and International City Management Association, Washington, D.C.

Kinasz, T. J. 1981. "Contempt of Court as an Alternative to the Exclusionary Rule." *Journal of Criminal Law and Criminology* 72:993.

Knoohuizen, R. 1974. *The Question of Police Discipline in Chicago: An Analysis of the Proposed Office of Professional Standards.* Chicago Law Enforcement Study Group, Chicago.

Krajick, K. 1980. "Police vs. Police: Fear, Loathing, and Mystery." *Police Magazine* 3:6–21.

LaFave, W. 1965. *Arrest: The Decision to Take a Suspect into Custody.* Little, Brown, Boston.

Laski, H. J. 1930. "The Limitations of the Expert." *Harper's Monthly Magazine* 162:101–10.

Law Enforcement Assistance Administration. 1973. *Equal Employment Opportunity Program Development Manual.* U.S. Department of Justice, Washington, D.C.

Lohman, J. D. and G. E. Misner. 1966. *The Police and the Community: The Dynamics of Their Relationship in a Changing Society.* President's Commission on Law Enforcement and Administration of Justice, Washington, D.C.

Lundman, R. J. 1980. "Police Patrol Work: A Comparative Perspective." In *Police Behavior,* ed. R. J. Lundman. Oxford University Press, New York.

———. 1979. "Organizational Norms and Police Discretion: An Observational Study of Police Work with Traffic Law Violators." *Criminology* 17:159–71.

———. 1974. "Routine Police Arrest Practices." *Social Problems* 22:128–41.

———, R. E. Sykes, and J. P. Clark. 1978. "Police Control of Juveniles: A Replication." *Journal of Research in Crime and Delinquency* 15:74–91.

McKeachern, A. W. and R. Bauzer. 1967. "Factors Related to Disposition in Juvenile Police Contacts." In *Juvenile Gangs in Context,* ed. M. W. Klein. Prentice-Hall, Englewood Cliffs, N.J.

Mark, Sir R. 1970. "A Police Point of View." *Criminologist* 5:82–92.

Matthews, A. R., Jr. 1970. "Observations on Police Policy and Procedures for Emergency Detention of the Mentally Ill." *Journal of Criminal Law, Criminology and Police Science* 61:283–395.

Medalie, R. J., L. Seitz, and P. Alexander. 1968. "Custodial Police Interrogation in Our Nation's Capitol: The Attempt to Implement *Miranda.*" *Michigan Law Review* 66:1347–1422.

Mehlman, M. P. 1972. "Police Initiated Emergency Psychiatric Detention in Michigan." *Journal of Law Reform* 5:581–98.

Meltsner, A. J. 1971. *The Politics of City Revenue.* University of California Press, Berkeley and Los Angeles.

Milner, N. 1970. "Comparative Analysis of Patterns of Compliance with Supreme Court Decisions: *Miranda* and the Police in Four Communities." *Law and Society Review* 5:119–34.

Mosher, F. C. 1982. *Democracy and the Public Service.* Oxford University Press, New York.

National Advisory Commission on Criminal Justice Standards and Goals. 1973. *Police.* U.S. Government Printing Office, Washington, D.C.

National Center for Health Statistics. 1979. *Violent Statistics.* U.S. Public Health Service, Chevy Chase, Md.

National Civil Service League. 1973. *Models for Affirmative Action*. National Civil Service League, Washington, D.C.

National Criminal Justice Information and Statistical Service. 1981a. *Expenditure and Employment Data for the Criminal Justice System*. U.S. Department of Justice, Law Enforcement Assistance Administration, Washington, D.C.

———. 1981b. *Sourcebook of Criminal Justice Statistics*. U.S. Department of Justice, Law Enforcement Assistance Administration, Washington, D.C.

———. 1980. *Sourcebook of Criminal Justice Statistics*. U.S. Department of Justice, Law Enforcement Assistance Administration, Washington, D.C.

National Criminal Justice Reference Service. 1980. *A Community Concern: Police Use of Deadly Force*. U.S. Department of Justice, Law Enforcement Assistance Administration, Washington, D.C.

New York City Police Department. "Charges and Trials." *Rules and Procedures of the New York City Police Department*. New York City, New York.

Oaks, D. H. 1970. "Studying the Exclusionary Rule in Search and Seizure." *University of Chicago Law Review* 37:665–758.

Office of Federal Contracts Compliance Programs. 1980. *Federal Contractor's Compliance Manual*. U.S. Department of Labor, Washington, D.C.

Parsons, T. 1951. *The Social System*. Free Press, New York.

Pastor, P. A., Jr. 1980. "Mobilization in Public Drunkenness Control: The Legal Approach." In *Police Behavior*, ed. R. J. Lundman. Oxford University Press, New York.

Paulsen, M. G., C. Whitebread, and R. Bonnie. 1970. "Securing Compliance with Constitutional Limitations." In *The Rule of Law: An Alternative to Violence*. Aurora, Nashville.

Pederson, B. 1977. *Police Discipline Report*. International Association of Chiefs of Police, Gaithersburg, Md.

Perrow, C. 1972. *Complex Organizations: A Critical Essay*. Scotts, Foresman, Glenview, Ill.

Peterson, D. M. 1972. "Police Disposition of the Petty Offender." *Sociology and Social Research* 56:320–30.

———. 1971. "Informal Norms and Police Practices: The Traffic Quota System." *Sociology and Social Research* 55:354–62.

Piliavin, I. and S. Briar. 1964. "Police Encounters with Juveniles." *American Journal of Sociology* 70:206–14.

Police Chief Executive Committee of the IACP. 1976. *The Police Chief Executive Report*. Law Enforcement Assistance Administration, Washington, D.C.

"Police Complaints—A New Look." *New Law Journal* 75:9–10.

"Police Discretion and the Judgement That a Crime Has Been Committed—Rape in Philadelphia." 1968. *University of Pennsylvania Law Review* 117:277–322.

Potts, L. W. 1981. "Higher Education, Ethics, and the Police." *Journal of Police Science and Administration* 9:131–34.

———. 1980. "Integrating the Chief of Police into the Municipal Administrative Process." *Criminal Justice Review* 5:12–21.

Preiss, J. J. and H. J. Ehrlich. 1966. *An Examination of Role Theory: The Case of the State Police*. University of Nebraska Press, Lincoln.

President's Commission on Law Enforcement and Administration of Justice. 1967. *Task Force Report: The Police*. U.S. Government Printing Office, Washington, D.C.

Regan, D. E. 1971. "Complaints against the Police." *Political Quarterly* 42: 402–13.

Reiss, A. J., Jr. 1971. *The Police and the Public*. Yale University Press, New Haven.

Report of the Board of Enquiry Appointed by the Prime Minister to Investigate Certain Statements Affecting Civil Servants. 1928. Her Majesty's Stationery Office, London.

Roethlisberger, F. J. 1964. "Contributions of the Behavioral Sciences to a General Theory of Management." In *Toward a Unified Theory of Management*, ed. H. Koontz. McGraw-Hill, New York.

Rosenbloom, D. H. 1971. *Federal Service and the Constitution*. Cornell University Press, Ithaca.

Ruchelman, L. I. 1974. *Police Politics: A Comparative Study of Three Cities*. Ballinger, Cambridge, Mass.

Russell, K. 1977. *Complaints against the Police: A Sociological View*. Milltak, Glensfield, Leicester, England.

Salas, L. P. and R. G. Lewis. 1979. "The Law Enforcement Assistance Administration and Minority Communities." *Journal of Police Science and Administration* 7:379–99.

Savitz, L. 1970. "The Dimensions of Police Loyalty." *American Behavioral Scientist* 13:693–704.

Sayre, W. 1948. "The Triumph of Technique over Purpose." *Public Administration Review* 8:134–37.

Schlesinger, S. R. 1979. "The Exclusionary Rule: Have Proponents Proved That It Is a Deterrent to Police? *Judicature* 62:404–09, 457–58.

Schmidt, W. W. 1976. "Recent Trends in Police Tort Litigation." *Urban Lawyer* 8:682–92.

Seeburger, R. H. and R. S. Wettick, Jr. 1967. "*Miranda* in Pittsburgh: A Statistical Study." *University of Pittsburgh Law Review* 29:1–26.

Selznick, P. 1957. *Leadership in Administration: A Sociological Interpretation*. Harper & Row, New York.

———. 1949. *TVA and the Grass Roots*. Harper & Row, New York.

Shafritz, J. M. 1978. *Personnel Management in Government: Politics and Process*. International Personnel Management Association, Chicago.

Shawcross, Lord H. 1965. "Police and Public in Great Britain." *American Bar Association Journal* 51:225–28.

Shearing, C. D. 1974. "Dial-A-Cop: A Study of Police Mobilization." In *Crime Prevention and Social Control*, ed. R. L. Akers and E. Sagarin. Praeger, New York.

Sherman, L. W. 1981. *The Study of Ethics in Criminology and Criminal Justice Curricula*. Joint Commission on Criminology and Criminal Justice Education and Standards, Washington, D.C.

Sholl, R. 1968. "Problems of Criminal Law Administration: An Australian Lawyer's Impressions in the U.S.A." *Australian and New Zealand Journal of Criminology* 1:137–46.

Skolnick, J. H. 1975. 2d ed. *Justice without Trial*. Wiley, New York.

Snibbe, J. R. 1973. "The Police and the Mentally Ill: Practices, Problems and Some Solutions." In *The Urban Policeman in Transition*, ed. J. R. Snibbe and H. M. Snibbe. Charles C. Thomas, Springfield, Ill.

Spiotto, J. E. 1973. "Search and Seizure: An Empirical Study of the Exclusionary Rule and Its Alternatives." *Journal of Legal Studies* 2:243–78.

State Employment Security Division. Annual. *Manpower Reports*. Federal Bureau of the Census, Washington, D.C.

Steer, D. 1970. *Police Cautions: A Study in the Exercise of Police Discretion*. Oxford University Press, New York.

"Suing the Police in Federal Court." 1979. *Yale Law Journal* 88:781–824.

Sullivan, D. C. and L. J. Siegel. 1972. "How Police Use Information to Make Decisions: An Application of Decision Games." *Crime and Delinquency* 20:119–28.

Talarico, S. M. and C. R. Swanson, Jr. 1980. "Policing Styles: Notes on an Empirical Synthesis of Wilson and Muir." *Journal of Criminal Justice* 8:327–34.

Territo, L. and H. J. Vetter. 1981. *Stress and Police Personnel*. Allyn and Bacon, Boston.

Terry, R. 1967. "The Screening of Juvenile Offenders." *Journal of Criminal Law, Criminology and Police Science* 58:173–81.

Theilens, W., Jr. 1958. "Some Comparisons of Entrants to Medical and Law School." *Journal of Legal Education* 11:153–70.

Thompson, J. D. 1967. *Organizations in Action*. McGraw-Hill, New York.

Tifft, L. L. 1978. "Control Systems, Social Bases of Power and Power Exercise in Police Organizations." In *Policing: A View from the Street*, ed. P. K. Manning and J. Van Maanen. Goodyear, Santa Monica.

Uniform Guidelines on Employee Selection Procedures. 1978. Equal Employment Opportunity Commission, Washington, D.C.

U.S. Commission on Civil Rights. 1975. *Federal Civil Rights Enforcement Efforts*. U.S. Government Printing Office, Washington, D.C.

Wald, M. 1967. "Interrogations in New Haven: The Impact of *Miranda*." *Yale Law Journal* 76:1521–1648.

Walker, S. 1980. *Popular Justice: A History of American Criminal Justice*. Oxford University Press, New York.

———. 1977. *A Critical History of Police Reform*. D. C. Heath, Lexington, Mass.

Wallace, S. C. 1930. "Nullification: A Process of Government." *Political Science Quarterly* 45:347–58.

Watson, N. A. and J. W. Sterling. 1969. *Police and Their Opinions*. International Association of Chiefs of Police, Washington, D.C.

Weber, M. 1973. "Bureaucracy." In *Perspectives on Public Bureaucracy*, ed. F. A. Kramer. Winthrop, Cambridge, Mass.

———. 1952. "The Essentials of Bureaucratic Organization: An Ideal-type Construction." In *Reader in Bureaucracy*, ed. R. K. Merton, A. P. Gray, B. Hockey, and H. C. Selvin. Free Press, New York.

Westley, W. A. 1970. *Violence and the Police*. MIT Press, Cambridge, Mass.

Wilensky, H. L. 1964. "The Professionalization of Everyone?" *American Journal of Sociology* 70:137–58.

——— and C. N. Lebeaux. 1965. "The Emergence of a Social Work Profession." In *Industrial Society and Social Welfare*, ed. H. L. Wilensky and C. N. Lebeaux. Free Press, New York.

Wilson, J. Q. 1978. "Dilemmas of Police Administration." In *Policing: A View from the Street*, ed. P. K. Manning and J. Van Maanen. Goodyear, Santa Monica.

———. 1975. *Varieties of Police Behavior*. Atheneum, Boston.

Wilson, J. V. and G. M. Alprin. 1971. "Controlling Police Conduct: Alternatives to the Exclusionary Rule." *Law and Contemporary Problems* 36:488–99.

Wilson, O. W. 1963. *Police Administration*. McGraw-Hill, New York.

——— and R. C. McLaren. 1977. 4th ed. *Police Administration*. McGraw-Hill, New York.

Wilson, W. 1887. "The Study of Administration." *Political Science Quarterly* 2:197–222.

Wisconsin State Committee. 1972. *Police Isolation and Community Needs*. U.S. Commission on Civil Rights, Washington, D.C.

Index